I0338288

VJ

VJ

The unplugged adventures of MTV's first wave

Nina Blackwood, Mark Goodman,
Alan Hunter, and Martha Quinn

with Gavin Edwards

ATRIA BOOKS

New York London Toronto Sydney New Delhi

ATRIA BOOKS
A Division of Simon & Schuster, Inc.
1230 Avenue of the Americas
New York, NY 10020

First Atria Books hardcover edition May 2013

ATRIA B O O K S and colophon are trademarks of Simon & Schuster, Inc.

For information about special discounts for bulk purchases, please
contact Simon & Schuster Special Sales at 1-866-506-1949 or
business@simonandschuster.com.

The Simon & Schuster Speakers Bureau can bring authors to your live
event. For more information or to book an event contact the
Simon & Schuster Speakers Bureau at 1-866-248-3049 or
visit our website at www.simonspeakers.com.

Designed by Kyoko Watanabe

Manufactured in the United States of America

10 9 8 7 6 5 4 3 2 1

Library of Congress Cataloging-in-Publication Data

VJ: the unplugged adventures of MTV's first wave / Nina Blackwood . . . al.].
     p. cm.
   Includes bibliographical references and index.
  1. MTV Networks—History. 2. Video jockeys—Biography. I. Blackwood, Nina.
   PN1992.8.M87V585 2013
   791.45'611—dc23
   2012034425

ISBN 978-1-4516-7812-3
ISBN 978-1-4516-7814-7 (ebook)

For J. J.

contents

VJ

introduction

by Gavin Edwards

Western civilization began on a Friday night in November 1982. The occasion was marked by spies in trench coats, hypodermic-wielding dancers in leather teddies, and a bullet cutting through the jack of diamonds. At least, that was what I saw the first time I turned on MTV. I was a thirteen-year-old who had stumbled onto the video for "Twilight Zone" by Golden Earring, but it felt like all music, art, and film had just served as a preamble to this moment in history.

If you grew up when MTV was a logical acronym instead of a cruel joke, you probably had a similar epiphany. It might have involved Michael Jackson teaching two street gangs to dance, Duran Duran trekking through the jungles of Sri Lanka, or even the Buggles singing, "Video killed the radio star." But no matter how you discovered MTV's quick-cut mash-up of surrealism, new-wave music, and extreme haircuts, when you turned your TV off, suddenly ordinary life seemed a bit, well, banal.

Faithfully guiding us through this 24/7 rush of sensory overload were five stalwart VJs: Nina Blackwood, Mark Goodman, Alan Hunter, J. J. Jackson, and Martha Quinn. Together, they were a five-headed Virgil, taking us through MTV's Inferno, past the circles of slow-motion table-flipping, girls in cages, and arty black-and-white cinematography. MTV was more fun when you watched with a friend, trying to figure out what was going on in "The Safety Dance" or "Total Eclipse of the Heart." The presence of the VJs meant you *always* had a friend watching with you.

This book is the story of the pioneers: the original VJs. Before Alan, J. J., Mark, Martha, and Nina, the term *VJ* didn't exist. They didn't invent MTV, but without them, the channel wouldn't have become the cultural powerhouse that it did. They were proxy members of the audience—music fans that we could laugh with, learn from, or lust after.

They call themselves brothers and sisters, and being with them feels like visiting your family at Thanksgiving: they trade stories, bicker cheerfully, and elbow for position to get the first serving of mashed potatoes. After everything they've been through, it would be understandable if they couldn't stand each other, but they treat each other with deep understanding and love. When they worked together on this book, only one thing cast a shadow on their collaboration: the absence of J. J. Jackson, who died in 2004 and is still very much missed.

These days, Martha resides in Malibu, California; Alan in Birmingham, Alabama; Mark in New York City; Nina in coastal Maine. But for a few years, they lived in the center of the universe—a better, shinier universe.

cot my back against the record machine

Close Encounters with David Lee Roth

Mark Goodman:

David Lee Roth was convinced that he was the hottest rock star in creation. Dave was the funniest guy on the planet—to him. He laughed at all his own jokes. But his mind worked at three hundred miles an hour. These phrases would just fall out of his face—he'd be talking about people who were idiots, and he'd say, "You know, speed-limit IQ." Or regarding other bands that weren't as amazing as Van Halen: "Here today . . . gone later today."

Martha Quinn:

When Dave was doing publicity for Van Halen's *Diver Down* album in 1982, MTV assigned me the interview. I was ecstatic—I couldn't wait to be the one to cut through Dave's razzle-dazzle façade of one-liners and reach the true person underneath. I was determined to stay strong, and not fall for his schtick. I didn't get that his schtick *is* his genius. During the interview, he threw out his best Daveisms—"What you see onstage with Van Halen is what you're gonna find underneath the stage"—and I remained stone-faced. I *refused* to jump into the hot tub of fun that was Dave.

At one point, he said, "If you take a Van Halen record and you stick it in your collection, it'll melt all your other records."

Cut to me, dead silent. Finally, I said, "I'm trying to think what my Van Halen records are next to."

I thought if I didn't fall for his trickery, he'd reveal his soul to me, and we'd live happily ever after.

Mark:

Before MTV, Van Halen were already pretty big—they were playing arenas by then. But videos took them to another level. Pete Angelus had been Van Halen's lighting director, but he started directing the band's videos. And that let people see the band's attitude: They were badass guys, they were cool, they were funny. The sense of humor was there in the songs, but you had to pay attention. The videos hit you over the head with it.

> *Five highlights from Van Halen's "Panama" video:*
>
> 1. *David Lee Roth swinging over a stage, suspended by a cable, listening to a boom box.*
> 2. *Diamond Dave being dragged down a hallway by two cops, wearing only a towel, white athletic shoes, and handcuffs.*
> 3. *Eddie Van Halen sitting at a piano in a white tux, blowing smoke rings.*
> 4. *The lyric "Model citizen / Zero discipline."*
> 5. *David Lee Roth wearing a T-shirt decorated with a picture of David Lee Roth.*

Mark:

Dave's lyrics had a Tom Waits vibe: a storyteller with this weird attitude. He was great at painting a picture with a sentence, like in "Panama," when he did that monologue: "Reach down between my legs and ease the seat back . . ." It was rock 'n' roll, it was about sex, but it was also poetic and had a noir feel. Sure, there was a ton of ego, and he had a teenage boy's sense of humor and fantasy, but I always believed that he was deeper than he cared to let on.

Martha:

He was one of my big crushes. I interviewed him a couple of times, and I always used to wonder, "Why doesn't Dave ever ask me out? Doesn't he see how much I *get* him?" I wanted to be Mrs. David Lee Roth, but I had no idea how to make that happen. Recently I saw a picture of one of our interviews: I was wearing a Boy Scout shirt, buttoned up to the top, and a tie! *A Boy Scout shirt!* What was I thinking? With that shirt, and my hair super-short, I looked like a boy. No wonder Dave never asked me on a date. A magazine—*Circus*, or maybe *Creem*—printed an item that Dave and I were romantically linked. I cut that out and pasted it in my scrapbook. A rumor to treasure.

Mark:

I connected with Dave at the US Festival in '83. Van Halen had a compound: They were paid around a million dollars to play, and they basically spent it on the compound. It was all kinds of trailers, and tons of booze. Dave was totally hammered: coked up and drunk. We did this interview where we just sparred back and forth. I asked him what he wore under his spandex pants, and he made an allusion to circumcision: "All Jewish boys have this. You know about that, don't you, *Goodman?*" And I was like, "Yeah, *Roth!*" The two Jews recognized each other and tacitly agreed that we were members of the same species. Still, he was being outlandish Dave, dancing with a drink on his head.

> *Excerpts from the US Festival interview, on May 29, 1983.*
> *Mark Goodman is in a yellow mesh shirt, while David Lee Roth*
> *sports tiger-print spandex pants and a torn fishnet top:*
>
> DAVID LEE ROTH, CHANNELING ROD SERLING: *"Dave Roth, trapped*
> *in a desperate struggle against time. Will he be able to take the*
> *stage, armed with nothing but a microphone and the will to*
> *survive? Dave Roth, somewhere at the US Festival."*
> MARK GOODMAN: *"Have you learned what software is?"*
> DAVID LEE ROTH: *"I have! I just learned that a floppy disc isn't*
> *a record you left in the sun. . . . In about ten minutes, the*

tailor lady will come in and suck all the air out of my pants at the cuff. We'll seal them off and be fully prepared for tonight's presentation."

MARK GOODMAN: *"When you come to the US Festival, the whole theory is camaraderie . . . and here's Van Halen in their own private compound. Why is that?"*

DAVID LEE ROTH: *"With the private compound, it's not so much that we build walls to keep people out, but that when people get inside walls, they feel more comfortable. . . . You're inside someplace, as opposed to merrily under the stars with your sleeping bag. Although there will be a few people under the stars after tonight." (Roth laughs and leers at the camera.)*

Martha:

Van Halen picked up where Black Sabbath and Blue Oyster Cult left off, but with sex appeal. Van Halen's audience doubled because girls wanted to see them as much as guys. For one blond reason: David Lee Roth.

Nina Blackwood:

The classic Van Halen video would have to be "Jump." It captured the dynamic of the band, and David Lee Roth's performance could have been in the circus. Eddie looks adorable, with that little smile he gives while he's playing his butt off, and you felt like you were in the audience watching them, only you got really good seats.

Martha:

Eventually, I did get to see the real Dave—when I least expected it. At the very first Video Music Awards, in 1984, they had me stand on a hydraulic set, warming up the crowd. The plan was that I'd finish my speech, the stage would lower, and the show would start. I looked out into the crowd at Radio City Music Hall and saw luminaries like Herbie Hancock, Rod Stewart, and Quincy Jones. I gave a dramatic "Let the show begin!" and threw my hand up—but nothing happened. I stood frozen with my hand in the air, like the Statue of Liberty. Still nothing. Finally I walked offstage—and as I reached the edge of the proscenium, the hydraulics kicked in. Teetering on the edge of a dropping platform, I tried to leap to safety, but tripped and fell.

I was crushed. I had wiped out in front of the whole music industry! All night long, it was all I could talk about, to anyone who would listen.

David Lee Roth was sitting in the front row; I was sent down to interview him for a bumper into commercials. Before the camera started rolling, I said, "Oh my God, did you see what happened?"

With great compassion, Dave said, "Aw, darlin', you know how many times I've done that? Welcome to the Rock and Roll Hall of Fame." I'm eternally grateful to him—in the middle of a live broadcast, he pieced me back together. And he gave me a coping mantra I've called on many times since then: "Welcome to the Rock and Roll Hall of Fame."

From the broadcast of the Video Music Awards on September 14, 1984:

Martha Quinn is wearing fingerless white opera gloves. David Lee Roth sports sunglasses, a bright red jacket, and a bleary smile.
MARTHA QUINN: *"David, congratulations on your award. How do you feel?"*
DAVID LEE ROTH: *"Hey, Martha. Life, after all, is really a kung fu movie. . . . Like my daddy said when I was real little, he said, 'Dave, if you ever get in a contest, it doesn't matter whether you win or lose, it's how good you looked.'"*

Mark:

Off camera, Dave was a smart, interesting guy. He liked to cut his own path by doing all that crazy macho shit—on the cover of *Skyscraper,* that was really him climbing the rocks. He traveled to the Amazon and he was into martial arts—he was like a rock 'n' roll Hemingway. Dave was in amazing shape. He could drink and smoke nonstop, but it didn't ever affect his performance onstage.

Alan Hunter:

I went to a rock festival in New Jersey; Van Halen and a bunch of other people were playing. Daryl Hall and John Oates were onstage, but I was hunting around for Mark. I walked around backstage, going from trailer to trailer. I knocked on a door, opened it up, and Mark was in there with David Lee Roth. "Hey, come on in, close the door." I walked in and they were sitting at a little table—Dave had a big vial of coke. They invited me to join them.

I said, "I didn't mean to horn in, but okay."

We partook of the coke and had a grand time. And then people started knocking on the door: a producer or a friend or something. And one by one, they came in and sat in another part of the trailer while the three of us stayed seated, chatting, having a beer, doing another line. Before we knew it, the trailer was packed. No one was sitting with us, because they didn't know David—we did. And they were all just watching us do blow. It was like we were royalty; we were completely nonchalant about fifty other people watching us do blow. People in the TV world, publicists, people we didn't know. Any of them could have gone out and said, "Man, we're watching two VJs sit there with David Lee Roth doing blow." It was like people at orgies watching other people have sex.

At a certain point, we were getting low in Dave's vial and he said, "Y'all have any?" When we told him we didn't have anything to contribute, he became less charitable.

Mark:

When things started to go really badly with my wife, I needed to get away. Dave was on his first solo tour, and I was friends with Pete Angelus, who had become Dave's manager. They invited me out on the road—I flew out to meet them in Detroit and rode the bus with them for a week or so.

Dave wanted to cheer me up. So in Buffalo or someplace, whatever hockey arena we were in, Pete sent me into the locker room. I thought Dave was going to be there and we were going to do some blow. I walked in and this girl came out of the showers. She was hot, in a slutty rock 'n' roll kind of way, and she started chatting with me. After a short time, she got onto her knees and started to unzip my pants. And I felt weird about it—I had to tell her, "I can't." I think that may have negatively affected my friendship with Dave; he just wanted to make me feel better.

When Dave was touring, both with Van Halen and solo, he had the barriers in front of the stage painted different colors on the side that faced him: red, blue, and green, to denote the different areas of the audience. He'd look for hot girls in the crowd, and between songs, go to his assistant Eddie on the side of the stage, and say, "Green, right, fourteen rows back, three seats in." The assistant would go out into the audience and stick a pass on her tits. So after the show, there'd be twenty-five girls in the dressing room who all thought they'd been singled out to be with Dave that night. In fact, a number of them would be. The others would end up with other band members—or, if necessary, the crew.

I would hear stories from these guys about the stuff they would do on the road. Pete told me about overhearing a band member with a girl on the back of the bus. She was saying, "I don't want to blow you." His line to her became a catchphrase with the band and the crew for the rest of the tour: "Just fucking do it." They thought that was hysterical, and I couldn't handle it. They would have girls do headstands in toilets—they thought it was the funniest thing ever, but it was just gross and sad. It wasn't lost on me that these girls were there by choice and at any time could have said, "Fuck off, I'm not doing that!" Still, I couldn't treat another human being like that. I wish I could have gotten it together for that girl who came out of the showers, though.

Another time, I was in L.A., staying at L'Ermitage. Dave met me at the hotel, and decided we would go to this kickboxing competition—he was into mixed martial arts way before anyone. I followed him over the hill from Beverly Hills to Van Nuys, and he pulled into a strip mall. We walked past the 7-Eleven to the dojo; Dave told me that we had to bow as we walked in. All the fighters shouted hello at Dave—he was just as comfortable there as when he was onstage or backstage. We watched a bunch of matches, and while these guys kicked the shit out of each other, Dave explained what was happening: who each fighter was, his history, and what he was doing right and wrong. He was doing color and play-by-play for each match as only fast-talking Dave could.

Afterward we went to a place called the 0-1 Gallery on Melrose. It was an art gallery, but it was really just an excuse for a club where you could drink after the bars closed. You paid to get in, but not for drinks—that was their workaround for the alcohol laws in L.A. Around four in the morning, Dave and I were in the bathroom doing a bump or two, when all of a sudden, we heard screaming. Somebody came running into the bathroom saying, "The cops are here! The cops are here!"

Dave immediately sprang into action. He tied his hair back and tucked in his shirt. He had a big vial that he dropped out the bathroom window. I threw my vial out and we casually strolled out into the club. The LAPD came in with their guns drawn. They were really over the top. There was a lot of shouting and pushing and gun waving as we tried to get out of the club without being noticed. That wasn't happening: They had all of us go out on the street. They lined us up on Melrose and were looking at us, literally shining flashlights in our faces. This was a rare moment where I saw Dave *not* trying to be David Lee Roth; he just wanted to blend. But nobody recognized him—the cops didn't, anyway. They made us disperse, meaning that they yelled, "Get the fuck out of here." I looked the other way for a second, and Dave had already taken off.

Nina:

Actually, I was more of a Sammy Hagar person.

2

changes come around Real soon, make us women and men

Life before MTV

J. J. Jackson (from a 1999 interview):

My mom was in Paris in the 1950s as a fashion model. She told me, "J. J., you acquire true sophistication experiencing the music and the food of the different cultures of the world. Doing so will enrich all areas of your life, wherever and whatever you decide to pursue."

She said this to me when I was just a kid and I always remembered it. She also practiced what she preached. She encouraged me to listen to everything. She took me to see everyone from Count Basie and Josephine Baker to Chuck Berry. I also got into Elvis Presley and Clyde McPhatter. She taught me that you didn't necessarily have to *love* everything you were exposed to, but the opportunity to experience it was what was most important. To have an open mind to what other people create and experience—that will make one's own life that much more rich and meaningful.

Eventually, I joined the Marine Corps. When I got back, I worked at the New England Data Systems. Computers in those days were mammoth and all the information had to be keyed into these monsters. Hugely intimidating machines they were! I was dating a girl I worked with. She was already a keypunch operator whose job was to enter data into these computers for the New England Board of Education. She had a real passion for music, and I enjoyed it as well. In particular, she got me interested in . . . I think it was the Jefferson Airplane.

I'm almost embarrassed to talk about it, but I enrolled in a correspondence course to become a DJ! Even though it's corny to talk about, it turned out to be one of the best moves I ever made.

I'll never forget the day that changed it all for me. This was 1967. I was in a three-piece suit at a school in Connecticut, working for the Board of Education, and I had all these computer cards that we would take and load into the computer. So I was driving back to Boston when I saw two hippies hitchhiking along the road. I stopped and picked them up in my station wagon. In those days, there was no quandary as to whether or not you would pick someone up. You just did it.

They asked me if I minded if they lit up a joint. I said, "Sure, go ahead," and we started to talk. They asked me if I'd heard of the hip underground station in Boston, WBCN. I hadn't, and when I heard it, it freaked me out! They were playing everything, right across the board. Anyway, those kids were going to the "Mods and Rockers Ball," which was going to be held the next day at a place called the Boston Tea Party. I dropped my new friends off and told them I hoped they would have a good time. I became extremely curious about what was going on in Boston on the music scene.

At my job at the computer center, there was a guy who wanted to take a computer operator's course at Tufts University in Boston. This guy was involved with radio. He wanted me to show him how to operate a computer, and he needed someone to do a radio show for him. I did the show, the program director liked what I did, and he kept me for six months! I worked all day at my day job and then did the radio show at night. I was playing and learning everything they had in their music library.

During this time, I became intrigued about that place on Berkeley Street in South Boston called the Boston Tea Party. I was always hearing about what a trip it was to be part of that scene. So I started to go there and experience what it had to offer. In particular, there was this dance—the band was called the Hallucinations, and Peter Wolf was playing. He was right into the R&B stuff. Man, he was the blackest, whitest kid on the block.

He saw from the stage how much my girlfriend and I were into it and he came over to see us. Wolf said he was a DJ at WBCN and they needed some help. Would I be interested in doing "whatever" at WBCN at night? I jumped at the chance. What it amounted to was me working my computer day job and being a WBCN gofer at night. I didn't care what I did—I would be around the hippest station in town and that was good enough for me.

It was a real crash course about how a radio station runs. I got my big break when one of the major DJs at WBCN relocated to the West Coast. They gave me a job doing the midday show and I just loved it. People seemed to enjoy what I was doing, I was enjoying what I was doing—it was a very satisfying experience.

Mark:

My parents weren't musicians, but they played a mean hi-fi. They turned me on to Sarah Vaughan and Billie Holiday and, of course, Frank Sinatra. My dad was a jeweler. He did manufacture and repair, but he was very creative. In later years, he became a jewelry designer. He taught me the trade. When I was thirteen, I made a ring that I still wear today. After the hot gold was poured into a cast, I had to carve out the rough casting with little saws and files. And because I was a thirteen-year-old boy, I picked a design with snakes running up the sides.

My mom wanted to make money and improve. She brought in all these clients for my dad: major department stores like Gimbels and Strawbridge & Clothier. We lived in the suburbs of Philadelphia—first in a row house, and then in a split-level. I could never figure out my parents' relationship. He was an artsy introvert; she was an outgoing businesswoman. He wasn't interested in debating philosophy or politics; she thrived on it. Where other guys had a strong father figure and grew up with a more macho attitude, I always saw the woman's side. My mom was a classic narcissist, and proud of it: Her motto was "Me first." When my sister, Maris, was a little girl, she asked my mom for the banana that she was about to eat with her lunch. When my mom said no, my sister asked why. The answer was, "Because it's mine!"

Maris and I were really close growing up. My sister, who is four years older than me, wasn't one of the popular girls in school: She was really shy, and she went through a dorky-looking phase. But I knew she was the coolest person on earth. She turned me on to great music, from Bach to the Band. It was a shock to me that Maris had trouble getting dates—and when she came home, she'd often tell me stories of how the guys mauled her, trying to get into her pants. I took to heart how those guys were assholes, and when I got older, I avoided being "the mauler" at all costs, because I knew what a drag it was for the girl.

I think I was a difficult kid. I was always getting suspended from school—I wasn't beating up other kids, just getting in trouble. I was probably just trying to get my parents' attention.

When I was in junior high school, almost all the kids at my school were into pop music, but I had five friends that I hung around with, and we were all into black music. We dressed the way black people dressed back then: super-starched highboy collars, bright blue pants, white alligator shoes, and Italian knit sweaters. We even had "black" names we used—Steve Stoll, who started the group, was Moe. Richie Slack was Tyrone, Ricky Abrams was Otis, and I was Leroy. I was into these cool soul bands like the Intruders and the Manhattans. I got to see Otis Redding, the original Temptations, the Supremes, all of those acts—some of them I saw down in Atlantic City, long before the casinos came in. This DJ on an AM soul station, Georgie Woods, had a dance TV show on a UHF station (remember UHF?), channel 17, called *17 Canteen*. I would cut school and go dance to Jay Wiggins's "Sad Girl" and the Mar-Keys' "Philly Dog."

I sold meth when I was in high school, making money to buy a stereo and clothes; I had been working in a deli before that, but I quit. My parents were blissfully unaware. A good friend of mine had this connection, Thierry, a French guy married to a nurse. I don't know where Thierry got it from, but he had garbage bags full of crystal meth, in chunks the size of basketballs. And my friend was an amazing marketer—at a time when people were just folding up drugs in a piece of paper, we were using beautiful little glassine envelopes. When we sold hash, my friend came up with the idea of putting in key filings, which we got from the local hardware store. When you make a key, you shave off some of the brass, and it looks like gold powder. We called

VJ 13

it "The King's Hash." When you lit up, the powder would disappear, presumably into your lungs, but because it was "The King's Hash," it was twice the price. And it sold like crazy.

I graduated from high school, Mitchell Prep, in 1970. I had been selling meth for two years, and the summer before I went to college—Pitt—we had one gigantic deal planned with Thierry. I had invested all the money that I had saved, thousands of dollars. I was planning to go to school with ten thousand dollars in my pocket. And then, boom, Thierry got arrested and deported. I still have the article from a Philadelphia newspaper, with a picture of this guy and his little dog Budeu, getting busted with all my money.

Five weeks after I got to college, my girlfriend broke up with me. I took it really hard—she was the first girl I slept with, the first girl I fell in love with. I didn't realize that when people go to college, things change. A month later, she was living with this lowlife idiot. He worked at a gas station that he ended up robbing. She and I would still talk, and because it was basically the '60s, I would be saying, "Hey man, it's cool," even though the whole situation was humiliating. And this guy turned her on to heroin. I thought, "Oh yeah? I can do that too." For a while, heroin was a big part of my life; my period of heaviest drug use was eighteen to twenty-five, and I did everything. Luckily, I don't have an addictive personality, so I never, ever had a habit—I was never strung out, and I never blew all my money on it. But I did see some of my friends die.

Once I realized that I didn't have the patience to be a musician, I focused on radio. After a couple of years, I transferred to Temple and moved back to Philly. I was a communications major and I worked at the school radio station. I wanted to get on-air experience, but the station played jazz. I knew nothing about jazz before I started working there, so I pulled out records and read the liner notes on the air. My senior year, I did two internships. At night, I worked in the news department at WMMR, the cool FM rock station. During the day, I was at WFIL, a huge AM pop station. They had me call people randomly from the phone book and ask them questions about what music they liked. "Callout research" was just being invented, but it would soon become the industry standard, contributing to the homogenization of radio. Research replaced the taste of DJs.

The WFIL program director, a guy named Jay Cook, took a liking to me. They bought an FM adult-contemporary station and he hired me to do weekend overnights. On Saturday, I would go until 4 A.M. and then I would play the religious tapes until 6 A.M. The first one was an hour, and then there were two half-hour tapes. One night, I fell asleep and got woken up by the guy who was on at 6 A.M. "I wondered why there had been thirteen minutes of dead air," he said. I was terrified, but they didn't fire me.

I also did afternoon drive at an adult contemporary station in Delaware and free-form radio in Allentown, Pennsylvania. All the time, I was sending tapes to WMMR. Finally, they hired me. The program director, Jerry Stevens, was one of my idols—he had programmed the original WMMR, left to pioneer the disco format, and then returned. What I didn't expect was that he was abusive and a huge egomaniac. My idol used to torture me on the air—I'd be talking on the mike and he'd be flicking the back of my head and writing on my sneakers. Around 1978, after Jerry had been replaced by a young whiz-kid programmer named Jeff Pollack, we explored the possibility of my hosting a video show, probably an hour long, on Friday nights, simulcasting on WMMR and on a UHF channel. I ended up not doing that because I got promoted to music director. Which was great, but I had to be at the station all day, plus I did my show from six to ten at night. We were kicking ass, though—number one in the ratings.

I used to say that it wasn't enough for me to have just my friends and family love me—no, I had to have the whole city love me. And ultimately, the whole country.

Nina:

I grew up in Massachusetts, and I was a pretty solitary kid. I had three imaginary friends: Jamie, Beanie, and Cold Cuts. I also had one little tomboy friend—she liked frogs so much, she'd pick them up and squeeze them until she killed them. But mostly I didn't like being around other kids; I thought they were smelly. I was shy then and I'm still shy.

When I was seven, we moved to the suburbs of Cleveland—my dad was an executive in the Defense Department, and he got offered a good position in Ohio. I liked writing poetry, and my poems were always about horses and trees and the golden waves of Ohio grain. I was studying piano and acting in children's theater: My favorite part was Wendy in *Peter Pan,* because I got to fly. As shy as I was, I blossomed onstage—I loved living in an imaginary world and pretending to be a character.

In sixth grade, I saw the Beatles on *The Ed Sullivan Show,* and I was hooked immediately, like millions of other people. I bought every Beatles album, every Beatles book, even all the Beatles cards with the chewing gum. I had three girlfriends, and we pretended to be the Beatles together—we'd talk with these phony Liverpool accents. I was Paul. And on sleepovers, we'd pretend that we were the Beatles' girlfriends, and try to do our hair like Jane Asher and Pattie Boyd did.

Before I was born, my mom was a clothing buyer for a boutique in Massachusetts, so she used to order my clothes from New York. She always complained about the clothes in Cleveland—her expression was "The clothes here are from hunger." She's Italian, not Jewish, but she got that from the *schmatte* business. She was ahead of the curve, and she bought me two pairs of Beatle boots before the Beatles even came to the States. At first other kids teased me, but suddenly, the boots were really cool.

There was always lots of music at my house. When my dad was younger, he had been a drummer in a jazz band. My mom loved Rodgers and Hammerstein musicals, and I did too. When I was thirteen, I started playing harp. I had a friend named Susan who played, and whenever I went to her house, I'd sit down and pick out songs on her harp. The sound was so beautiful; the instrument connected with me on a profound level. There was a two-year waiting list to get an orchestral grand harp, so we rented a smaller troubadour while we waited for my personal instrument. I'll never forget the day it arrived in its *huge* wooden crate.

I was a good student in high school. I was shy, but I was also popular—I was a cheerleader and I was on the student council. I played harp with the school orchestra. Normally, they have the harpist at the back, but they put me in front by the cellos. Later I realized that was probably because I wore short skirts.

I had a couple of high-school boyfriends: One of them gave me my first Doors album, *Strange Days,* but he opened it and played it before he gave it to me. Typical musician. I went on dates where I didn't know what to say: One guy told me, "Just talk about anything—current events." My junior year, I went to a teen club to see this band of brothers called the Tree Stumps, and I met the father of the band, who was also their manager. He thought I would be perfect for one of his other sons, Kevin. I didn't feel shy around the family, and Kevin ended up being my high-school sweetheart.

After I graduated high school in 1970, Kevin and I lived together for a little while—he was going to college, studying urban planning. He was one of the first people to be in that field; years later, he ran for mayor of Atlanta. I was pursuing music with my harp, modeling for painting classes at the Cleveland Institute of Art, and working at the Cleveland Playhouse. One day, a gorgeous boy with Lindsey Buckingham hair and green eyes came to the playhouse and told me, "I'd like to do a painting of you." I bought that line, and suddenly, I wasn't with Kevin anymore. That was my first real downfall with my choice of men—I was such a sucker.

One night, I went to the Viking Saloon to see Eli Radish, this great country-rock band. I decided I'd love to jam with them. Even though I was trained classically, I wanted to do more rock 'n' roll. I tried to figure out who was the boss, and decided it was the bass player, Danny—I told him I wanted to jam with them on harp. He said, "Okay, come next week." So I borrowed a van from a girlfriend of mine, and when I got there, I asked the roadie, Airborne, to help me with the harp. He looked at me strangely—when I said "harp," they all thought I was going to play the harmonica. The gig was a disaster—you couldn't hear the harp, and I played so hard just to hear myself, my fingers started bleeding.

I tried playing with Eli Radish again a couple of weeks later, in Kent. It was the middle of winter, so I wanted to keep the harp warm in the van: Extreme temperatures put a lot of stress on the strings, and sometimes they can snap in the cold. My brilliant solution was to wrap up the harp in blankets to keep it warm in the van. Well, that doesn't work—a harp has no body heat. I got straight A's in my high-school science classes, but sometimes I look back at things I did, and I can understand why people thought I was a dumb blonde. The Kent gig was canceled, so we all went to a party. I talked to Danny for a while, and we hit it off—he seemed so worldly to me. When he was fourteen, he had a band called Spontaneous Corruption that got a major-label deal, and opened up for the Who and the Doors. Danny and I became a couple, and he ended up being my manager. I was so malleable. "Go play this gig." "Sure, Danny, whatever you say."

Danny and I developed this technique of using a butter knife on the strings of the harp—it made it sound like a slide guitar. We moved around for most of the '70s, trying to do music in different towns: Nashville, back to Ohio, Massachusetts, Tennessee, then back to Cleveland. I wanted to live in New York, but Danny hated the cold, so we went to L.A. We drove across the country in June 1979 in an MG Midget with a big trunk on the back. We took the southern route; I cooled off with a spray bottle the whole way through the desert.

Alan:

I grew up in Mountain Brook, which is kind of the Beverly Hills of Birmingham, Alabama. I lived on the other side of the tracks; my mother and father got divorced when I was seven, so we led a very middle-class life. I didn't know until I was an adult that my parents got married twice—to each other. The first time, they lasted about a year, until my dad moved to New York to pursue his dreams of being the next Perry Como. After a year, he felt guilty and came back. They got remarried and stayed together for the next fourteen years.

I was class of '75 at Mountain Brook High School. It was all white, and full of cliques, starting with the cool kids who smoked cigarettes out back and wore braided leather belts and penny loafers without socks: They were the future lawyers, doctors, and frat-boy ne'er-do-wells. There were also the jocks/cheerleaders, the band/choir kids, and the Jewish contingent (hardly outcasts, but definitely in their own pod). I wasn't a member of any of the tribes, but I got along with all of them because I participated in everything, starting with sports: base-ball, basketball, football. I was a star football player—wide receiver, punt returner—and I dated the head cheerleader, my first love, Mary. But I was also in the school choir and all the theater productions, shows like *Paint Your Wagon*.

Mary and I dated for three years, starting in tenth grade. I was the envy of my friends because, to be perfectly honest, I was getting some.

My senior year, Mary and I broke up for about three weeks. I needed to sow my wild oats, but none of the other girls in school would date me, because they loved Mary too much.

My senior year, the Spartans had a great football season. The last game, the coaches told us, "This is the last game you'll ever play in your life—you think about that when you're lollygagging around the field." We got killed in that game—but I caught the last touchdown and was quite pleased about that. Everybody was weeping in the locker room, but I had a bigger perspective.

I applied to eight colleges and got into all of them. I had spent forty dollars a pop of my mom's money to apply to these schools, and didn't get off my ass to visit any but one: Millsaps, in Jackson, Mississippi. Mary's sister went there, so we took a road trip to visit. It looked fine to me.

Mary wanted to follow me—that was my first experience with will-fully saying goodbye to somebody. I didn't know what I wanted to do with my life. My mom made me take a vocational test in high school; the results said I was best in social sciences, I had a creative spirit, and I had very low marks in organization. I took that to mean I should go into something like psychology, so that's what I majored in. I didn't have any desire to go into the entertainment business—my father's failed singing career spooked me a little bit.

I had a lot of fun at Millsaps. Like in high school, I was into every-thing: the choir, theater, student government. I checked out the local ballet school for the exercise—and because there were hot chicks there. They gave me a scholarship and I stuck with it for a couple of years. It was an internationally known school, run by a Russian lady. I was the only guy who could lift the women, and she would tell me, "You are strong as bull."

I met my future wife, Jan, early on. We didn't like each other at first; I thought she was a bitch, and she thought I was a pervert. I've always been a joker, and I had a reputation for saying inappropriate things—or, from my perspective, voicing what everyone else was thinking. Jan told me later, "You talked about sex all the time. We all figured you weren't getting any and that was why you talked about it so much." One night we had a real conversation outside the local beer joint, and connected. She was pretty and vivacious and theatrical—we had a common bond in our love of movies and musicals. And we were in the Troubadours together, which was the school's elite special-forces singing group. The music was square, and we had to wear these black Elvis jumpsuits with rhinestone piping, but I liked the discipline of it all. Some of the members were devout Christians—which didn't inhibit them at parties when we started drinking and playing spin-the-bottle.

Jan and I started dating my sophomore year, and my senior year, we got married. We honeymooned in New York City, spending a week in a friend's apartment. We went to see *A Chorus Line,* my first Broadway musical, and I was smitten; I started considering a life in the theater.

We spent another year in Birmingham, doing children's theater, and then came back for a summer in New York, attending the Circle in the Square drama school. Jan was a musical-theater person; she wasn't into the angst of Method acting classes like I was. I thought being a "serious" actor meant diving headfirst into life, whether it was good, bad, or ugly. It wasn't easy to do that if you were married, so my De Niro goals were hobbled from the start. But then, I was never going to be De Niro.

Back then, you could live in New York for five hundred dollars a month. We were subletting an apartment on Seventy-second and Broadway, and I could smell this restaurant downstairs, the Copper Kettle. We were living on grits and oatmeal—I wanted so badly to be able to afford a meal at that restaurant. But at the end of the summer, we committed to pursuing our dreams in New York.

Martha:

I grew up in Ossining: home of Sing Sing prison, about an hour north of New York City. My best friend Carol and I, pretty much every day after school, would go to one of our houses and play Beatles albums over and over. Every single Beatles song, I know the harmonies by heart.

If you ever hear me say, "I got the music in me!"—well, I got it from my mom, Nina Pattison. She started playing piano in 1931 and is still playing today—she can sight-sing any piece of music, with perfect pitch. My dad, David Conrad Quinn (my middle name is also Conrad), was a trial lawyer who knew everything there was to know about Shakespeare. Completely self-taught: Not many of his neighbors in the Bronx were into *King Lear.* A World War II rescue pilot, he was funny and charismatic—at a wedding or a graduation, he was the guy making a toast. My brother Dave is a lawyer; my brother Chris was a navy pilot; I'm a performer. We all took aspects of David Quinn as our life paths.

My parents divorced when I was five years old. They sat me down in the living room and told me my dad was going to move out. I knew just what to do: I ran to the front door and locked it so he couldn't leave. Isn't that sad? My dad moved into New York City and got an apartment; I visited him every other weekend. It was the '60s: I was the only kid I knew with divorced parents. When I went to Carol's house, I would see her dad's red leather chair in the living room, and wonder what it would be like to have a father around.

A few years later, my dad married a young writer named Jane Bryant Quinn. She wasn't a bestselling author and financial expert yet—she was working in the mailroom at *Newsweek.* Later, she got a column at *Businessweek,* but had to use J. B. Quinn as her byline because they didn't want people to know she was a woman. Jane had a son, Matthew (my stepbrother), and she and my dad had a child together, Justin. Jane worked her ass off to be successful. Whenever I hear people say a celebrity is "lucky," I think of Jane and I know it ain't luck.

When I was in eighth grade, my sister-in-law Barbara saw me walking down the street in a granny dress and a sweatshirt and boots. (There was actually a period of time where gingham and calico *Little House on the Prairie* dresses were popular.) Barbara said, "Oh my God. She needs help." She whisked me off to Bloomingdale's and picked out a powder-blue leotard, a light coral skirt, and a sweater that had *both* powder blue and coral in it. This was a revelation. Looking back, Barbara was my first stylist—I'm still much better off when someone else pulls together clothes for me!

I'm proud to be an Ossining High School girl. When OHS made the national news for race riots, my dad begged me to move to the more genteel Chappaqua school district, but I stayed. I was decent in language arts and history, but got a genuine F in geometry, and in science, I was a lost cause by the time I hit chemistry. I wasn't concerned, because I always assumed I was going to be an actress. I did all the school plays, from the chorus of *Damn Yankees* to the lead role of Anna in *The King and I.* Then for a class, I started to work on the school radio station, WOSS, and I loved all nine watts of it. I thought, "Whoa, I can just sit here and play music and talk. This is much easier than studying lines!"

I hung out with the Zappa-lovin' musician crowd, and didn't think of myself as being popular. That said, I was class president my junior year, and vice president my senior year. (I didn't want to have to plan the prom!) But, oh, the sadness—I tried out for the cheerleading squad and didn't make it.

I'd had a crush on a boy, Tony, since third grade, when I looked over at this new kid and thought he looked like a rock star. I spent many years chasing Tony's approval, while he broke my heart again and again. I kept going back to him, no matter how many times he broke up with me; my entire sense of self-worth hinged on this guy's opinion of me. I would sit on the OHS stairs leading down to the cafeteria, crying because he didn't love me.

When I was in eleventh grade, Richie—this guy from Tarrytown, the next town over—took me to see Paul McCartney at Madison Square Garden, the Wings over America tour. It might have been a date in his mind, but nothing ever happened with Richie. In fact, after the concert, I had him drive me to Tony's house. I was so bad—but I really wanted to see Paul McCartney. Sorry, Richie!

J. J. moved to Los Angeles in the early '70s, where he was the afternoon "drive time" DJ at KLOS-FM for nine years, and then held the same slot at KWST-FM. He also worked for the local ABC-TV affiliate, and was credited with conducting the first TV interview ever with Bruce Springsteen. He was good friends with many major rock bands, including the Who, Queen, and especially Led Zeppelin.

J. J. (in 1999):

I saw them in Los Angeles at the Inglewood Forum in 1973. Led Zeppelin wanted to play their very best wherever they went, but L.A. was always extra special to them. They really tore up the house that night.

And then it was party time, at the home of a prominent L.A. radio station owner. We got out of the Forum in a big hurry, which was going nuts, demanding more encores when we were going down the road, I'm sure. When we got there, all in high spirits, of course, it was a beautiful home, complete with a swimming pool, and everyone was partying like crazy.

I was standing in the kitchen, talking to some people. The place was packed inside and out. Suddenly, it sounded like there was a riot going on and then a big splash. Bonzo [Zeppelin drummer John Bonham], who loved to play pranks, and some others were starting to throw people in the pool. Everyone was laughing hysterically at the hijinks. I was wearing a new suit that night that I had just bought. I wasn't making a lot of bread in those days as a DJ, so there's no way I could afford to have it ruined.

I could see Bonzo was whirling around, looking for new victims to get hold of and throw into the pool. So I quickly ducked out of sight by hiding behind the kitchen curtains, hoping he wouldn't set his sights on me! I hid there for quite a while, praying I wouldn't have my new clothes ruined by going for an unwanted dip. I managed to escape him, but I was pretty anxious behind the curtains for quite some time, let me tell you!

Nina:

I found a job playing harp six nights a week at the Hyatt near the L.A. airport. It was a beautiful room with stained glass and a round bar—they had me up on a pedestal in the middle of the room, under a gorgeous stained-glass skylight. I also played weddings and parties. That was my main source of income, along with voice-overs and commercials for clients like Dodge and JCPenney. I was just starting to get my acting career together. I wasn't on camera; my commercial agent told me I wasn't salable because I looked too much like Janis Joplin. I didn't think I looked like Janis, but welcome to Hollywood.

Danny and I put together demos for two radio shows that we were trying to get syndicated. One was *Teen Tips*—I was a lot closer to being a teen at the time—and the other was a talk show called *Woman to Woman*. I also took acting classes at the Lee Strasberg Institute:

Amy Madigan and Rebecca De Mornay were in my class. My favorite part that I played at Strasberg was Laura in *The Glass Menagerie.* That character resonated really deeply with me. I don't think I'm damaged like she is, but I related.

I wanted to do acting with substance, but people kept warning me that lots of casting agents would just want me for hooker parts. And sure enough, the first feature film that I was in, I played a hooker. It was in *Vice Squad,* which became a cult film. My character was Ginger, a naïve hooker who gets killed. Her pimp Ramrod comes by her hotel room—after he throws her across the room five times, she just asks, "You gonna beat me again?"

I met a brilliant, eccentric guy named Michael Seinhardt, an avant-garde video artist. He had a gibbon named Opal—at the time, it was legal to keep a gibbon as a pet. That ape was like his daughter, and she'd flirt with men, but she was very jealous of females. Michael and I started putting together a pilot for a TV show called *K-Punk.* We filmed in Chinatown—that's where all the new-wave and punk bands were. We showed videos and I did man-on-the-street interviews with the punks. It was the early seeds of being a VJ. I rolled up the sleeves on my T-shirt, and I had a fake tattoo that read BAD. Watch out! Nina Blackwood, she's *bad!*

Mark:

Carol Miller was a DJ at WMMR, doing weekends. She had been a student at the University of Pennsylvania; she applied for a job at the station on a dare, and promptly got hired. Not long after, *Philadelphia* magazine voted her the sexiest woman in Philadelphia. By the time I got to MMR, she had moved back to New York. I knew about her, but we didn't actually meet until 1980, when I was offered a job at WPLJ, the top rock station in New York. Carol had been working 10 P.M. to 2 A.M. at WPLJ; they juggled the schedule, moving her to 6 P.M. to 10 P.M., and hiring me to do her old shift.

The first time I saw her in person, I was with my attorney—we were working out some parts of the job offer, and they were giving me a tour of the studio. I was twenty-nine, but I was the wide-eyed kid: "Wow, this is a New York radio station." Carol waved at me from behind the glass. I didn't realize who it was at first—but I felt good about the fact that I'd be following her on the air every night. She was stunning. She had black hair and green eyes, and big white teeth, and perfect skin. She told me later that when she waved at me, she said, "I think that's the guy I'm gonna marry."

WPLJ was the number one rock station in the number one market in the country. There are jocks who work their entire careers and never make it to that level. I was in radio basically four years, and it happened. Living in New York changed everything for me—it felt like home, and it felt like I'd hit the big time.

I started at WPLJ in the summer of 1980. Radio stations take on the personalities of the program director, and the guy who was running WPLJ was an uptight sphincter muscle. But Carol and I started hanging out—we'd see each other late at night, and on weekends. Saturdays were the worst, because I would be on until 3:30 A.M., until the public-affairs guy came in. Carol used to wear this perfume called Tea Rose, and she would leave a dot on the microphone before she left. I never knew that—I just knew that the studio always smelled like her, and the engineers would say, "Fucking Carol, this whole studio smells like Tea Rose, it's driving me crazy."

At the time, Carol was going out with Jimmy Iovine. He was producing Tom Petty's *Damn the Torpedoes* and Stevie Nicks's *Bella Donna,* so he was out in California all the time. I really had to fight for her. Although Jimmy wasn't right for her, he was a good guy and she didn't want to hurt him. To make things more complicated, ABC Radio, which owned WPLJ, had very strict guidelines about employees going out—but within months, we were living together. If they had known, they would have had a problem with it, especially because we were right next to each other on the air. But I stayed at WPLJ less than a year before MTV happened.

Martha:

I graduated high school in 1977, and when I went to college, I was deciding between Vassar and Colgate. (I know what you're thinking: "How could she have gotten into Vassar or Colgate?" What can I say? Extracurricular activities meant a lot back then!) Here was my in-depth calculation: Vassar had four girls to every guy, Colgate had four guys to every girl. Guess where I went?

At Colgate, I lived in a dorm right down the hill from the school's radio station, WRCU, so in my first week, I wandered over there. Other than WRCU, Colgate wasn't for me—there were way too many cows in Hamilton County. I wanted to do journalism or radio, and my stepmother, Jane, gave me some great advice: "Be in the life. Go where the action is." So my sophomore year, I transferred to NYU.

I actually majored in radio at NYU. I always say "communications," but it's not true. There were twelve of us in the radio major, and our advisor, Irving Falk, had been a production assistant on *The War of the Worlds* with Orson Welles in the 1930s. Our "professors" were DJs like Richard Neer, from WNEW-FM, a big rock station in New York. A typical day in the classroom: "Well, if you play Led Zeppelin at ten-twenty and there's a news break, this is how you make the transition."

I took some other classes, but mostly I worked at the WNYU radio station. I was on all the time with different shows: *Just Plain Folk, Jazz Expansions, The Afternoon Show* (where I played Duran Duran's "Planet Earth"), and my baby, the R&B-oriented *Getaway*, named for an Earth, Wind & Fire song. I played Shalamar, the Whispers, and Parliament-Funkadelic—on the air, I called myself Tiffany.

I lived in NYU's Weinstein dorm, and I worked there as a front-desk clerk, putting mail in everyone's mailboxes, taking phone messages, and handing out lightbulbs and other supplies. Future superstar producer Rick Rubin lived there at the same time—I didn't pay any attention to him, but I'm sure I gave him toilet paper many, many times.

I had a roommate, Becky, who was a model with the Wilhelmina agency. She was tall, blond, and very cute, like a young Christie Brinkley. She did commercials, and I decided I wanted to do them too. I got my on-and-off boyfriend Tony to take photos of me, and I sent them out to every talent agency listed in the phone book. Two responded, one of which was the Mary Ellen White Agency, a kids' agency. They signed me up, and I started booking auditions. Becky never let on if she was bummed, but in her shoes, I probably would have been!

I did a lot of commercials: Clearasil, Campbell's soup, a deodorant soap. I was the Chicken McNuggets girl for McDonald's, promising, "You'll go nuggets for McNuggets." (Ironic for a girl who went on to be a staunch vegetarian!) I was making a ton of money—my senior year, I got thirty thousand dollars for being in a Kellogg's commercial. (I had something like six hundred dollars in my bank account. I had a drawer full of checks, most of which I threw out because I mistakenly believed they had expired.) I did a Country Time Lemonade commercial with Jeff Daniels; I think he played my dad. We filmed it at a barn on Staten Island, frolicking around, enjoying the sun, being wholesome and lemonade-y. Years later, I interviewed Jeff for *Arachnophobia* and told him we did a commercial together. He said, "Really? Was it for hemorrhoids?"

My senior year, I got an internship at WNBC-AM, which was the biggest pop station in New York City. In 1980, AM stations were still relevant in the musical world—NBC, pronounced "NnnnnnnBC," was the home of Don Imus (Howard Stern arrived soon after). I considered myself a radio pro by this time, and was genuinely surprised when the music department didn't let me, a college student, help decide what records to play! I spent a year alphabetizing the ratty old singles they stored in the back closet, putting little stickers on their dust jackets. I spent a year in that closet—except when they sent me out to pick up dry cleaning for Imus.

After graduation, I moved into Tony's apartment. He proceeded to spend all his time in Ossining. At first I pretended not to notice, but within a few weeks I knew I had to get out. Finding an apartment in New York ain't easy, but luckily, Jane knew a guy who had an apartment to sublet on the Upper East Side, on Eighty-eighth Street between York and East End. It was a fifth-floor walk-up, and I had to take care of a big, mean parrot. This guy also collected African erotic art, so there were all these carvings of people with erections. It was totally odd, but I was desperate. I moved out of Tony's place over a weekend, not even telling him that I was leaving. I was hoping he'd discover I was gone and run wildly through the streets like Stanley Kowalski: "Martha! *Marthaaaa!*" My family carried my furniture up five flights of stairs, I pushed all the erection art to the back, and I tried to figure out what I was doing with my life.

Alan:

Jan and I found a rent-controlled apartment in New York the night before we went back to Birmingham to get our stuff, and gave the broker all our money. That night, we stayed on the floor of our new apartment, ecstatic about how our life was unfolding, if weirded out by the late-night sounds of the big city: a couple making mutual death threats, a dog barking until dawn, a baby wailing loud enough to drown out a saxophone. The next morning a young couple knocked on the door and said, "Y'all are in our apartment." *Whaa?* The apartment was double-booked—to another couple from the South—Alabama, no less. I suggested we could share the joint, but no luck.

We went back home; several weeks later, I came back up and found a studio with a kitchen in the closet at the Woodward Hotel on Fifty-fifth and Broadway. It was a transient hotel—okay by me, but guys can wear the same socks for weeks. I knew Jan wouldn't be happy: she wanted at least a one-bedroom with a real kitchen.

She drove up from Alabama in a U-Haul for seventeen hours with my brother Randy, who was coming to New York to be a musician. To stay sharp, he smoked dope and did coke most of the way. When they arrived in the early evening, Jan looked stunned, like she had been shot out of a circus cannon. She went up to the tenth floor on the rickety elevator, walked into the apartment, and burst out crying. "This is our apartment? It sucks."

"Yes, honey, but the price is right," I said—with no conviction.

We sat there for the first couple of weeks, not believing we were really in New York. We'd watch *The David Letterman Show*—this is when he was on in the morning. My brother would slurp his coffee and smack his lips; Jan was getting increasingly irritated. One day, I looked at the two of them and said, "Fuck it, somebody's got to get a job." I walked down the street to a restaurant that was owned by the Mafia, and got us jobs waiting tables. The job didn't last long for Jan: She locked horns with the manager and he fired her. She found another waitress job at the Magic Pan on Fifty-seventh Street; they had a better-paying job for me as a bartender, so I told the manager to fuck off and followed Jan to the land of the crepe.

I auditioned for the part of Lysander in a new-wave/punk-rock version of Shakespeare's *A Midsummer Night's Dream,* at the New York Theater Ensemble on East Fourth Street in the East Village. I didn't get the gig, but the director called me up and said, "Do you move well?" He cast me as one of the spirits of the forest—there were eight of us, four guys and four girls. The director was named Lester and he was flamboyant, to say the least: "I want the spirits of the forest to be *sexual animals.* I want you always in the background as the scenes between the earth people and the gods unfold, groping and hanging on and just *being sexual.*" We had tights and makeup and music was playing: Joan Jett, Talking Heads. I did well because of my dance background, but there was a problem: because of all the groping I was doing with my cute girl dance partners, I had a constant hard-on! I was wearing tights, so it wasn't a secret. Lester was enthused; hopefully, the audience thought it was a prosthetic for effect. And I was married—that didn't make me bitter, just conflicted.

I had a bit part in the movie version of *Annie,* playing one of fifty ushers at Radio City Music Hall. I had a line; it got cut. But I got to spend three days on a huge-ass production with John Huston directing. Huston sat in a corner with his emphysema tube, watching a monitor, barking orders to his assistant director. I got my SAG card based on that.

Once I had my union card, I qualified for a better class of auditions—I went on casting calls for industrial videos or extra parts in movies. I showed up at one of those, and they told me that it was for a David Bowie video. Look at the camera, say your name, turn sideways, get out. I didn't have to do a dance audition; I just told them I danced. I got a call two days later: "You got the video."

There were six of us; the other people were dancers except for one, a guy named Obba Babatundé, a black guy who, a year later, got nominated for a Tony in the original production of *Dreamgirls.* We had two days of rehearsal. The choreography was very experimental, and I was feeling very non–Martha Graham. We had to make these specific moves with our arms to our foreheads and our chins; we were voguing years before Madonna did it, and I didn't know what it was.

We showed up at the fabled Mudd Club in lower Manhattan: every rock band played there in the '70s. It had a reputation as the raunchiest of clubs, where people vomited, pissed, and defecated all over. It reeked! When the time came for our little squad to do our weird signature moves, I was self-conscious about it and chose the statue pose: My choice as a dancer was to be still, like a John Cage performance of silence. The choreographer said, "That's great, because that's weird—that's the new dance."

I looked over and saw David Bowie watching us flail around. A couple of sycophant extras were bugging him, but he was very gracious. On a break, I found an opportunity to ease up next to him, and he said, "Good job, mate." I said, "Oh, thanks, but it's not really what I do." I was trying to explain that I was an actor. When Bowie got onstage for his performance in the video, he did the moves that we had been taught and I realized, "Oh, we're mirroring what *he's* doing." It was a new kind of dance, invented by Bowie himself.

A month later, the video played on Wolfman Jack's *Midnight Special,* which was a late-night music show on NBC. I stayed up till midnight to watch it—it was insane and fabulous to see myself on TV.

3

welcome to your life

MTV Hires the VJs

Nina:

I read an article in *Billboard* saying that there was a new twenty-four-hour music channel, owned by Warner AmEx Satellite Communications, that was looking for hosts and hostesses who knew about music. I sent them my résumé and an eight-by-ten picture. I wanted it to look punk, so I started coloring the picture with crayons. Danny came by and said, "What are you doing?" I told him and he said, "Nina, there are such things as color Xeroxes."

They came out to L.A. and held auditions. I went down in my little MG, dressed all in black. I was dying in the heat, but I had to look cool. A few weeks later, they came out again. This time they wanted me to interview a "celebrity." It was Robert Morton, who went on to be Morty, the producer of David Letterman's show—he was pretending to be a smart-alecky Billy Joel. It went well, but I didn't hear from them for a while, and I thought that was weird. I'm not the cockiest person in the world, but I kept thinking, "If they don't hire me, who are they looking for? In the whole United States, how many people are working on this sort of thing already?" And I had rock 'n' roll in my heart.

So I called them up, and the phone number went to a hotel, I think the New York Sheraton. I hung up and told Danny, "Oh my God, they're a fly-by-night organization using Warner's name. How are they getting away with it?"

He said, "You should call back."

It turned out they were the real thing—they were working out of a hotel room—and they wanted me to come to New York for the final verdict. I went out, and they said, "We want you, but you have to move to New York." Because the company's name included "satellite communications," I had assumed the job was going to be in L.A.

I couldn't decide, so executive producers Sue Steinberg and Robert Morton said they would show me the highlights of New York, hoping I would want to move and take the job. They took me to the public library—hey, I like books. And we went to lunch at the Tavern on the Green. I was nervous, and when they brought out the crusty rolls, I inhaled one. It lodged in my throat—I was choking to death. Luckily, Morty knew the Heimlich maneuver. He jumped up and saved my life. After everybody calmed down, he said, "You owe me."

I said, "Yeah, you're right. I'll take the job."

Mark:

I got a call from a friend of mine in Philadelphia. We both knew a guy named Richard Bencivengo, and he said, "I heard that Bencivengo's working on some sort of music video channel." I was unhappy at WPLJ, so I called them up. It turned out they were seeing everybody in the world. A bunch of people from PLJ went in—I saw them at the auditions. The first audition was in a forty-eight-degree studio. It was pitch-black, with a stool and a spotlight. Freezing cold, with a spotlight in the face, the vibe was interrogation: *Answer our questions or we're going to pluck out your eyeballs.* I talked into the camera about Eric Clapton going on tour. There was a one-way window in the studio; it felt like a sci-fi movie where they do an experiment and the alien overlords watch through the window, waiting to see if your head explodes.

It was a few weeks before I heard anything—I guess they were scouting for talent in other cities. I had a second audition, at a different, warmer studio. They had two areas set up. One had a big white card with pictures of the Eagles taped on it, perched on an easel. They wanted me to back-announce an Eagles video, and then walk from the board to this other area, which had a ratty couch and a chair, sit down there, and throw to the next video. They were literally seeing if I could walk and talk at the same time.

There were a couple of camera guys, and a bunch of producers, and cue cards. I had never worked with cue cards before, but I knew what I was supposed to be saying. At one point, I was so far off the cards, the producer had no idea what to hold up next. I just said, "Next card, please." I found out later that went a long way toward getting me the job—when I needed some information, I didn't stumble through it like a standard TV host. I spoke to the people off-camera and asked for it.

The next section was interviewing "Billy Joel," as played by Robert Morton. Billy Joel is the nicest guy ever, but Robert was being cantankerous, giving yes and no answers to questions. At the end, I talked to Sue Steinberg. I'm six foot one, and Sue is approximately four foot nine. She looked up at me and said, "I think you'll be hearing from us." There was something in her face that said, "I can't tell you this, but you so have this job."

Nina was the first one they hired, and then maybe a day later, J. J. I got the call very soon after that. I had a three-year contract with ABC, which owned WPLJ, but I really wanted to do MTV. I booked a vacation, went away for ten days, and let my lawyers hash it out.

Nina:

They wanted me right away—this was the middle of June. I asked if I could stay in L.A. for the Fourth of July. At the time, there were wonderful fireworks up and down the coast, and I really wanted to see them. I watched them from my favorite spot, Topanga Beach, and left for New York City on July 5.

MTV was a gamble. Vicki Light, who was my agent, and Danny, who was my manager, figured it was some little cable show, and if I didn't like it, I could come back in three months. We weren't even sure it'd still be on the air six months later.

MTV put me up in a beautiful hotel, the Berkshire. After the incident at the Tavern on the Green, I was really scared about choking when I was by myself. For about two months, I would order room service and eat right next to the phone so I could call the front desk in case anything happened.

The first weekend I lived in New York, I had maybe one friend outside of the people at MTV—and I didn't really know them either. Mark kindly said, "You want to go to Central Park?" I got into a cab to meet him and immediately got into a car accident. Not a big one, but there was lots of screaming and yelling. After I finally made it to Central Park, Mark and I were walking around when a bush came alive.

Mark:

There was some commotion in the bush, and I said, "Oh, that's probably rats fighting. No big deal. There must be some garbage there." Nina completely freaked out. She was so not a New York person. I thought Nina was really hot, and I was definitely attracted to her, but I was in love with Carol, so I didn't try to instigate anything between us—and today, we're like brother and sister.

After a format change at KWST—it went from classic rock to top 40—J. J. was without a job. At his MTV audition, he also interviewed "Billy Joel"—and did well, despite not caring for the actual Billy Joel. When the producers told him that the job meant moving to New York City, he said, "You see that beautiful black Jensen Interceptor sitting out there? You see those mountains, that blue sky, those big, puffy clouds? All that goes away if I go to Manhattan. But I'll go, 'cause I need the gig."

Nina:

I met J. J. in the lobby of the Berkshire, where MTV had put us both up. He commanded your respect immediately, but he was a very sweet man. We were both Angelenos, so we talked about the sports cars that we had left behind. I had an MG; he had a Jensen Interceptor, which was a hand-built British car. He always pronounced it "Intacepta." It wasn't so much of a Boston accent as it was a J. J. accent. MTV gave the two of us tickets to see Judas Priest. Our seats were right in front of the speakers, so we lasted maybe thirty seconds and then went out to dinner.

MTV had hired one other VJ, Meg Griffin. I knew she was an FM jock, and I thought she was really cool. I didn't get a chance to talk to her very much, because she quit almost immediately.

Mark:

Meg had been at WNEW-FM for years, and was next in a long line of jocks who were being groomed for a full-time spot. She was great—I was happy she got the MTV job. Meg was a very cute all-American girl next door, bangs and freckles, a Martha Quinn type. One day, before we launched, Meg did an interview with the Equators. At the end, Meg was supposed to get up: They would play some Equators music and she would dance with the band. For some reason, they had to do a few takes, and she was really uncomfortable with the whole thing. In her mind, that sealed the deal. We shared a cab uptown together after we were done for the day, and she said, "I'm going to quit."

I told her, "Meg, don't do this. You will regret this. Do not leave—you'll work this out."

Later, she told me there were other factors: Bob Pittman, who ran MTV, didn't want her to keep a part-time job at WNEW. He said, "You're going to work harder if this is your only job." He wanted her to have the fear that comes with no backup plan. That was Pittman—he always wanted to keep his foot on our necks.

Meg was at MTV for the same reason I was—she was passionate about music. It became clear to her that wasn't why they hired her: *Do they want me here because I love music, or because I look like whole wheat?* So she quit, and got that full-time position at WNEW. That was what made room for Martha.

Martha:

Even though I'd graduated from NYU, I kept my desk clerk gig at Weinstein. (Some clerks stayed there for years—the most famous being Ric Menello, who wound up directing videos for the Beastie Boys.) One afternoon in July, I was sitting on the city bus, heading back uptown to my weird apartment. Around Rockefeller Center, the traffic got really bad. The bus wasn't moving, so I jumped off to visit my friends at WNBC. Purely by chance, a guy named Burt Stein was also visiting. He used to work for A&M Records in California, and he was hanging out at WNBC that day for no particular reason. A bunch of us were shooting the breeze in the music office. Then Burt randomly asked, "Hey, what's Bob Pittman doing?" Bob had been the youngest-ever program director of WNBC—he left before I got there, but he was a legend.

Buzz Brindle, assistant program director at WNBC, and a former professor of mine, said, "Oh, he's doing this MTV thing." And then Buzz looked at me and uttered the words that changed my life forever: "Martha, that's what *you* should do. You should be a VJ on MTV."

"What's a VJ?" I practically scoffed.

Buzz said, "It's like a DJ on the radio, but on television."

This sounded like *WKRP in Cincinnati* to me, so I asked the logical question, "What do I during the records?" I was thinking they'd film a DJ studio.

"No, it's videos," he explained. "They're playing these clips."

I said, "Oh, I can't do that. You know who should do that? Evan Davies, he's really good at music." Evan was another radio major from NYU.

Buzz said, "No, I really think you should do it." He picked up the phone and called Bob Pittman. It turned out it was the last day of auditions. Buzz said, "You gotta get down there—they're closing up shop at five-thirty."

It was already 5 P.M., and I didn't know how I would get to Thirty-third Street and Tenth Avenue in time. I knew I'd never get a cab, so I called my friend Adam, the only person I knew who had a car. Adam picked me up, dropped me off on Thirty-third Street, and went to get a pizza. I walked into the studio and said, "Hey, I'm here to audition." And they were like, "Uh, who are you?"

Nina:

As I was running out the door, in came this young woman, barely five feet tall. As I remember it, she had a flower hat, and a T-shirt that said I LOVE COUNTRY MUSIC. I thought, "Hmmm, not very rock 'n' roll." Not being judgmental—I just didn't think she was what they were looking for.

Martha:

I was in the outfit that I'd put on that day to go work at Weinstein—I was dressed for sorting mail and handing out toilet paper. I had a T-shirt with an iron-on glitter transfer that said, of all things, COUNTRY MUSIC IS IN MY BLOOD. My junior-year roommate (not the Wilhelmina model—this one left school when she got pregnant and married a Bible salesman) gave it to me. And I was in a white tennis skirt and Keds. Not one speck of makeup. I didn't even have a brush for my hair.

After they figured out that I was supposed to audition, they sat me in a barber chair in front of a camera. I read the teleprompter for a bit, and then they said, "Okay, now tell us about a concert that you've been to." I talked about an Earth, Wind & Fire show at Madison Square Garden. I had no idea what was at stake—if I did, I probably would have been too jittery to get the job! The audition was literally three minutes, but by the time it was over, I had a pretty good idea of what this MTV thing was about and I really wanted the gig. I called my brother and said, "I auditioned for something that is perfect for me."

A couple of days later, after getting my hair cut at the Plaza—courtesy of Jane Bryant Quinn—I checked my messages from the corner of Sixth Avenue and Fifty-ninth Street. That was back when you had to access your answering machine with a little beeper. There was a message: Sue Steinberg saying, "Come to the studio, we think we have good news."

I hailed a cab right away. When I got to the studio, I was escorted upstairs to a conference room with executive producers Sue Steinberg and Julian Goldberg. They asked, "So how would you like to have a job where you fly around the country and interview rock stars and go to concerts and be on TV?"

I said, "Okay, I'll take it." I didn't even ask, "How much?" I was twenty-two years old.

Mark:

We were doing run-throughs, practicing as we led up to the channel's debut on August 1. Martha and Alan joined very late, in mid-July. I watched Martha and thought, "Who is this kid? She has no idea what she's doing." Neither did I, but I did know music. It was clear to me that they were desperate as we got closer to the launch: They wanted five VJs, and they didn't have them.

Alan:

In the summer of 1981, I went to a "Way Up North in Mississippi" picnic in Central Park, an event for anybody born, bred, or educated in the state of Mississippi. There were hundreds of people at the picnic, eating watermelon, spitting seeds, doing the barbecue thing. They even—oh, Lord—sang "Dixie."

Bob Pittman showed up in a jacket, snazzily dressed for a hot summer day in New York City. I was wearing some grungy shorts. Bob's father was friends with my father-in-law; they were both Methodist ministers. So I was introduced to Bob; I didn't know a damn thing about him except he was big in radio. I told him I was a struggling actor, bartending at night, going to auditions, trying to catch a ride somewhere. He told me he was working on a new cable channel for Warner AmEx: music video, twenty-four hours a day. "Really? I was just in this David Bowie video." I told him about "Fashion." I couldn't imagine how spinning videos twenty-four hours a day would work, but I was polite about it. Bob was a nice guy, but aloof. A very cool cucumber.

Two weeks later, I got a phone call from Sue Steinberg. I don't know how she got my phone number, but she said, "Bob bumped into you at the park and thinks you should audition for this thing we got going, called The Music Channel."

I went to the audition totally blind. I had to read some teleprompter copy, no problem. I was a good cold reader, if a little stiff. When it came time to describe a recent concert I had seen, that was trouble: The last show I had seen was the Doobie Brothers, about a year earlier, hardly a target band for the channel. I would get halfway through my extemporaneous chitchat, and not know where I was going. I laughed and giggled a lot. Lots of flop sweat, but I was jovial enough in my embarrassment. I ended up doing three torturous auditions, and each one, I just wasn't good at it. I couldn't even pronounce my own name correctly. I kept hitting a hard *T* instead of a soft *t:* "Alan Hun-TER."

A few weeks later, I came home from some other audition, about to go work at the bar. I hadn't heard a lot of good feedback that summer—I had been in the Bowie video and *Annie,* and that was about it. Rejection, that's the actor's life. I checked the messages on my answering machine. Sue Steinberg had left a message, saying they wanted to offer me the job. It made no sense at all.

In a state of total disbelief, I went to meet with Sue. It didn't appear to be a joke or a mistake: She told me how much they would pay me and gave me an envelope with five hundred dollars cash in it to buy some clothes. Totally overwhelmed, I walked home to Jan. I shuffled across the room like a zombie, collapsed on the bed, and said, "Oh my God, Jan, this is fucking real." We both cried: I had a steady gig in New York. The weight of the world was off our shoulders. We could buy a new couch.

Mark:

Carol auditioned for MTV—pretty much anybody who was in radio in New York went down and tried out. Carol was a big star in New York, and beautiful, and smart. It seemed like she would have been perfect. But as it turned out, she was stiff on camera. I think part of the friction that developed in our relationship was that I got the gig and she didn't.

I found out many years later that they cast us as types. According to Sue Steinberg, my niche was that I was the hunk. Which I didn't necessarily agree with, but thank you for the compliment. J. J. was the benign black guy, Nina was the video vamp, Alan was the jock, and Martha was the girl next door that every executive wanted to fuck.

Meg Griffin told me that the day she was supposed to sign her contract, she overheard Bob Pittman on the phone in the next room, only his list was a little different: "We've got our black guy, our Jew, our vixen, and our jock."

4

step right up and don't be shy

MTV Blasts Off

Martha:

The first week I rehearsed with the VJs, we practiced news segments. I'd say, "Here's Billy Joel talking about his new album," and then they would roll one of the audition tapes, where everybody had pretended to be interviewing Billy Joel. But the tape they rolled was always this one particularly goofy audition, done by a guy with longish blond surfer hair.

Then they hired Al—I was shocked when I met him, because he was the guy in the goofy audition tape!

Alan:

I met the other VJs at dinner, downtown at Odeon with some of the executives: Sue Steinberg, who hired us; John Sykes, who was the director of promotion; and John Lack, who came up with the idea of MTV. J. J. was extremely gracious and big-hearted, a fatherly huggy-bear type: "Welcome aboard, kid, let me show you the ropes." Mark seemed pompous—maybe because he didn't know what to make of me. Martha had a coy quality, so I connected with Nina much quicker. That's partially because Nina is Nina and she engages everybody with love and energy. But it was also because we were both actors and we were able to talk about that.

Soon after that, Les Garland took us all out for a "get to know me" dinner—he was second in command under Bob Pittman, our head honcho. Les was a wild man, a big schmoozer. His big early triumph was convincing Mick Jagger to join the "I Want My MTV" ad campaign. When Mick asked what was in it for the Stones, Les whipped out a single dollar bill. Years later, Les became the answer to a trivia question by being the voice of the DJ on Starship's "We Built This City." And, like Pittman, Les had one good eye and one glass eye.

Martha:

I honestly thought the other VJs were the coolest people that I'd ever met in my life. I was starry-eyed and felt so lucky that they had to hang around with me. I have two older brothers who I always thought were the coolest guys around. Being with the VJs made me feel like our mom forced them to babysit me; I was the thrilled little sister.

Mark:

In the earliest days, I thought Martha was just a kid. I was like, "Wow, what is she doing here?" It wasn't really her age that bothered me—it was that she had no sense of the history of rock 'n' roll! It made me question the direction of the channel.

I was so serious and pompous back then. It was because I loved music so much—but geez, Goodman, lighten up. It's only rock 'n' roll.

Alan:

Martha was immediately really good at what she did. Nina was doing great and she was obviously loved by the brass. In the beginning, she was the one they were banking on—a hot rocker girl. She was sexy and she read the prompter well. She was a very good ambassador for the likes of the Scorpions.

Nina:

Alan seemed like an actor, a musical-comedy guy. I thought he had talent, but he didn't seem very rock 'n' roll.

There was a lot of experimenting in the studio, and a lot of kinks to be worked out. You could feel the anticipation because the deadline— August 1, 1981—was coming fast.

Mark:

It was easy and full of excitement—it never crossed my mind that there would ever be a problem. That was my naïveté, I guess.

> *Other news stories on Saturday, August 1, 1981:*
>
> *Air traffic controllers announced they would strike on Monday if they didn't receive a new contract (a strategy that didn't turn out well for them); the Reagan administration announced a plan to intercept boats carrying Haitian refugees. In sports, a seven-week baseball strike was settled, while the Detroit Pistons signed their number one draft pick, Isiah Thomas (in a four-year deal that paid him a total of $1.6 million). Movies released that weekend included the POW drama* Victory, *directed by John Huston and starring Michael Caine and Sylvester Stallone, and* Under the Rainbow, *a comedy about the little people playing Munchkins in* The Wizard of Oz, *starring Chevy Chase and Carrie Fisher.*
>
> *The top five singles in the United States:*
>
>   1. *Rick Springfield, "Jessie's Girl"*
>   2. *Air Supply, "The One That You Love"*
>   3. *Joey Scarbury, "The Theme from 'The Greatest American Hero'"*
>   4. *Kenny Rogers, "I Don't Need You"*
>   5. *Oak Ridge Boys, "Elvira"*

Mark:

For the launch, everyone at MTV, which can't have been more than a hundred people, got in a school bus and went across the river to

Fort Lee, New Jersey. We weren't on the cable system in Manhattan, so we had to go to Jersey to see the network. The launch party was at a blue-hair restaurant called the Loft. There were a lot of old people upstairs, and we were downstairs in the basement. We watched on a television—not a big screen, just a TV wheeled in on a cart like a high-school AV club project. I don't think we even had it in stereo—and they had us plugging the shit out of how MTV was in stereo.

MTV launched with public domain footage of the Apollo 11 mission— a rocket taking off, and then astronauts cavorting on the moon. After a couple of videos, the VJs were introduced in prerecorded clips, touting the awesomeness of MTV. Due to a technical glitch, the clips were played out of order: Mark was supposed to be first, saying "Just moments ago, all the VJs and the crew here at MTV collectively hit our executive producer Sue Steinberg over the head with a bottle of champagne and behold, a new concept is born." Alan ended up being first, saying, "I'll be with you right after Mark," and even today, he playfully touts his "first VJ" status.

Martha:

At 12:01 A.M., the rocket went off and you heard John Lack—one of the network's executives—say, "Ladies and gentlemen, rock and roll." People in the room were sobbing. I had been at MTV for only two weeks, and it was amazing for me. There were people in the room who had started the channel in a hotel room and had been fighting for it for years.

Mark:

I cried. I was so overcome with the fact that we were all there at the beginning of this big thing.

Alan:

We bonded that night. The rocket blasted off, and we looked at each other and realized we were the only five people on the planet doing what we were doing.

The first fifteen videos MTV ever played:

1. *The Buggles, "Video Killed the Radio Star"*
2. *Pat Benatar, "You Better Run"*
3. *Rod Stewart, "She Won't Dance with Me"*
4. *The Who, "You Better You Bet"*
5. *Ph.D., "Little Susie's on the Up"*
6. *Cliff Richard, "We Don't Talk Anymore"*
7. *Pretenders, "Brass in Pocket"*
8. *Todd Rundgren, "Time Heals"*
9. *REO Speedwagon, "Take It on the Run"*
10. *Styx, "Rockin' the Paradise"*
11. *Robin Lane and the Chartbusters, "When Things Go Wrong"*
12. *Split Enz, "History Never Repeats"*
13. *.38 Special, "Hold on Loosely"*
14. *April Wine, "Just Between You and Me"*
15. *Rod Stewart, "Sailing"*

Mark:

People stayed for at least an hour, watching videos. I had seen "Video Killed the Radio Star" and the Pat Benatar video before, but I don't think I had seen .38 Special. There was a fair amount of drinking. It was one of the few times that people at the company all felt that we did this thing together. The company was small enough that everybody was doing all they could for the channel, and their job was important to the final product. I didn't know any of these other people, so I was hanging out mostly with Carol.

Nina was wearing a fishnet top. It wasn't a fine net, and I believe she had no bra on. I thought, "Wow. Okay."

Nina:

I can't believe Mark remembers that. You could have given me fifty million dollars, and I wouldn't have been able to say what I was wearing that night. I owned only one fishnet top: a blue shirt that originally belonged to Kevin, my high-school sweetheart. But if I was wearing it that night, I'm sure you couldn't see through it—because if you could, I wouldn't have left the house.

Mark:

That night, after the launch, I thought about how now MTV was on forever. That was in my head all night: *"Now we have to feed the beast."* Over and over and over again, and it's never, ever, ever, ever going to stop. Shit. How are we going to do that?

5

Let's Make Lots of Money

Contracts and Paychecks

Nina:

My MTV salary wasn't extraordinary—I know the second generation of VJs got way more than we did. But it was enough to live comfortably in Manhattan. I was able to go out to eat and treat my friends. We could have made a lot more money, except MTV had exclusive contracts with us. Procter & Gamble came to me once: They wanted me to endorse a skin-care product, and they were going to buy time on MTV. I was excited, and I took it to John Sykes, one of the top executives. I felt like the cat that brought the mouse home—in the early days, we were hurting for advertisers. John was really nice, and he went to bat for me. But Bob Pittman's philosophy was that he never wanted the VJs to be bigger than the channel. I'm not greedy, but that sucked. It would've been a nice chunk of money to put away for my retirement.

Alan:

In the beginning, I made $27,500. I had been bartending and auditioning for shows, so my criterion was that I wanted to make as much as a chorus boy: On Broadway, they made about $550 a week. I was paying $550 a month in rent. Looking at the apartment buildings across the street that cost $700 to $1,000 a month, I dreamed of living there—if I could just make chorus boy money.

When I got the job at MTV, I didn't have a lawyer. I called Bob Pittman, the executive at MTV who brought me in, and asked if he could suggest a lawyer. I knew it wasn't the smartest move, but he was a family friend and I had no other connections in New York.

Bob was amused but helpful. He said, "Call this guy—he'll take care of you."

I went with Bob's lawyer. He was a good guy, but whose interest was he protecting? My first year was $27,500, then there was a bump in the second year to $35,000, and then $40,000 the third year. I was making $520 a week—it was close enough to my chorus boy goal.

Martha:

When they first signed me, it was a three-year deal. It was $26,000 my first year, then $28,000, then $32,000. I didn't have an agent—my dad was my lawyer.

Alan:

Martha making less than me was pure discrimination—we were equally inexperienced.

Mark:

I think I started at $75,000, maybe $80,000. Because when I was working at WPLJ, I was making about $50,000.

Nina:

I knew how much Mark made, because they accidentally sent his contract to my house. I thought it was mine and opened it—oops!

Martha:

After I signed my MTV contract, I had a whopping 26K coming in. I started looking for apartments so I could move out of African erotic art central. I found a place I liked, and my stepmother, Jane, came to look at it. Being the personal-finance guru that she was, she recited the formula that my rent should be one-quarter of my income. The rent was $750, so I was very close. My own apartment!

I moved into One Astor Place, back in my beloved Greenwich Village, just blocks from the Weinstein dormitory. I had a job, I could pay my own rent—I could even get a kitten without having to ask anyone, "Can I keep it? Can I?" I went to the Elmsford Animal Shelter and got the first of my Beatle-named cats, Prudence.

I *loved* that apartment. It was a tiny studio with a sleeping loft— you climbed up there on a wooden ladder. To me, it seemed like a one-bedroom apartment, even if the bedroom had a three-foot ceiling! I bought a mattress from 1-800-MATTRESS—two, actually, because I used the second one as a couch. I bought a giant TV from Crazy Eddie's, a discount electronics chain in New York. It had a push-button channel-changing panel, which felt very high-tech. I do not believe it had a remote. I got cable courtesy of a guy who hot-wired my Manhattan Cable. I felt guilty afterward, paranoid I would be exposed: "Cable Star Arrested for Stealing Cable!"

Alan:

As soon as I got the job, we went to our creepy German landlord and got a new apartment on the same block. Life picked up from there. I could afford new tennis shoes.

A couple of months into the whole thing, J. J. and I were talking about money. Laughing, he said, "Ah, these cheap bastards. I'm sure you made a pretty good deal with them. I mean, I've been in the business for a while, so I'm at a certain level, but you're new to the game. I hope they're doing right by you." We weren't saying numbers at first, but then J. J. got specific: "If they're not paying you at least 40K, then you're totally getting ripped off."

I laughed awkwardly: "Ha ha ha—no, I'm good." That was the first time it dawned on me: I should have asked for more money. And if J. J. said forty for me, he had to be making eighty.

Martha:

After a year or so, they told me they'd rip up my old contract and give me a new three-year deal for $40,000, $50,000, and $60,000. I would have stuck with the first one—they didn't have to do that. A couple of years later, they tore it up again and I got an even better deal.

Alan:

Six months in, the company told me, "We like what you're doing—we want to renegotiate your contract." Now I can see that they were staggering the contracts. Hire everybody at the same time, and then space out when the contracts expire so you can control them a little more.

Mark:

I would have loved to rip up my contract. By the end of my time at MTV, I was making something like $150,000. I got an agent, and I turned Alan on to him. Many years later, I found out Alan ended up making more money than me.

Alan:

I made almost $200,000 at the end, which was good money for 1987. I had a contract for three years; it would have been $225,000 and $250,000, but I only took advantage of one year. I heard that after us, VJs like Carson Daly and Duff were well into the seven figures. That's okay—we were like the early sports stars.

Mark:

I was astonished that Alan had a better deal than me. I thought I was hot shit—I'm the guy with the history in radio and the knowledge and he's getting more than me? I couldn't believe I didn't even get a favored-nations clause. In retrospect, Alan was the future of MTV: someone who could be wacky and fun, not a music fanatic.

Alan:

With all of us, our fame far outstripped what we were getting paid. If I was traveling on my own dime, I'd be in coach, because I didn't want to pay for first class—I was too cheap. But during the prime of MTV, people would have funny reactions, clearly wondering, "Why are you back here with the cattle?" It made some of the other VJs uncomfortable, but I didn't care. I was going on vacation with my wife, so what was the difference? But people who knew me from TV couldn't figure out how to respond. The stewardess would bring me a bottle of champagne, even though I was sitting in row 32.

6

There's always something Happening and it's usually quite Loud

The First Days of MTV

Alan:

We filmed at a place called Teletronics, in the worst part of Manhattan, near the corner of Thirty-third Street and Tenth Avenue. Before we came there, they were doing commercials and industrial films and talk shows. It was a small studio, so all five of us had to share a single dressing room. Being physically confined like that forced us to relate to each other.

Mark:

I couldn't have cared less that there was only one dressing room. That felt punk rock to me.

Nina:

I didn't mind sharing, but before I went on the air, I would go into the bathroom and lock the door, just so I could have some solitary headspace. I needed some quiet time.

Mark:

It was an unusual situation—a whole new staff, and suddenly we were together all the time, at the studio from seven in the morning to eleven at night. Martha was like a little girl; Nina was spacey but cool; J. J. was pompous, but at least he knew what he was talking about! And I thought Alan was an idiot. Just a buffoon, possibly gay—even though he was married. And we were all changing clothes in front of each other.

Alan:

Inevitably, there was dressing room exposure. It's not my fault that the makeup mirror reflected Martha and Nina trying to get ready behind me.

Martha:

I loved that we were all sailing together on the SS *MTV*. I had no life, so I didn't give a rat's ass about working until eleven at night. We didn't really have any place to sleep, but sometimes I would lie down on a couch at the back of the control room.

Alan:

We were working sixteen-hour days, mainly because nobody, from the crew to the office to us, had a good handle on the job. The whole machine was incredibly inefficient—with the exception of the props guy at the studio, who was this old union guy that I loved, named Leo. Behind the scenes, we kept getting memos changing the strategy, because nobody knew how anything was going to turn out. "Get rid of the green plants, they look too corporate." "Forget the scripts." "Tell the VJs to stand on their heads."

Mark:

Everybody was so young. We had technical limitations, and we didn't even know that we needed to invent what we needed. One of the big things for me was that we couldn't really segue. There was no machine that did that yet—going from one video to another was handled with the fader bar, and it felt very stiff. It killed a lot of momentum.

We had people on staff who had never directed TV before or floor-managed before—they could have been interns. Everybody was just trying to figure it out.

Alan:

J. J. and Mark would come into the studio with a *New York Times* and sit there reading it while they waited for their shifts. I would think, "How can you even read the paper? Why aren't you prepping?" They weren't being cavalier; they knew how to do the gig. I was serious about it, because I had to be: sweating over everything, doing my homework, trying to make every segment brilliant. In the beginning, they rarely were.

Mark:

Alan and Martha had challenges that J. J. and I didn't have. Nina hadn't done this sort of gig, but she had a background of being a fan of rock 'n' roll. I thought J. J. did a great job. He was like, "Well, all right, here we are, it's MTV, how you doing?" And I would be doing this intense whisper. Viewers used to think I was high on the air—my eyes always looked like slits. That was bad makeup application, nothing else. I was never high during VJ segments.

It took me a while to get to where I felt comfortable enough to say what I wanted and be relaxed the way that I was by myself in a radio booth. I was experienced enough in relating to a microphone, knowing that on the other side of that were people. I knew I had to do the same sort of exercise for a camera.

Alan:

I sucked in the beginning. I didn't know what to do without a role to play! I was just supposed to talk and be natural, but I was watching my southern accent really carefully, and I ended up with this weird, almost Shakespearean accent. I was being diligent about my diction, and every day, they'd say, "Just loosen up and be yourself." I'd go home and tell Jan, "They're going to fire me. This is not good."

Martha:

J. J. was the top dog. And Mark, he'd been on WPLJ, so he was second. They were the pros—they knew about music, how to deal with executives, all the ins and outs of the business. Alan, Nina, and I were far less experienced and way more starry-eyed. We called ourselves the Junior VJs. Nina actually came up with the "Junior VJ" term, but she might not have felt like she belonged in that club. She had a lot of history in music, but it wasn't as high-profile as those guys'. She's like me—confident on the outside but not on the inside.

Nina:

I think I was in the middle. Mark and J. J. were too cool to say they were the Senior VJs, but when I was with Martha and Alan, we were the JVJs—the Junior VJs.

Alan:

I wasn't particularly in league with the women, but I did feel shunned by Mark and J. J.—I wasn't part of the boy team.

Mark:

I hated Alan. He seemed like a nice enough yokel, I guess. But I was totally precious about whether something or somebody was rock 'n' roll. I was completely passionate about music—that was all I cared about. So I resented people who got into the business for different reasons. And I knew that Alan and Martha didn't know anything about music. Martha did a rap early on that included the line "Hey, it's all rock 'n' roll, from Helen Reddy to Abba." I was watching in the control room, thinking, "*Whaaaat?* Are you fucking kidding me?"

Martha:

In the early days, I would write down every little piece of information that I wanted to talk about in my "off-the-cuff" segments. So I was constantly studying, reading *Billboard* magazine, *Trouser Press Record Guide,* biographies, anything I could get my hands on. I wish I still had my copy of *Lillian Roxon's Rock Encyclopedia*—I thumbed through it so much, it was totally dog-eared. We saved our *Rolling Stone* magazines, and our *Creem* and *Kerrang!* magazines, because there was no Internet or Wikipedia. You either had the information in your hand, or you had to make five thousand phone calls. Every day, it was like we were cramming for finals. I wasn't partying—I was just a studious little VJ.

Nina:

Martha really put her nose to the grindstone. To this day, we are both meticulous with our research.

Martha:

Nina and I would sit in the library, surrounded by rock encyclopedias and magazines: "Oh, look, here's the Random Note on Adam Ant." We actually held the scripts in our hands and read them. Nina used a clipboard, but I went with index cards. We didn't have a teleprompter.

Alan:

We didn't have electronic teleprompters—but early on, they got us paper teleprompters. Cutting-edge, right?

Martha:

That's right—the script would be typed out on sheets and then they put it through a conveyer belt, basically. They put us on teleprompter, and then they took us off teleprompter.

Alan:

That was another flip-flop. In the beginning, it was totally scripted, and we all came off very stiff, so Bob Pittman said, "Throw the scripts out, no teleprompters." That was a crisis for me, because I didn't have the knowledge to improvise about all the music: "Uhhhh, Def Leppard's concert was really neat." But after a while, the only things that were scripted were the news segments.

Martha:

I can't believe how smooth I was back then, just talking from bullet points. I don't think I could do it now.

Alan:

Martha was very good extemporaneously, and Mark had it down pretty well. Nina wanted the total script, the way I did. She would pore over every word.

When I got home at night, the packet for the next day would be waiting by the door of my apartment, delivered by car service. It had the music log for my shift, which was the list of videos I'd be playing, and the scripted news segments. I'd do my homework, buzzed or not: I dutifully went through it and underlined everything, and then I went to bed.

Nina:

Sometimes I'd take a break from the next day's script and go to Radio City Music Hall. I lived on Fifty-sixth Street, so it was easy to walk over there, and I always had tickets. I'd see a couple of songs and walk home. It was like walking to the corner bar, except it was Radio City.

Mark:

At the time, we thought our set was so relaxed and funky, but really, it was just a brick wall with a tennis racket leaning up in the corner. It was supposed to be like a kid's rec room, I guess, but it looked like a bare, empty loft. There was almost nothing there: A bicycle, a barber's chair, two steps up to a wooden platform, and a bay window that looked out on nowhere. It took them a long time to figure out we needed more stuff in there.

Alan:

It was a pretty basic set. There were three or four different areas you could do setups.

Mark:

Alan always seemed to be by the brick wall, which had a monitor built into it. They could move that in and out. Either that, or he was doing stupid shit up on the platform. There's footage of him literally falling off the thing.

Alan:

It was a fun little playground for a while.

Mark:

I was having the best time ever. I was out of the WPLJ job, which I hated. I was making a little more money, and I believed in MTV's potential. I had been doing the WPLJ job on autopilot, but now I was coming to work every day feeling passionate about what I was doing, and that was phenomenal.

> *Excerpts from a September 1981 memo (four pages, single-spaced) from Mark Goodman to Sue Steinberg, on the subject "Ideas":*
>
> *The audience of MTV will not be like the average TV audience. They will be, in many cases, more musically aware than many people involved with this project. The fact that some of our audience may not notice some of the fine points of our presentation is no reason for*

us not to strive for perfection in that area. All people involved in the research for scripting and on-air presentation must be authorities. In a time when cable TV means specialization and precise targeting of audience, we cannot afford to fall back on lowest common denominator programming. All of us must have a clear picture of who we are and want to be if we target on the demo.

We should strive to involve our listeners at every turn. Make the channel one-to-one. Never refer to "all of you watching." Instead of asking for comments, let's ask a question of the week and offer bumper stickers or one of our other fabulous promotional items to all who respond.

If we are, in fact, a new and alternative entertainment form, then let's do something new with music on TV. We've got 24 hours a day, 7 days a week to do it. Wild idol humor and "in-jokes" are not new, nor do they represent an alternative. With the immediacy of video, we can thrust the excitement of rock 'n' roll into living rooms like never before, not just with video performance tapes.

The concepts I have mentioned here are essential for success against our inevitable competition. We have the chance now to position ourselves as the standard for the genre, the ones to emulate, or face the possibility of being the ones who took that bold first step and stumbled.

don't talk to strangers

The Wages of Semi-Fame

Martha:

J. J. almost quit a couple of weeks after we started. It might have been because it was John Lee Hooker's birthday. He wanted to mention it on the air, and the producers said, "Oh, who cares about that?"

Nina:

It was because J. J. wore his beloved black jumpsuit. I wasn't in the studio at the time, but I heard he was told in no uncertain terms by one of the executive producers never to wear it again. This didn't sit well with J. J., who thought he should be able to wear what he wanted.

Alan:

Was the jumpsuit showing too much of his package? Or was it that he was wearing it with some tan Beatle boots?

Mark:

Jumpsuits were kind of cool back then, I guess. Pete Townshend used to wear them. J. J.'s wasn't flattering—he was a little chubby—but it wasn't horrible either.

Nina:

I thought he looked just fine in it. The jumpsuit fit his personality. And management can't have taken offense with jumpsuits per se—I wore many of them during my time at MTV, and can even be seen in them in some promo photos. But the whole incident was so unpleasant for J. J., he seriously considered bailing from MTV.

Martha:

After work, I passed by J. J.'s hotel on Madison Avenue, and thought, "I'm going to talk to him." I can't imagine how I got the nerve, but I called him from the house phone in the lobby and he let me come up.

He had a huge suite in this fancy hotel, and he was in a spa bathrobe, like Hugh Hefner. For some reason, that didn't seem weird. I said, "You were right about what you said today, but I think that maybe you're blowing it out of proportion. If you don't mind me saying so, you might be a little homesick. But you should stay—if you leave, I think you'll wind up regretting it." I thought MTV was the greatest situation ever, and I couldn't imagine how anybody else might not feel the same way.

At the end of our conversation, he said, "Okay, I'm going to stay." Then he took me out to dinner at some seafood restaurant. MTV pulled people together—here I was, just graduated from college, and I was hanging out with a fortysomething black guy, ex-marine, rock history out the wazoo. There's no other situation in a thousand years where I would have come in contact with J. J., but that night cemented our friendship. From then on, he treated me like his little sister—he always looked out for me.

Alan:

Everything I do, sports or acting or dance, I either get it the first time and it's totally natural to me, or I get a handle on it around the thirtieth take. Everything in between is this awful purgatory. And the second scenario was happening to me at MTV. I didn't know what I was doing and I felt miserable.

One day, Nina took me across the street to a bar called Sam's. She was so diplomatic. She said, "Al, you're doing really good." And then she told me just to think about it as an acting job. I was looking at her sideways, thinking, "You're trying to tell me something, aren't you?" She didn't say, "They're going to fire you"—she just said, "I think we all need to step up the game a little bit."

I said, "Am I on thin ice?"

She said, "I don't know. But there's ways you can work this. Just use that acting."

Nina:

I was coming from the Strasberg school of acting that you help your fellow actor. I didn't know they were upset with Alan, but I was concerned for him—he was bouncing off the walls of the studio, and what he was doing just wasn't rock 'n' roll.

Martha:

A few days after I started, the producers told me, "You're going to do your first interview. How about you interview Daryl Hall and John Oates?"

I panicked: "Oh, no, I can't do that. Don't you have an intro artist for me to interview? You should give them to Mark or J. J."

MTV insisted—I guess it was a trial-by-fire philosophy.

Nina:

I liked doing interviews because I could keep quiet. I liked being able to listen.

Mark:

In the early days, one of the big questions we had to ask everybody we interviewed was "Have you done a video?"

Alan:

One of my first interviews was with Paul Simon and Art Garfunkel, when they reunited for a free concert in Central Park. I was excited—I used to listen to my big brothers' Simon and Garfunkel albums and I dug their music. I studied, and wrote questions with the producer. When they sat down, Paul Simon pegged me right off the bat as a twenty-four-year-old pup. Every question I asked, he answered yes or no or "Why do you ask that, Alan?" I was sweating, and Art was embarrassed because Paul was beating up on me so bad. He kept saying, "Come on, Paul, be nice."

Martha:

Another interview I did early on was with Rick Springfield. When MTV launched, he had the number one single in the United States, with "Jessie's Girl." Not long ago, I asked Rick what his first impression of MTV was, and he said, "Well, actually it was you, Martha." He told me that when he came in, he looked around and thought, "Who is this kid talking to me?" I'm sure his interviews before then had been with actual journalists. He must have thought, "What kind of operation is this? Can't I talk to an adult?"

I had a huge crush on Rick—who didn't? I had visions of being Mrs. Rick Springfield. I was hoping he'd ask me out, or whisk me away in his limo. But I did that interview wearing a big cowl-neck sweater, with yards of fabric wrapped around my neck. Cleavage did not enter the picture in any way.

Mark:

Rick's a good friend of mine now, but back then I thought of him as a soap star who wanted to sing. I always loved great pop tunes, and Rick delivered them pretty consistently, but soap operas meant nothing to me. The only connection I had with him at the time was that Alan used to do a hysterical impression of how Rick played guitar in the "Jessie's Girl" video, with that extra-wide stance and a guitar strum that looked like he was sawing wood.

Nina:

Adam Ant visited MTV in August, the first month we were on the air. I thought, "He's not really a handsome guy, but he's beautiful." He had exquisite lips and skin. Adam invited me to his show—New York used to have summertime concerts on the Pier, which was an actual pier on the Hudson River, near the *Intrepid* aircraft carrier. I didn't feel like Adam was making a move on me, so I went to the show, and then hung out backstage afterward. He asked me to go back to his hotel—he wanted some rice pudding. So we sat in the restaurant at the Sheraton and ate rice pudding.

Afterward, everybody at MTV was convinced we had a thing going on, which wasn't true at all. The most intimate thing we shared is that he told me how he got his lips to look so good: He used gold lip gloss. So I started using gold lip gloss on top of everything else.

But from then on, every morning in the dressing room, our stage manager would knock on the door and say, "It's Adam, ship's here." I never heard the end of it.

Mark:

Early on, the plan was to do a Saturday night concert, live, from somewhere every weekend. So in September 1981, MTV sent me to Houston to introduce Journey. It was an arena show, eighteen thousand people or so, and we weren't on most cable systems in Texas yet. The crowd had no idea who I was; Journey had no idea who I was. But we were on in College Station, which is about a hundred miles away from Houston. I went onstage and my rap was something like, "Look, you people don't know who I am, but hopefully, you're going to be watching MTV in the future." And I said, "Anybody here from College Station?" There were about a hundred people, making a lot of noise, and it was shocking to me that they recognized me. Of course, the other 17,900 people didn't.

Martha:

Cable TV had no cachet in 1981. Cable meant HBO and Ugly
George—he resembled MTV's "Moon Man" in that he was always
dressed in silver, a tinfoil outfit. Somehow Ugly George could convince girls to take their clothes off.

Mark:

At the time, cable in New York was basically Robin Byrd, a porn actress who hosted her own program, and this other guy Al Goldstein,
who had a naked talk show. That blew my mind when I moved to
New York—naked people on TV talking about politics. And this guy
named Ugly George had a show on one of the public-access channels.
He walked around Manhattan in a tinfoil suit—it looked like a giant
oven mitt—and a portapak for his camera on his back. And he would
talk women into getting undressed in alleyways or the vestibules of
apartment buildings. They wouldn't have sex, they would just get
naked on camera. I had tons of respect for the guy. I couldn't speak to
anybody, and this guy would walk up to hot women, total strangers,
and regularly convince them to get undressed on camera.

One day, Carol and I were walking on Eighth Avenue; we looked
up the street and saw Ugly George. He had just begun this conversation with a woman, and they hadn't gone into the vestibule yet. Carol
jumped in front of the camera and said to this girl, "Don't listen to
this guy, he's a fucking asshole. You'll make a fool out of yourself in
front of the three people who are watching his show." We watched the
show later that week and he did a funny voice-over about "Oh, here
comes Miss Tight Ass walking up the street, watch her, she's going to
be trouble." So Carol was on his show, and she was great.

Alan:

Even after MTV launched, I kept my bartending job. I told my coworkers, "I've got this job—I go down to the studio on Thirty-third
and Tenth and I do television." They'd say, "Oh, good, you got a gig.
You're keeping this job, right?" Cable was all about public access,

where pretty much anybody with a camera could get on the air. On channel 10, you had Ugly George, Robin Byrd, and the crank-call show. When I told people I was working on a music channel, they were happy for me, but they had no idea what I was talking about—MTV wasn't on cable in New York City at that point, so they assumed I had to be doing some sort of porno thing.

Mark:

We had these MTV bumper stickers—our slogan at the beginning was "You'll never look at music the same way again." Every single cab I got into in 1981, I slapped one of those stickers on the partition. Normally, when you work at a radio station, you never, ever wear the radio station T-shirt. But I wore the MTV T-shirts because I was really proud to be associated with the network and I wanted to spread the word.

Nina:

Because we weren't on in New York, we weren't aware of how popular we were in other parts of the country. They used to send us on personal appearances—one of my early ones was in San Antonio, Texas. I was in a limousine with my minder, going to a record store in a mall. We drove into the parking lot, and there was a line around the block. I figured there was some rock star in town doing autographs at the same time and I asked, "Who's here?"

He said, "You."

Alan:

I was bartending at the Magic Pan, the cabaret where Jan was performing. I wasn't a very good bartender—I was a one-drink-at-a-time kind of guy. I couldn't line up five glasses and pour 'em all down, and I'd always have to look up how to make a Rob Roy or a Manhattan. But I could make a mean daiquiri, because that's what the place was famous for.

I was working fourteen- and sixteen-hour days at MTV, but I kept bartending on weekends. It wasn't that I thought MTV was going to go away, because it seemed like there was a lot of money involved—I just convinced myself that I was ensuring the success of MTV by keeping that job. I thought that if I said, "Fuck the bartending job," the next day it would all blow up.

One night, about a month after MTV launched, I was at work making daiquiris, and this dude from New Jersey was sitting at the bar, looking at me funny. He'd already had a couple, and I had no idea why he was at this cabaret by himself. Finally he said, "You look familiar."

I didn't help him out, because it didn't dawn on me. "I don't know, do you want another daiquiri?"

Then he said, "There's this music show all the time on my cable station. You look like one of those guys."

I said, "Ohhhhh, you watch MTV."

"Yeah, MTV, that's it. You look like that guy—Mark." I swear he used Mark's name.

"Actually, I'm Alan Hunter."

"Yeah, that's it, Alan Hunter! I've seen you on MTV. What the fuck? Why are you here?" He was confused, and for the life of me, I could not figure out how to explain why I was there mixing daiquiris. I thought, "Wow, I don't think I'm going to be a bartender anymore." I finished my shift and quit.

sometimes you tell the day by the bottle that you drink

Life in Hell's Kitchen

Alan:

Thirty-third and Tenth was a pretty scenic area—we were right at the bottom of Hell's Kitchen, just before you hit Chelsea, and we had hookers on the street right outside the studio. There was a dive bar and grill next door to Teletronics called Sam's—we all repaired there during lunch and after hours. If you bellied up to the counter, there'd always be some working girls hanging out.

Mark:

The only reason we took breaks when we were shooting was because we had a union crew. So when they had their contractual rest periods, we'd all go hang out at Sam's and have some beers.

Nina:

The waiter was named George, and he always seemed harried and hurried. His hygiene was a bit on the fragrant side, and he had a serious scar down one of his cheeks—it looked like he had been sliced by a switchblade. He would get orders wrong, and then he'd get mad at us. The attitude was a lot like the John Belushi sketch on *Saturday Night Live:* "Cheeseburger, cheeseburger, cheeseburger."

Mark:

I loved that neighborhood—it was like nothing I had ever seen before in my life. On one of those late nights, I was upstairs on the second floor, looking out the window. A girl in hot pants was in this guy's parked car. He had his pants around his ankles and she was going down on him. And while she was doing that, she was also going through his pants pocket, looking for his wallet.

Carol and I used to rent cars every weekend to get out of town. One Friday afternoon, after I finished shooting, I picked up a car somewhere in the neighborhood. I stopped at Thirty-third and Eleventh; I was about to turn right to go uptown, and I was futzing with the radio. Just as I was about to make my turn, I heard a knock on the window. I turned, and there were two giant black tits pushed up against the glass, belonging to a three-hundred-pound woman with no shirt. That was the neighborhood.

Alan:

When Joe Cocker came to the studio, he arrived in a taxi, nobody with him. Afterward, he was hanging around. I was a big Cocker fan, so I was chatting him up. I asked him if he needed us to get him a ride or a taxi—"No, mate, I'm all right." Somebody mentioned something about going next door and getting a drink. Well, of course he'd like a drink. A bunch of us went to Sam's.

We sat there and hung out with Joe Cocker for an hour while he drank his Scotch whisky. And I thought, "This is pretty good." I don't know what his reasons for hanging out with me were—I was pretty sure he didn't sit around watching MTV all day long. Honestly, it was probably alcoholism—if somebody's buying, you'll find a friend wherever you can. He had some interesting stories, and I thought, "Wow, this is a cool job." He wouldn't have left if I hadn't said I had to go.

Nina:

Joe Cocker had a little crush on me. I guess I flapped my hands around a lot on the air, and he told me that he had never seen anybody gesticulate more than he did. And that's pretty serious: The first time my mother saw Joe Cocker, she honestly thought he had Saint Vitus's dance. I decided to take it as a compliment.

He invited me to see him play, and there was a party afterward. He was clean and sober at this point, but Marianne Faithfull, who was also there, wasn't. I love Marianne, just love her, but she was getting worked up. She wanted Joe to go out on the back deck at this party, and he wouldn't. He wanted to be with me. It wasn't a date, but he liked me.

She thought I was stopping him from going out to the back deck with her—which I wasn't—so she deliberately knocked over her wine on me. I had idolized her since I was a little girl, so I thought, "Wow, Marianne Faithfull dumped her wine on me! That's pretty cool."

9

ain't Nothing Gonna Break My stride

Early Triumphs and Tribulations

Alan:

One day, I was in the greenroom on lunch break, joking around. A producer, Liz Nealon, said, "That's what we need you to do on camera." She got me walking and talking, so I wasn't stationary in a chair like a news anchorman—a simple thing, but it liberated me. I started using props the way actors do sometimes, to get themselves out of their heads by having a physical object to focus on. I brought in sock puppets, or pictures of the other VJs for the cut-a-hole-in-the-mouth gag. The crew made suggestions: "Here's a pumpkin. You'll carve it up and we'll pretend we've got the camera inside it looking out." I was finally having fun; everything was flowing. Much to the chagrin of Mark, who couldn't believe my clown schtick was working.

Mark:

One show in particular, Alan was doing something with finger puppets. I was on right after him, and I was watching him, completely disgusted with his cluelessness. Of course, I couldn't let it stand. When I went on air, I picked up the tennis racket that we had leaning in a corner of the set for no apparent reason, and I grabbed the finger puppets that Alan had left on a shelf. I said, "So, Alan Hunter. Thanks, Al!" And *boom!*—I started whacking the finger puppets with the racket, serving them off the set.

Alan:

Mark was definitely not passive-aggressive. I was in awe of him, and kind of intimidated by him, but I had to do what I needed to do to make myself comfortable in front of the camera. I'd start a segment lying down on the ground, upside down with my feet up in the air. It didn't make a lick of sense, but the camera guys and the crew were supporting it, because it was kind of fun. It was 24/7 cable, and I had the overnight shift, so I did whatever I could for somebody watching at 3 A.M. I don't think it was particularly good television, but it was different.

Mark:

I just thought "What the fuck is he doing here?" And I was an asshole back then, so I didn't think about hurting anybody's feelings. When it came to the job, I knew I was always right. But there were other aspects of Alan I wasn't aware of, or didn't care about. He's a talented actor, and he's really funny. And the sweetest guy you would ever want to meet. Over the years, we've become best friends.

Alan:

About a half year in, Mark and I started to bond. We'd make jokes in the dressing room—I could always crack him up with this schtick where I would pretend to throw up. One day, we were getting dressed, and the Police's "Every Little Thing She Does Is Magic" was playing on the monitor. We looked at each other and agreed we had a very cool job. I told him, "I hope this MTV thing lasts." It was a good moment.

Martha:

The great thing about those early days was that everyone on the crew had a role. Everyone felt important and everyone was inspired. The audio guys, the video guys, the cameramen—if anyone had an idea, it was tossed in the mix and experimented with. It really was, "Hey kids, let's put on a show." The VJs were part of the team like everyone else. There were tons of times when I would go into the control room and time the VJ segments. Usually a production assistant would do that, but if there weren't any PAs around, I'd sit next to the assistant director with a stopwatch and write the times in the shift log.

Alan:

We started stretching for anything to fill up the segments. Sometimes it would be a gag with chroma-key—green-screen technology—that put us in front of some weird picture or made us look like we were three inches tall. When we weren't reporting the news, we would do anything to make our segments mesh with the fun of the videos.

Mark:

One day, Alan dressed up like an actual clown, in full costume and whiteface. This gave him license to act like an even bigger dick. He came on Martha's show and did this bum-clown schtick, saying, "Show us your nipples!" You could hear through the cameramen's headsets that everybody in the control room was going crazy and applauding.

Nina:

I had lost my grandfather a year earlier, and then my dad died. Having the work kept me going. But I guess one day I wasn't as sparkly as usual. Cameraman Michael Pelech wanted to cheer me up, so he created "runaway camera."

Alan:

One day, out of nowhere, Pelech thought up this gag in which the camera had gone rogue. He gave me and the director a heads-up, and when we came out of a video, he screamed *"Runaway caaaaameraaa!"* and pushed the camera hard enough that it rolled through the set, between me and the other camera. He ran behind it as if he were trying to catch up with it.

The runaway camera became a regular bit that happened with all the VJs. The rest of the crew—floor producers, set guys, interns, whoever was available—would all run behind Michael after the camera gone loose. The jock on air would placidly continue with the business at hand.

I'm not saying that David Letterman copied us, but when you look at his early shows, you can see him doing the same mess-with-the-camera schtick. Clearly, something was in the air.

Martha:

When I see runaway camera now, it just looks like love. We were all together, fighting for this unified goal: a dynamic rock 'n' roll environment on TV. Once a lighting guy streaked behind me on camera.

Mark:

Stark fucking naked, bounding across the set behind Martha, who was shrieking.

Nina:

Sometimes we flagrantly misbehaved by locking the doors to the studio and having epic water fights. That would happen around ten at night, when everybody had been there for fourteen hours.

Martha:

Sometimes on long days, the crew could see that the VJs were getting tired, and would do whatever they could to wake us up: wear hats, sing songs, tell jokes, anything to make it work.

Nina:

Every morning, our two main cameramen, Jerry and Michael, would give me a "cameraman sandwich"—they'd come on each side and squeeze me as hard as they could. Being an only child, it felt like having brothers.

Martha:

We were really lucky that MTV wasn't on Manhattan cable for the first year. The executives and their friends couldn't see it, which gave us an opportunity to bond and figure out how to make our segments work, without 127 outside opinions.

Mark:

Radio is an individual sport and TV is a team sport. The hierarchy on the set when we were shooting segments wasn't really clear. My sense of the situation was that I knew what I was doing, so I was the boss. But I was working with the associate producer on the floor, who would come to me before a segment and say what was planned. "Okay, you're going to some music news and then we're going to these graphics for the concert dates. Okay? Great, count him in. Five, four, three, two . . ." The structure of the segment was determined by what visual elements they had set up in the control room.

Nina:

The three associate producers rotated on the floor. Each of those producers clicked with different VJs. I always felt that Liz Nealon was a Nina producer—she knew how to handle me. And maybe Brian Diamond was more of an Alan and Martha producer.

Mark:

At the time, I was about thirty, and everyone was younger than me, except for J. J. And in some cases, a lot younger—right out of college. I could get along with them just fine, but I didn't really want to take orders from these associate producers. Brian Diamond was a cool rocker kid, funny and knowledgeable, and straddled the line between getting the job done and being easy to work with. Whereas Liz Nealon was a nut-crusher who knew that she was in charge. She was really smart, and kind of terrifying. Alan did a great impression of Liz getting disgusted with a segment: She'd throw up her hands and walk away. But I trusted her feedback. I didn't know that she was helping Alan out with how he should present himself; she never said anything like that to me. I guess she thought I was all right and I did my job.

Martha:

The best-kept secret about MTV was that the VJs weren't actually watching the videos. It doesn't pay to have a television crew sit around and watch "Hungry Like the Wolf" fifty times. So we would just say, "Hey, that was Pat Benatar, 'Hit Me with Your Best Shot.'" Cut. Move. "Oh my God, Quiet Riot, aren't they amazing?" Many times we would introduce videos that the channel hadn't received yet. We were working a couple of days ahead of the broadcast, and then the videos got delivered straight to the satellite uplink center on Long Island. We'd say, "Wow, that was the new Rolling Stones video," hoping that it didn't end with babies being decapitated or something else that we should be reacting to.

Nina:

We didn't reshoot very much—sometimes if a producer thought we could do something better, we'd do it again. We tried to avoid burning back the tape, unless there was a big problem. Early on, we played a video by Carlene Carter, June Carter's daughter (not with Johnny Cash). She was married to Nick Lowe, and she had put out a rockabilly country album. I did a segment, sitting on the set in the barber chair, and I said, "Carlene Carter, she came out with that album and said she's the one who put the 'blank' in 'country.'" To this day, I have never said that actual word—years later, I did *The Vagina Monologues,* and I made sure to pick the pieces that didn't have that word in it.

We shot the segment, the floor producer was cool with it, and everyone thought it was fine. Then it got out to Smithtown, the broadcast center in Long Island, and the guys at Smithtown freaked out. I got in trouble and we had to reshoot it, but I didn't actually say anything! Carlene Carter could have been the one who put the "tree" in "country"!

Martha:

When we first started MTV, we'd finish a segment—"I'm Martha Quinn, and right now, Split Enz"—and wait for the light to go off, indicating we were off the air. And you'd get panicked and sweaty while you were waiting, staring at the camera.

One day, Mark came into the studio on fire, and said, "Guys, I saw Dan Rather do something. We have to do it too. At the end of the segment, turn and look as though you're looking at a monitor." It sounds obvious, but it was huge. It was a godsend.

Mark:

I was always trying to figure out how to bridge the gap between the segments and the videos. The videos were so amazing, and I always felt like our segments would bring everything to a screeching halt. The other thing I came up with was us moving as the segments opened— that ended up being overkill.

Martha:

Walking and talking? I thought that was helpful.

Mark:

What wound up happening was we ran all over the freaking set, like little Energizer bunnies. Eventually one of the executives told me, "I'm getting exhausted watching you. Stop running around all over the place. Where are you going?"

Alan:

I did a cartwheel into the shot one time. I was always trying to break free of that "Three, two, one, go be a talking head" routine. So I suggested, "Why don't I start the segment off-camera? And then enter with a back handspring."

Everybody said, "That sounds good to me, I'm bored too, let's go." I came crashing into the shot and slammed into the camera. I broke the teleprompter and glass went flying all over the place. I sprang up and said, "Well, there you go, and here's the Go-Go's."

Martha:

My senior year in college, when I heard John Lennon got shot, I went up to the Dakota with all the other devastated Beatles fans and left flowers. If you check the front page of the *New York Times,* you can see the back of my head in a photo, in my Eddie Bauer parka. Six months later, in June 1981, I went back to the Dakota, but this time as a VJ interviewing Yoko Ono. It was surreal walking past the area where I'd stood and grieved with hundreds of other mourners. I kept telling myself, over and over, "Don't cry." No one knew what to think of Yoko at that point—some people were still nursing the "she broke up the Beatles" resentment. But she was 100 percent lovely, and even invited me to one of Sean's birthday parties.

December 1981, on the first anniversary of Lennon's death, I was taping a segment in the studio, and I was going on and on about John and what he meant to me, practically having an emotional breakdown on the air. The director stopped me and came out to talk to me. He was trying to console me, but the message boiled down to "You're going on way too long."

Nina:

My worst moment was interviewing Frank Zappa. There's nothing else even close to it in my whole career.

Mark:

Three months in, Nina hosted a show in New York that was broadcast live, a concert with Frank Zappa on Halloween. Zappa ripped her to shreds and she didn't even realize it.

Nina:

He gave me trouble from the rehearsal on. He was just condescending and rude the whole time. I came in wearing a beautiful hand-made poncho from Argentina, and he kneeled down in front of me, like he was pretending to be a midget, because I was shorter than he was! He sarcastically called me the "little MTV lady." I had some experience interviewing the punks in L.A., but they were nothing compared to that obnoxious guy: He asked me to jump up and down on camera. If it happened today, I could put him in his place, but back then, I did not know how to handle it. As soon as the camera went off, I ran into the bathroom, not wanting to come out. I just was not ready for him.

Alan:

People loved Nina's vulnerability and her sweet nature. She didn't do well with people who were being dicks—she got flustered and gave everybody the benefit of the doubt. She wasn't made to be around people with a mean or cynical spirit.

Nina:

J. J. probably should have done the interview. Zappa never would have acted that way with him. Mark, possibly. Al and Martha, it would have been the same as me, if not worse.

Martha:

When I hosted a show with Zappa years later, he was a doll. Maybe he liked that I could quote from the Mothers' *Fillmore* album, or maybe he was comfortable because we were shooting at his house up in the Hollywood Hills. I'm sure if he met Nina in different circumstances, they would have gotten along great.

Alan:

It wasn't a fair match. Afterward, J. J. said, "He's a beast for anybody."

I was a big Zappa fan, but when I interviewed him, a few years later, he was a total jerk. "Yes." "No." "Why would you ask that, Alan?" "Well, that's a stupid question." Two weeks later, he came back to the studio with his daughter, Moon Unit Zappa. She was doing a guest VJ spot and she told him he owed me an apology. He said, "I was just feeling ornery that day."

Mark:

When Nina was hired, she was the video vamp, she was a hottie, and she was going to be the number one jock. She was perfect for what they had in mind, and they gave her a great time slot. That Zappa show was a big black mark on her record, and after that, she was on from 4 A.M. to 8 A.M. Everyone else had longer shifts and better times. They really kicked her hard for it. She was so insecure after that, and I don't think she ever really fully recovered from it.

Alan:

We all felt really bad about Nina's fall from grace.

Nina:

Years later, Mark told me about how it affected my career at MTV, but I was blissfully unaware of it at the time. Nobody in management ever said anything about it to me. Nobody ever said, "Well, next time, if you run into somebody like that, you should do this." Not that there was anybody else quite as obnoxious as that.

I just knew it was a fiasco. I had never been publicly humiliated like that, and it undermined my confidence. I wanted to hide forever. I wish there had been somebody there to support me, or a producer to slap him around. What were they doing? Because I know I was running into the bathroom by myself.

10

Here in my car, I feel safest of all

Rental Cars and Limousines

Martha:

All five of us used to go to concerts together at the Brendan Byrne Arena, which was part of the Meadowlands complex in New Jersey. MTV had just started, and they weren't paying for limousines, but they'd spring for a rental car. I would always volunteer to drive: I'd go to Hertz, then drive all over Manhattan, picking up the VJs. I didn't care that it took an extra hour—I felt privileged that I was spending time with the other VJs. I was in heaven.

First, I'd get Mark—he lived at 3333 Henry Hudson Parkway, in Riverdale in the Bronx, and I would drive all the way up there. Then Nina from her apartment in Midtown, Al from his transient hotel/ apartment building, and J. J. from his pad in the West Village. I wish I could go back and eavesdrop on one of those rides.

When we got to the parking lot of the Brendan Byrne and climbed out, people would freak, because New Jersey cable had MTV.

Nina:

It was like we were getting out of a clownmobile. We used to go see a lot of concerts at the Brendan Byrne, but after a while, we were getting mobbed in our seats, so we had to sit in private boxes.

Alan:

Early on, I didn't care if they were toting us around town in cars or not. But J. J. got incensed about it. He would say, "It's bullshit that they don't give us car service." I was still taking the subway, and I was glad to have five tokens in my pocket, unlike the year before, when I was broke. But he got me pumped up about the issue, and then I became relentless.

Mark:

I took the position with the MTV executives that it was bad image management, not only for the five of us, but also for the company, for us to show up at these concerts in a rented Ford. I said, "We should be in a limo." Much to my surprise, they went for it.

Alan:

Once we had car service, we totally abused it. They gave us a big stack of vouchers and told us to go for it. I got arrogant about it. Literally, if I had five blocks to walk, I would call the service and wait ten minutes for the car to show. My perspective got really skewed. When the first bill came in, it was humongous, but they didn't tell us to lay off.

Martha:

I took the subway everywhere, even after MTV gave us cars. If it was raining, I knew I'd get to the studio faster if I just grabbed the subway at Astor Place.

Excerpts from a Mark Goodman letter to the XYZ cab company, dated December 28, 1981:

On the morning of December 24, 1981, an incident occurred between myself and the driver of cab number 46.
    I called XYZ that morning and rushed out of the house, late for

*the television studio where I work. As we began heading for 503
West 33rd Street, I realized I had left my home on West 72nd Street
without a voucher. I told the driver that I had made this mistake
and began to suggest the obvious alternative: Deliver me to my
destination, leave the meter running, and allow me to go into the
studio and obtain a voucher.*

*The driver raised his voice immediately, not even letting me finish
my sentence, saying, as he began to swerve toward the curb, that he
would have to have a voucher. He threatened (loudly) at this point
to take me back to West 72nd Street. When I protested, he radioed
for instructions. The instruction from the base was to ask me to pay
the $3.50 over the meter. The driver, refusing to hear any logical
alternative, or suggest that to the dispatcher, told me what he had
been instructed to do. All the while, his manner was loud, rude, and
threatening.*

*As we approached the studio on West 33rd Street, I pulled out my
wallet and realized that I did not have as much cash as I thought. I
began to say that I didn't think I could pay the fare plus the $3.50
and have any money to make it through the rest of the day. I had
not gotten more than half of the sentence out when this driver wildly
stamped on the gas pedal, hurling me back against the seat. He locked
the doors and began shouting, as we passed my destination, that he
was taking me back to West 72nd Street. He was screaming that he
would not let me out of the cab until I paid.*

*As we raced along 33rd Street, I tried desperately to make him
understand my problem, raising my voice myself to try and be heard.
By the time we reached a stoplight at the end of the block, he was
threatening to kill me, poking a screwdriver at me over the seat
back.*

*By this time, I was trying to get out of the cab—not to escape
paying, that idea is obviously ludicrous in this situation—but to
protect myself. Finally, when it became clear to me that this driver
was incapable of any reasonable discourse, or any logical thought,
I threw $20.00 on the front seat, trying to avoid the screwdriver.
Cursing at me as he counted my change (the wrong change—it was
$1.00 short), the driver continued to act not just unreasonably,
but uncontrollably and irrationally—he seemed truly dangerous. I*

am thankful that this driver did not have a gun. Indeed, I wonder whether a man like this should be permitted to drive.

Please let me know in writing how you have dealt with this situation.

Sincerely,
Mark Goodman

Mark:

I didn't even live that far from the studio.

11

I Hope That When This Issue's Gone, I'll See You When Your Clothes Are On

Nude Photographs

Mark:

Never in my life was I able to pick up a girl in a bar, just walk up to somebody and be that macho dude. But once MTV started, pretty girls started coming on to me. Alan and I were getting pictures in the mail, and we started having a contest.

Alan:

In the beginning, our fan mail came in dribs and drabs. Nina got lots of it, and Martha had a lot too, and I had a scant few envelopes. But it didn't take long until the mail started to stream in from Middle America, and I didn't have anything more important to do than to read it. So Mark and I had a contest as to who would get the first naked picture—because we could feel that they were coming.

One day I got a fat envelope that smelled of perfume. I opened it up—Mark was there with me—and there was a five-page letter and a picture: a buxom naked woman built like a brick house. I was celebrating: *"Yes, I'm the winner!"* So I read the letter: "Dear Alan, I love

MTV. I love watching you—you're so sexy." Sweet, this is great. "But my biggest fantasies are for Journey—they're the best band ever. I've given you this picture hoping that you can get it to Steve Perry."

Mark was shouting, "You don't win! That's not for you! You can't be a pass-through!" We were making up the rules as we went along. I argued for a little while, but honestly, it was deflating. It emphasized that we weren't actually stars—we were just the conduits.

Mark:

If you ask me, I was the winner. I got one card—a beautiful personal note with a wax seal on the back. It didn't have a picture attached, but it was very feminine. I opened it up and it said, in lovely cursive handwriting, "Wanna meet a girl who can suck the chrome off a trailer hitch?" And there was a P.S.: "If you can't come, send Al."

Alan:

We had heard that Nina had posed for *Playboy*, and we were all curious to scope it out, but nobody had a copy. Then I was doing a personal appearance for the channel, and when I was signing autographs, some guy came up to me with a copy of the magazine. I couldn't really react in the middle of a thousand people, but I checked it out as discreetly as I could. I came back and told Mark, "I saw the mother lode, man." And then I looked at Nina sideways for the next two weeks.

Nina:

After high school, I signed up with a modeling agency—I did some photography, but I was too short for the runway. I also modeled for art classes at the Cleveland Institute of Art. I was taking my clothes off for painting classes, but I wasn't thinking of it as being sexual. I loved the artistic atmosphere of the art school, even the smell of the turpentine and paint. As lame and corny as it sounds, I did it because I was inspiring artists. I couldn't draw, but I always enjoyed hanging out at museums.

Playboy came to Ohio in 1978 to scout for a feature on "Girls in the

Office," and Danny, my boyfriend and manager, heard about it. He said, "You really should do this." My modeling agent said, "You really should do this." My friends all said, "You really should do this." The money was decent. I don't remember the exact figure—but I believe if you did the centerfold, that was a hundred grand.

I didn't have to send in naked photographs. I actually submitted my senior picture from high school. For some reason, I had posed for that picture in a curly ringlet wig. It was a very Victorian vibe—I sent that in instead of a bikini shot. They looked at me for the centerfold, but according to Hugh Hefner, my chest wasn't big enough. That was fine—I never thought I had a voluptuous build. They treated me well, the money was good, the photographer was wonderful. I did a lot of yoga, so I could hold poses like there was no tomorrow.

> *From "The Girls in the Office":*
>
> *It's a fact that the world is run by secretaries. Without them, thousands of seemingly important men would spend most of their time hunting down pieces of paper and punching out letters on the typewriter with two fingers. And, as anyone who has one knows, a secretary who's not only skilled but pretty is more than valuable; she's priceless—far better than coffee to get one's eyes open in the A.M. . . . Nina Blackwood, who works for an Ohio music publisher, also plays the harp and does voice-overs for commercials.*

Nina:

After it came out, this guy Gary, one of Danny's friends, came up to me and said, "Yeah, there's going to be a lot of stuck-together pages, huh huh huh." I didn't understand what he meant. Honestly, on my life, I had no clue how guys related to *Playboy*. That's how dumb and naïve I was.

Not long after that, Danny and I moved to Sewanee, Tennessee—he was playing with the country singer David Allan Coe. It was a little town, but the University of Southern Tennessee was there. And I thought, while Danny was out on the road, that I'd do some modeling for a sculpture class. I lasted one day—I couldn't do it anymore. The whole thing felt tainted.

After MTV launched, *Playboy* reprinted the photos. I was mad. They don't ask you if it's okay—they just do it. Executive producer Julian Goldberg called me into his office and asked, "So how are we going to handle this?" I said, "I don't know—I didn't put it out." I don't know if it was real or just in my mind, but after that, I always felt like the executives saw me as the bad sister of the VJ gang. It wasn't pleasant to be called into the principal's office. I'm left of center in a lot of ways and I have a rebellious streak, but intrinsically I really am a good girl.

Alan:

Nina was embarrassed by my bringing it up, and I got frustrated because I thought she was being coy. False modesty is annoying—you posed for *Playboy,* so why do you disown that now? I had the stereotypical man's opinion: A woman who poses nude is secure in her body and sexually easy. Now I know Nina better and I know she wasn't being disingenuous.

Nina:

I have very few regrets in my life, but posing for *Playboy* is probably my biggest. For over thirty years, I've had to put up with a preconceived notion that I'm something that I never was. And I still have to talk about it all the time, because almost every interview I do, especially with male radio jocks, they love to bring it up. It pisses me off, because I have to explain it so much and it's the antithesis of who I really am. Sometimes after one of those interviews, I'll call up Danny and say, "I'm still talking about that darn thing!"

Guys just won't let it go. If I cured cancer, they'd probably touch on that: "Oh, you cured cancer, but let's talk about how you posed in *Playboy!*" And when I complain about it, they say, "Well, you should be honored." You know what? I'm not.

i'm a cool Rocking Daddy in the u.s.a. Now

The Mighty J. J. Jackson

Mark:

J. J. was a big name-dropper. But he didn't come off like a putz—I loved hearing about him and Rod Stewart or him and Freddie Mercury, because he was a great storyteller. He used to go to Rod's house in Bel Air, and he always called him "the Duke of Bel Air" on the air. And one of J. J.'s big claims to fame was that he was the first person in the United States to play Led Zeppelin on the radio. He was genuinely close with those guys—he called Robert Plant "Percy." And *nobody* called him Percy except the guys in the band, and Peter Grant, their manager. J. J. talked about hanging with the guys in Led Zeppelin at the "Riot House"—the famous rock 'n' roll Hyatt on Sunset Boulevard in Los Angeles. He told me that he introduced the band to some girls that he knew.

Martha:

Robert Plant wouldn't talk to anybody at MTV except J. J. Same with Roger Daltrey.

Mark:

We all quickly came to love J. J. That said, he was a little pompous and he acted like he was royalty. There were times when I thought, J. J., just reel it in. Please, not another story about you and the Duke of Bel Air. Over the years, I realized he was one of the most secure people I ever knew. He was smart and honest, he had diverse interests, and he was totally comfortable with himself.

Martha:

I didn't realize at the time how much weight J. J. carried. He wasn't some kid off the street, the way I was. Only later did I hear some of the stories about the things he did, like introducing Jimi Hendrix onstage in Boston, or showing all the guys in Led Zeppelin around Boston in his station wagon. Can you imagine? Plus, I was young and self-involved. Okay, he broke Led Zeppelin in the United States, fine, I have to go worry about my boyfriend.

Alan:

Sometimes stories would roll out of J. J.'s mouth that we'd never heard before. He'd say, "I was a marine," and I'd expect the sentence to finish with "on the sands of Iwo Jima."

Nina:

He didn't talk about the marines much. I know he was a seagoing marine and he worked in air traffic control while he was in the service.

Mark:

In retrospect, he kept certain things to himself. He would tell these stories, and he liked to present a particular profile, but he only let us know a certain amount.

Nina:

He didn't like the way Rod Stewart had changed in his career from being a rock 'n' roller to the spandex-wearing disco stuff. I guess he told Rod that once, because they had a bit of a falling-out.

Alan:

I loved Howard Jones and I was surprised that J. J. liked HoJo too. J. J. and I had interesting overlaps in our musical tastes.

> *Asked toward the end of his MTV tenure to name his top ten albums of all time, J. J. compiled this list:*
>
> *1. Roxy Music,* Avalon
> *2. U2,* The Unforgettable Fire
> *3. Led Zeppelin,* Physical Graffiti
> *4. The Rolling Stones,* Let It Bleed
> *5. The Jimi Hendrix Experience,* Electric Ladyland
> *6.* The Beatles *(aka "The White Album")*
> *7. The Who,* Who's Next
> *8.* The Pretenders
> *9. Prince and the Revolution,* Purple Rain
> *10. David Bowie,* Station to Station

Alan:

I couldn't tell exactly how old J. J. was, but he did seem to be nervous about his age. When we launched, just about everybody working at the channel was thirty or under, including Bob Pittman, who was twenty-seven at the time. And here's J. J., who had to be around forty-five. He was playing a young man's game, and he seemed nervous about that at times.

Mark:

I met J. J.'s mom years later. She confided that he was older than he said. Tell me something I don't know.

According to an MTV obituary, J. J. was born on April 8, 1941, making him forty years old when the channel launched.

Alan:

The entire time we were at MTV, it seemed like J. J. was an older guy stuck at the same age. He never aged, never got younger. His bald spot was always there, but for a long time, we didn't realize he was painting it over with a jet-black spray. I would get undressed in front of anybody and put on makeup wherever. But J. J. would go off in his own little world and come out all prepared. Secretly, he was very vain.

Nina:

J. J. went to all these underground clubs—rock, dance, after-hours—he was the one doing what people thought all five of us did. We called him Club Man.

Mark:

He would roll into the studio from the clubs to do a show, looking all puffy. He put Preparation H under his eyes to bring down the swelling.

Nina:

He said he learned that trick from a soap opera actress.

Mark:

The MTV studios were just around the corner from Plato's Retreat, the famous swingers' club. I never went there, but J. J. visited the Hellfire Club, another sex club. He'd been there a few times, and he told me crazy stories about the shit he would see there: group sex, girl-on-girl-on-guy, everything. The way he described it, it sounded like a Fellini movie. People would be having sex in these little alcoves with veils over them, like an exhibit. J. J. wasn't a particularly religious guy, but he said it made him feel like God was going to strike this city down.

Alan:

On the air, J. J. was inconsistent. Some days, he'd be nervous and sweaty; we'd watch the monitor and know that he was still fucked up from the night before. And then there were days when he was spirited and eloquent. When J. J. was popping, he literally would say, "Bingada-bada."

Everyone tolerated a lot more from him—he had earned the right to be a bit of a diva. He was the elder statesman, the most concerned about all of us. If Nina was emotional or having a tough time, I might feel uncomfortable giving her a hug, but J. J. would be in her dressing room and she was in his arms. So we gave him a lot of latitude.

Nina:

J. J. radiated a lot of love. Like me, he was an only child—which is kind of funny, because we represented the two extremes of that. I'm happy being alone, and when push comes to shove, I'll just hang out with my animals. But J. J. was the opposite—he was extremely outgoing and made everybody into his family. When he was talking to you, you felt like he was only thinking of you. And he treated everyone the same, whether it was the bell cap at the hotel or the head of the hotel corporation.

Martha:

J. J. and my dad got along great, maybe because they had both been in the military. And J. J. was amazing in those situations—when he met somebody's dad, there was no rock 'n' roll funny business. "Hello, sir, how are you doing? It's great to talk to you." He acted like the quarterback of a football team, and showed respect.

Alan:

Sometimes the other VJs would go out to a show, and invariably J. J. would already be backstage in the VIP area. He'd come out: "Hey, Al, come on back." He'd already swung the deal.

Martha:

I couldn't get into any clubs, I couldn't get backstage, I couldn't get good tables at restaurants, I couldn't get behind a single velvet rope. But doors would fly open for J. J.

Alan:

J. J. was tight with lots of people. If you wanted to go to a restaurant, he knew the maître d'. He was practically the pope of New York City.

Mark:

J. J. had pockets of people that he knew. All of us MTV folks were one pocket, and then another pocket would be these bikers that he was friendly with. There was one morning when some Hells Angels saw him in the Village, waiting for a car so he could get to work, and one of them gave him a ride to the studio on the back of his motorcycle. J. J. also hung around with some Mafia dudes—he was able to have his birthday party on a weekend night at the Palladium because he knew some people who knew some people. He told me Mick Jagger couldn't get the Palladium on a weekend night! He loved that. J. J. wasn't a thug himself; he just had the amazing ability to be a part of whatever group he was with. He could talk music and he could talk literature—he was especially into Chinese art and literature.

Most of the people J. J. hung with were white, and he was into rock 'n' roll and that's mostly white. But it wasn't like he was trying to pass as white. He just had a benign, cuddly vibe.

Martha:

One time, talking with J. J., I used the expression "It's the pot calling the kettle black," and he stopped me cold. "Don't say that, MCQ." (Most of the VJs called me Quinski, but J. J. liked to call me MCQ.) I asked him why—I thought the saying was just because cast-iron pots and kettles are black. He said, "No, no, it's assigning the color black a negative connotation."

Mark:

J. J. was very in touch with being black. It wasn't the main way he identified himself, but he had a smooth-black-guy vibe that the women loved. And he was good with that.

Nina:

J. J.'s most famous line ever on the air was the time he said, "This is brown Jackson here with news of Jackson Browne."

> *Excerpts of J. J. Jackson, in an iridescent blue double-breasted shirt, giving the music news on September 9, 1982:*
>
> *"Former Eagle Don Henley with 'Johnny Can't Read,' preceded by Joan Jett and the Blackhearts with 'Crimson and Clover.' My name is J. J. Jackson, you can call me Triple J. I got the music news for you here on MTV.* Brimstone and Treacle—*it's the film starring Sting of the Police—shared the Grand Prize at the World Film Festival in Montreal last month. Unfortunately, Sting was not capable of attending the awards ceremony, not because he didn't want to—when we talked to him out at the US Festival he reiterated that he was quite proud to receive that honor. He's a fine actor. If you ever get a chance to see him in* Quadrophenia, *do that as well, because he does a really fine job.*
>
> *"Brian Eno, who has produced Talking Heads and Devo and was one of the founding members of Roxy Music, well, he has made a unique video documenting twenty-four hours of the New York City skyline,* Mistaken Memories of Medieval Manhattan. *Love that. What's*

really unusual about the piece, though, is that you must turn your tele-
vision set on its side. Can you imagine if you've got a big combination
set? 'Okay, Dad, let's get it over.' No way. Anyway, he's off the wall, has
been for some time, but he does some very creative stuff.

"Got concert information for you right now: Fleetwood Mac is on
the road. Get ready for a Mac Attack—Stevie Nicks is just incredible
this particular tour. Christine McVie, all of them, the band is so tight.
Next hour, get concert information on Alex Lifeson, Neil Peart, and
Geddy Lee—Rush! A little later, we're going to check out Squeeze, with
'Black Coffee in Bed.'"

Martha:

I don't blame J. J. at all for feeling confined at MTV. He went
from launching Led Zeppelin to reading teleprompter copy about
Corey Hart. J. J. on MTV was like Jimi Hendrix opening up for
the Monkees.

Mark:

I sat in the control room, watching his technique when he had to
interview a performer he had never met. The artist sat down, and J. J.
said, "Okay, so here's where I'm at. I started at BCN in 1968, and
then I worked at K-West in L.A. and then I did ABC News. . . ." He
gave them his little bio so they would sit back and say, "Oh, okay, I'm
talking to the right person."

I thought it was funny, but I also thought it was a really smart
thing to do. I didn't think I would ever be able to pull that off—if I
tried, I'd sound like a dick. But with J. J., it was perfect. He just had
a commanding air.

Alan:

J. J. interviewed Public Image Ltd: Keith Levene and John Lydon, who
had been Johnny Rotten in the Sex Pistols. They were so snotty and
renegade, and smoking the whole time, and J. J. was just being cool.
J. J. adopted a light British accent in that interview—he was sort of a

chameleon, and every time he talked to an Englishman, he had a British lilt. J. J. didn't let them off the hook at all, and Johnny just smirked whenever J. J. would swat him.

> *The interview, conducted on September 16, 1982, was to promote an album* (Commercial Zone) *that never officially came out.*
>
> JOHN LYDON: *"It's very hard to get away from disco. It's not so bad, I quite like it. I like turning the radio on and hearing nonstop disco."*
>
> J. J. JACKSON: *"It's just a rhythm section, though, isn't it?"*
>
> JOHN LYDON: *"Yeah."*
>
> J. J. JACKSON: *"How much of that can you hear before—"*
>
> JOHN LYDON: *"Quite a lot."*

Martha:

Those guys came in the studio and were having a friendly chat with J. J.—then as soon as the actual interview started, they started with the snotty we-don't-like-to-answer-questions thing. I don't think they'd ever been interviewed by a marine before: J. J. stopped the spoiled-kid routine cold.

Alan:

J. J. and I would crack each other up. He loved doing funny Johnny Carson voices and old bits from *Sanford and Son* and *Amos 'n' Andy*. His laugh was contagious. He'd have tears streaming down his face, and he'd goad me into getting even sillier.

Mark:

He did Jackie Gleason voices too. I don't think too many MTV viewers got that reference.

Nina:

Early on, we were pushing MTV merchandise on the air; we had these little MTV pins for sale. J. J. was talking about the pin and trying to put it on his clothes, and it snapped in two. He went into his British accent and said, "Bloody hell, the thing broke."

> *J. J. Jackson, on December 12, 1983, in a proto-Cosby sweater, back-announcing a video where Loverboy ran through the desert in* Mad Max *clothing: "Loverboy, Paul Dean and the band, 'Queen of the Broken Hearts.' I love some of the ladies in that video."*

Nina:

J. J. was a ladies' man. He would always have hugs for girls, a kiss right on the lips. But it wasn't lascivious, it was just J. J. I ran into a female DJ that he had worked with, and she told me her nickname for him was Pillow Lips, because his lips were so soft.

Mark:

J. J. dated a lot of women. He dated the receptionist at the studio for a while. But there was a warmth to his casualness—it seemed like it was all very easy and comfortable. Whenever we went out, he never had a date—he would meet people at the clubs.

Martha:

Sometimes J. J. would come to work and complain, "People are leaning out of cars, calling my name. I don't get it—everybody's trying to talk to me. I can't even take the subway anymore. It's like I'm Elvis, I can't go anywhere."

Meanwhile, J. J. would go out wearing giant aviator sunglasses, a full-length rabbit-fur coat, and red cowboy boots, with a three-hundred-pound Akita on a leash. You could not miss this guy—from a million miles away, you could tell he was somebody. He just exuded moxie.

Mark:

J. J. told me that on the inside, he felt like Super Fly. For a year or so, he was wearing a floor-length fur coat—it was a full-on pimp coat. One day, I came into the studio and J. J. was upset—it turned out it was because a fan had written to him. She told him that he was her favorite VJ because he reminded her of Fozzie Bear. He laughed about it, but it was a reality check.

13

Hot in the city

New York City Serenade

Alan:

MTV was very much based in the New York scene. The record business was there, and Madison Avenue, and visual artists like Keith Haring and Jean-Michel Basquiat.

Martha:

I loved New York City. I could never understand why anyone would live in Minneapolis or Atlanta or anywhere else, when New York existed. When I walked down the street, I felt like John Travolta in *Saturday Night Fever.* Writing 10003 as my zip code gave me a thrill every single time.

Mark:

When I was sixteen, I got my driver's license. Three weeks later, I drove up the New Jersey Turnpike to New York. I can't believe my parents let me do it—that's insane.

Nina:

When I first came to New York, I felt very L.A., and I had a lot of West Coast pride. I was blond, I loved going to Topanga Beach, and I worked barefoot all the time.

Mark:

I used to call Nina "Hollywood" on the air, because she was so L.A.

Nina:

My acting teacher Marc Marno was from New York, and he worried about me moving to the city. He told me, "You have to be careful, because it could break you. You're fragile and it's a really tough city."

I could not believe the volume of the ambient noise in New York. Even in the dead of night, the city had a certain hum. After a while, I got used to it. Some nights, I'd sit in a restaurant with a pad of paper, drinking Courvoisier and writing poetry. My poems had turned dark, focused on broken spirits and shards of iron and steel—stuff like "and the broken glass that glitters, which pierces the soul of humanity."

Alan:

My favorite thing to do in New York was to sit in a coffee shop on a rainy day with a copy of the *Times,* and people-watch. It made me happy and lonely at the same time.

Nina:

I ended up loving the darkness of New York City. It was a great experience, because it didn't break me—it made me stronger. Because I didn't know anybody, almost every Sunday I would go to the Metropolitan Museum of Art. I would wander through the whole building, looking at everything, but I gravitated toward the Impressionists. I felt surrounded by the spirits of these artists.

Mark:

One of the first clubs that I went to in New York was Danceteria. I would dance, but sometimes I would go there just to hang out and listen to the DJ. One night, there was a girl walking through the place, and her only item of clothing was a belt. I asked her, "Aren't you uncomfortable like that?"

She said, "I have no negative emotions."

Alan:

I loved clubbing, but I wasn't a hound for it the way J. J. and Mark were. After a rock show, we'd sometimes go to the all-night clubs, on J. J.'s recommendation. In fact, any club, if they didn't recognize me, I'd throw J. J.'s name around—*whoosh!* I'd get right in. The Limelight, on Twentieth Street, was my favorite—it was a former cathedral, massively cool and ornate, and it had the best ambience around.

Martha:

The Limelight was pretty far north for me. I was one of those Village girls who rarely ventured above Fourteenth Street. With the exception of my summer sublet on the Upper East Side, my entire time in New York was five minutes from my college dorm. I never got a summer place on Fire Island or any other out-of-town vacation spot: I had a deck, and that was all the outside space I needed.

Nina:

MTV put me up at the Berkshire Hotel for a month. Since I had moved to New York with just a trunk of clothes, I figured it was a good idea to find a furnished apartment. It was eye-opening to discover how expensive it was to have such little space.

Eventually, I found an L-shaped studio on Fifty-sixth Street. It was a cute little gem: The walls were painted forest green, the sofa was upholstered in green and red plaid, and there was white lacquered furniture. It also came with an indoor tree. I lived there for most of my time in New York City. When I think of that apartment, I think of getting ready to go out. I'd play Joe Jackson's "Steppin' Out" and put on my perfume oils, which made me smell like the flowers I'd always check out when I passed by florists.

Alan:

I went to two or three live shows a week: Madison Square Garden, the Roxy, the Palladium, or my favorite, the Beacon Theater. Sometimes I would sneak off to a jazz show at the Blue Note or the Village Vanguard—I didn't really talk about that at work. At MTV, I was a closeted jazz fan.

Nina:

Danny came to visit me, to check that I was doing okay. It was during a garbage strike, which made the streets of New York stink like you wouldn't believe—as if he didn't hate the city enough already. I tried to convince him that the smell was soulful, but he wasn't having it.

One morning, I was running around, getting ready to go to the studio, and he was sitting on the sofa. I got a pitcher of water and poured the water in the tree's pot, and Danny said, "Nina, what are you doing?"

"It's dry in here—I'm watering the tree."

He said, "It's a fake tree." He was right—and I had been watering it for two months.

Mark:

I went roller-skating with Carol at a rink near the West Side Highway. I was terrified of roller skates—I broke my arm skating twice when I was a kid, in two separate summers. Heard it snap both times. But Carol was into it, and at that time, everybody was skating and listening to the R&B station WBLS. That's the scene that Mark Knopfler was singing about in Dire Straits' "Skateaway."

What I really loved was watching people skate in the park. People would set up orange cones and giant boom boxes.

Nina:

I didn't enjoy the cacophony of boom boxes and roller skaters that descended on Central Park in nice weather. That didn't just stress me out, it angered me—way too much noise.

I was in Central Park almost every weekend, no matter what the weather was. It is, to this day, my favorite place in the city. At the time, they hadn't cleaned it up, so there were some really funky areas: The duck pond was just a swampy mess with discarded food wrappers. But there was still nature all around and I marveled at how woodland creatures could survive in the middle of a giant hectic metropolis. In the spring, the hundreds of flowering trees made the park a mystical fairyland. As I journeyed through it, I would let my mind wander. Time travel is very easy in New York: I envisioned what the land looked like in the 1800s, before the park was built, and think back even further to the geological events that created the landscape of Manhattan.

Alan:

It was great to see *Sweeney Todd* on Broadway and not sweat the ticket price. Jan and I went to lots of theater: Broadway, off-Broadway, off-off-Broadway. Mark was intrigued, and eventually caught the bug. I could see he was getting interested in acting too: very ironic for Mr. Rocker.

Mark:

I liked going to the theater, but I didn't want to drop a ton of money on it. Carol and I would spend the price of theater tickets on dinner, though. When MTV started happening, a whole new side of New York opened up. I routinely got great tables at great restaurants.

Alan:

Bob Giraldi, who directed the video for Michael Jackson's "Beat It," opened an upscale Italian restaurant called Positano. I loved going there. Robert De Niro's joint on Columbus Avenue was also a fave. Or any bar on Bleecker Street.

Mark:

At Positano, they knew Carol and me. We had a particular wine that we loved—that was the only place we could find it. When we were seated, they'd just put a bottle of it on our table.

Nina:

I pretty much lived on the stuffed grape leaves from the deli around the corner. I usually went out to dinner—New York kitchens aren't that large, and it could feel claustrophobic being in the apartment all the time. I just wished I could find decent Mexican food.

Martha:

Every morning was the same for me: egg sandwich on a kaiser roll, a regular coffee in an Acropolis to-go cup, and the *New York Post*. I'd bring it all back up from the corner deli to my apartment, and would sit by my radio, listening to Howard Stern. I tried to time my mornings so I could run down to the car during a commercial break, and then ask the driver to turn Howard on for the ride to the studio.

Mark:

I loved the Cadillac Bar. Girls walked around the bar with two bandoliers across their chest. One of the belts had shot glasses, and the other one had rolled-up napkins. On their hips, in holsters, they had one bottle of tequila and one of 7Up. If you wanted a drink, they would slam down a foaming shot of tequila for you.

Nina:

My first year in New York, it was the Los Angeles Dodgers against the New York Yankees in the World Series. Our whole crew at MTV was from various areas of New York: the city, Long Island, maybe a couple of people from Jersey. So I had to be quiet about rooting for the Dodgers. I went to a couple of the games at Yankee Stadium—an early perk—and when the Dodgers won the Series, I won the office pool. I was not popular that day.

Mark:

Michael Pelech, one of the cameramen, discovered a strip club we called Shecky's Lap Emporium. Across the street from America, this cavernous restaurant I used to go to all the time, there was a little steel door. We went through the door, took an elevator up, and walked down a long dark hall to the box office, which was inside a glass booth. I slid my money through the little opening. The guy in the booth said, "MTV!" Not really the place I wanted to be recognized. Inside, it was not a typical lap dance place. In this small, dark room, music was playing, girls were taking their tops off, there was absolutely no "hands off" policy! It was a quintessential New York experience.

Nina:

There used to be a place called Claremont Stables in Central Park. I would go riding there, and I fell in love with a white horse named Mirage. He was on the small side, maybe fourteen-and-a-half-hands (slightly under five feet), but he had just enough of an attitude to make him feisty and a good ride. One time I was going to see him and I forgot to bring carrots, so I stopped into a deli and grabbed strawberry cookies. After I gave him the treat, his warm breath on my face smelled like strawberries. Riding him through the park was transporting—on a misty day, I would feel like I was on a vast estate, somewhere in the countryside of England.

Alan:

I shopped a lot at Macy's—that was how our apartment started to become more adult. We got rid of the thrift-store furniture, went to Macy's, and in one fell swoop, got bookshelves, couches, an entertainment complex, and a new TV. Every now and then, Jan and I would have a Thursday night with nothing going on, and we'd cherish an evening on the couch with popcorn, in front of NBC's lineup: *The Cosby Show, Family Ties, Cheers, Night Court, Hill Street Blues*. They hadn't started calling it "Must See TV" yet. Vegging out is at its best when you're squeezing it into your busy life.

Nina:

When I moved to New York, I thought I would do MTV and also have a harp gig—the way Woody Allen plays clarinet once a week. When I got settled in, I had my harp flown to the Teletronics studio, because the case was too big to fit in my apartment. I played it on the air—"Here Comes the Sun," one of my favorites. I stored the case in the MTV props department and took the harp home—it wouldn't fit in a cab, so Teletronics moved it for me with their van. It turned out there wasn't time to look for a New York City harp gig, let alone do it. MTV was 24/7, so the harp unfortunately got the back burner.

I played harp at a few weddings over the years—once for an MTV producer, and once for our director of marketing. And Tommy Shaw, the guitarist from Styx, asked me to perform at his wedding. That was a nerve-racking gig, just because there were so many professional musicians there.

Alan:

Jan started performing at the cabaret on the third floor of the Magic Pan restaurant at Fifty-seventh Street and Sixth Avenue. I went to her show every two weeks or so; sometimes I'd end up there at the end of the night after another evening activity. I loved watching my wife perform: She had the belting power of Ethel Merman or Liza Minnelli, and the comic timing of Lucille Ball. She was a real contender on the musical theater scene.

One night, I was feeling particularly happy with life at MTV and even more serene in the darkened warmth of a candlelit nightclub table, watching Jan sing her heart out on "I Can Let Go Now," a Michael McDonald song that I had helped her pick out. That song made me cry whenever I listened to it, no matter what the environment. But in that setting, on that night, I was a weepy mess. A few glasses of wine and an enraptured audience fueled my sentimental heart. Everything seemed to be in its place: my job, my love, my life.

Afterward, we went with the cabaret cast members to some late-night joint: theatrical types in full over-the-top extroverted display. Around three-thirty, we headed home in a taxi (which I could now afford). My dreams were coming true, and I was happy to share them with Jan.

14

Throw Your Arms around the World at Christmastime

Christmas Songs and New Year's Eve Shows

Mark:

One Christmas, MTV gave us all clipboards. I wasn't expecting a cash bonus, but once I got the clipboard, I was like, "What the fuck is this?" We were all looking at each other, thinking, "Why did they even bother?" And that was when I started thinking, "Wait a second, we *should* be getting something. Something better." Another year, they gave us all frozen turkeys.

Martha:

Every year, we taped a Christmas video, where we got a rock star to come into the studio and perform a Christmas song, with the VJs and the staff in the background. If I had to go back to one single day at MTV, it would be the day we taped our first Christmas video, Billy Squier's "Christmas Is the Time to Say I Love You."

Mark:

The worst of the lot.

Martha:

Really? I think it was the best. It captured everybody's enthusiasm and innocence and love of rock 'n' roll. Everyone still had stars in their eyes and fire in their hearts about MTV. It was a mash-up of Teletronics studio employees and MTV staffers—we were a team.

Mark:

We were one big happy family. Sort of.

Martha:

I wouldn't have cared if they said we had to do ten more shots, or fifty more shots, because I could've sat there all day. Everybody that I totally loved was right there, plus a rock star.

Alan:

"Reggae Christmas," the Christmas song we did a few years later with Bryan Adams, was kind of dorky. But it was always a big party for everybody to come down from the office and be part of the Christmas video. The concept for "Reggae Christmas" was that Pee-wee Herman fell asleep and dreamed the whole song, and I woke him up at the end. Whenever there was a pseudo-acting thing, they gave it to Al the actor—even though I was crappy too.

Pee-wee's Playhouse was huge in 1984—we all watched it every Saturday morning. It didn't matter how late we were out on Friday, we woke up to watch *Pee-wee's Playhouse* in the morning. Working with Pee-wee was like working with a wrestler: When we were staging the shoot, he was Paul Reubens. But when the camera came on, he did his Pee-wee thing.

Martha:

The first *New Year's Eve Rock 'n' Roll Ball* was in 1981, with Bow Wow Wow, Karla DeVito, and David Johansen.

Mark:

This was before Johansen had turned himself into Buster Poindexter. His next album was a live record, and for the cover he used a picture of his band onstage at the New Year's party. He covered up the MTV logo with the album title; the songs on the album were basically his set from that night.

Martha:

We taped in the ballroom at the Hotel Diplomat. We weren't on cable in Manhattan yet, but the party was still a big deal. My brother Chris snuck in with Bow Wow Wow's road crew, wearing the satin MTV jacket I'd given him.

Alan:

It was really cool to arrive for the show and see a line around the block. Over the years, it became the hottest ticket in town, but even on year one, I was sitting in a preproduction meeting at 5 P.M., when John Belushi came walking through the ballroom, getting a tour from one of our executives. Belushi stopped and leaned against a pole, to keep himself upright, and he just kept sliding down the pole.

Mark:

Belushi was hammered and obnoxious and falling over. I know, who'd have thunk it? But we were amazed he had turned up at our party!

Alan:

The notion that we were going to broadcast live was incredibly exciting and a little bit scary. All of the producers and people around us were neophytes, just like us. For a number of years, doing live events was sort of hell, because they didn't know how to handle it either.

Mark:

There was a technical glitch during the show—I think an artist took way too long to get on the stage—and then Alan was killing time on the air, bullshitting. Forty-five seconds is an eternity to fill on the air when you're not prepared. And this wasn't a minute, or two minutes—it was like five minutes.

Alan:

I was improvising at this little podium, getting a lot of hand gestures telling me to keep on yapping. There was actually a stack of blue cards in case we got into trouble like that, with little tidbits and facts, but nobody gave me the cards. Jan was standing next to me, watching me. Finally, having completely run out of things to say, I pulled Jan on camera and asked, "So, what kind of music do you like to listen to?"

"Oh, James Taylor."

Not Def Leppard, not Billy Idol—James Taylor. He wasn't a big part of our musical catalog, but I had totally put Jan on the spot. I didn't introduce her as my wife—I didn't want to be parading my family on camera. It was an extremely lame segment, and it didn't look like real TV, to be honest. It felt like a bunch of kids playing around.

Mark:

Alan was just rambling, talking about God knows what, stuff that didn't even relate to music. Live TV can be very scary.

Alan:

As time went on, the New Year's show became the best party on the planet. It was also an exercise in staying straight for four hours while everybody else was going to the bathroom and doing massive amounts of cocaine. It was weird to be at the center of the action and not be allowed to participate.

Nina:

Those shows were my favorite part of the whole year. I was doing what I loved, I had cool clothes that somebody provided, there was live music, and we were celebrating with the entire country. How do you top that?

Alan:

Every year, it got bigger. I'd go down to the ballroom where the show was going to be and find huge, lavish sets that people had been working on for months. We knew intellectually that MTV was getting big, but as VJs, we didn't really feel it. We had no handlers, no assistants, no wardrobe or makeup people—we were just doing our shows. But then we saw that other parts of MTV were spending lots of money.

Mark:

One year, Billy Idol was playing, and he was completely out of his mind. He could barely speak—I have no idea how he got up onstage and sang.

Alan:

Year three, we were at Roseland. Howie Mandel was wandering around the audience as the roving reporter. We had, for the first time, a miniature camera, which we called the lipstick camera. And Howie was shoving it up women's dresses, saying, "Whoa, look at that!"

Nina and I were doing a segment together, and once again, we had to stretch. We started the most banal conversation and before I knew it, Nina was talking about her cats. I don't want to blame this on Nina—I was equally at fault. I couldn't figure out how to get out of the cat conversation and segue into anything else. "Cats? How many cats do you have, Nina?" I felt like I was in an alternate universe. Nina was horrified herself, but she loved cats, and that was what came to mind.

Nina:

We were dying on camera. Where were the producers with the cards with all the information? They left us out there with egg on our face. They weren't inept, they were just inexperienced. And if Alan or I had been more seasoned, we would have broken the wall and yelled, "Give us some cards over here."

Alan:

It was ten scary, excruciating minutes. Finally, mercifully, we went to commercial.

> *From the script for the 1984* New Year's Eve Rock 'n' Roll Ball *(featuring performances by David Lee Roth, Joan Jett, and General Public):*
>
> MARK GOODMAN: *"It's New Year's Eve and I haven't seen this much hysteria since someone tied Pee-wee Herman's 'big shoe' laces together. Pee-wee?"*
>
> PEE-WEE HERMAN: *(Ad-lib & toss to J. J.)*
>
> J. J. JACKSON: *"I just found (Guest) out here in the crowd." (Q to come.) "Coming up, another $10,000 giveaway . . . and in a few minutes, 1985 in the Midwest."*

Alan:

The last couple of years, I inched back a time zone with my coke intake. We'd get to midnight in the Mountain time zone, the little coke vial would be burning a hole in my pocket, and I'd steal off to the bathroom. Mark and J. J. were adept at handling the bump to get through the show—pros that they were.

At two o'clock, our show was over. The rest of the world had been partying all night long; we'd jump into our limousines and join them. One year, I spotted Richard Belzer standing outside one of these clubs, looking around. I gave him a ride, and he was happy as a pig: "The VJ world's pretty good," he told me. I felt weird—you're Richard Belzer, and I'm just a VJ, but I've got the limo and you don't.

Nina:

After one of the New Year's Eve shows, there was a VJ party, and then an after-party, and then a bunch of us ended up at the Hard Rock Café, which was staying open through the night, going into breakfast. We were at the same table as Robert Palmer and his date, who was wearing a very tight green satin evening gown. We were all seated together, but we weren't really together. So the waitress comes around to take our orders, and his date kept answering, "Well, Robert will have this, and Robert will have that." Robert never got to say anything.

When it was my turn, I said, "I'll have whatever Robert will have." Robert laughed; his date didn't.

Mark:

By my last New Year's, I knew exactly how much I could enjoy myself and still keep it together on the air. I had a couple of vials of coke, a couple of bottles of Cristal in my sight, and a pack of Marlboros.

During a break, I had some champagne, and I was lighting up a cigarette. Along came this crew of people, including Ian Astbury of the Cult, who had just come from the bathroom with the Beastie Boys. I was about to light up the cigarette when Astbury came strutting by and snapped it out of my mouth. I grabbed him by the shirt and pushed him down on the floor. I was about to punch him in the face, but somebody pulled me off.

That's so not me. I've never had a fight in my life. I heard, many years later, that Astbury remembered the incident, felt bad about it, and apologized.

Alan:

I was hanging around with Ron Wood and his girlfriend in one of the greenrooms. They were both fucked up. Keith Richards came by the doorway, propped himself against the door, and said something unintelligible: "Hey, mate argle, what we do now yaaah." Then he giggled, lit a cigarette, and moved on. Sometimes, there were moments I couldn't believe I was even in the mix.

15

τake My τears and τhat's Not Nearly all

Romance and Its Discontents

Nina:

Even before I got the MTV job and moved to New York, my relationship with Danny was starting to chafe. He was the type of guy who took care of everything. He always told me that I didn't have to worry about the business end; I should just play my harp and do what I do. In a lot of ways, he created the Nina Blackwood thing. I hadn't been out of my parents' house very long before I met Danny—but in the decade since then, I had grown up.

I don't want to paint him as a bad guy—I still feel very indebted to him. And I was not good with business stuff. Sometimes Danny would be on the phone with me, talking about contracts, and I would get so upset, I would get the dry heaves.

Danny wanted to keep the personal relationship, but it would have ended, even if I had stayed in L.A. We went through a rough transition—sometimes I threw my phone across the apartment. I'm not a coldhearted person. I would go over to Alan and Jan's place, and I'd be sobbing on their couch. More than anybody else, they got the brunt of what I was going through with Danny. It was very emotional, but even after we broke up, Danny stayed on as my manager—and he's still my manager today.

Just before I left L.A., I was in the process of buying a white MG sports car. They were discontinuing them, and I was getting it as a collector's item. I got to test-drive it once, and then I left it in California. I gave it to Danny, as a big commission. I guess it was a consolation prize: I'm gone, but here's the car.

Martha:

During the first year of MTV, Tony resurfaced and we started dating again. One time, we even drove out to Jones Beach with Nina. I was thinking that now I had the MTV gig, maybe it would make Tony want me the way I'd always hoped for—it took me a long time to break out of that cycle. My being on MTV didn't impress Tony at all. He was a cameraman, and he was always working on big movies; my job was just a little weirdo cable thing.

We went on vacation to Club Med, on the French island of Martinique. On the beach, tons of women were sans tops. Wildly throwing caution to the wind, I took my bikini top off—the first and only time I ever went topless. Within ten minutes, this couple came up to me: They were from some town in New Jersey, one of the few towns in the entire United States that had MTV, and they recognized me. I was saying, "Hi, yes, I'm Martha Quinn, nice to meet you"—topless.

Soon enough, things fell apart with Tony. One night, I came home to find he had dropped off a paper bag. My doorman handed me the bag: It was filled with objects that had significance in our relationship, like a blanket that I had crocheted for him, and a picture of me from high school. He had stabbed the eyes out of the picture. I was so upset, I threw the whole bundle in the incinerator. The whole thing with Tony was a life lesson: If he doesn't think you're indispensible, then he's dispensable. I'm borrowing a concept from Honeymoon Suite's "Feel It Again," but it's still true.

Mark:

Carol definitely suffered the brunt of my fame, or my alleged fame. In a lot of ways, she was an innocent bystander who got shafted.

Martha:

When we started at MTV, I would hear Mark on the phone with Carol in that tiny VJ dressing room. He was begging her to move in with him, saying stuff like, "You'd make me the happiest guy in the world." I was jealous, in a moony way—like how Beatles fans felt when Paul McCartney got married.

Mark:

We ended up living in Carol's place, on West Seventy-second Street next to the Dakota. After a while, we bought an apartment up in Riverdale, in the Bronx—in Willie Mays's building. I never saw the guy, but I often parked right next to his car: It had a personalized license plate that said SAY HEY.

There weren't so much cracks in our relationship as there were cracks in me. I loved Carol like crazy: She was beautiful, she understood what I did, plus she flat-out loved music. It didn't hurt that she was kind of famous. Springsteen loved her, Stevie Nicks adored her, and Carol was great friends with Tom Petty and his wife Jane. But I just wasn't ready to be with somebody. I was completely unaware of my own psychology. When I was a kid, my parents tried to send me to a shrink, and I never wanted to go. As time went on, it became evident that I didn't know how to function in a relationship.

I proposed to Carol on the New Jersey Turnpike, just south of Newark. We were driving to Philly to see my parents. The gist of the proposal was "I'm not ready for this. I really love you but I don't know if I can handle one person for the rest of my life. I'm just not sure. But I love you, let's get married."

Carol was like, "What?" She totally thought I was going to break up with her. What must that proposal have sounded like? But she accepted right away. She was really centered and she knew who she was. She had her share of insecurities, which ultimately contributed to the demise of our relationship, but she was more together than I was.

We got married in December 1982. MTV had been around for over a year, but I didn't invite any of the other jocks to the wedding.

The VJs were in the studio together for hours on end, but we hardly ever saw each other outside of it, except at music events. It was a relatively small wedding, maybe a hundred people, in a beautiful room at the Tavern on the Green with sparkling lights.

Walking down the aisle, I thought to myself, "You're not ready for this now, but you will be."

Martha:

I passed by the Tavern on the Green in a cab the night of the wedding. There were lights in all the trees, and I thought, "Wow, that's Mark's wedding party." Mark had Carol, and Al had Jan, and J. J. was an adult, and I didn't have anybody. I was on my own.

16

i'll kick you out of my home
if you don't cut that hair

Makeup and Hairstyles

Alan:

The extreme hair and makeup mostly came from the other side of the Atlantic. While some American bands early on were getting used to the idea of wardrobe and the camera, we got exceptional videos from British bands no one had ever heard of like Ultravox, because the lines between music and trend were already blurred for them. The most memorable haircut was probably A Flock of Seagulls: The lead singer was Mike Score, who was a former hairdresser. He came up with a style that was Mohawk meets mullet. On both ends.

Martha:

I didn't think twice about Mike Score's hair. When you're young, you just think that everything your fellow young people do is cool. And anybody who doesn't think so just doesn't get it, right?

It seemed normal for male rock stars to be wearing makeup. In the '70s, we had David Bowie and the New York Dolls, and even Kiss. But I interviewed Boy George and was struck by the amount of pancake he had on. He even plucked his eyebrows, which I'd never seen up close before.

Nina:

I was sent out to MC a show by Eddie Money—in New Haven, I think. Guys were starting to wear makeup in videos, and Eddie wanted to get in on it. He asked me to put makeup on him. I did, but it was not good—some faces should not have eyeliner on them. He had those sweet eyes, like a basset hound.

Mark:

Before we went on the air, they brought in a woman to teach us how to do makeup. She had worked on David Letterman's morning show, and was waiting for *Late Night* to start. We had one lesson and we never saw her again. They gave us each a makeup kit.

Nina:

I loved that kit! I still have it. It was a big kit, with three layers to it, filled with brushes and powders and eye shadows. I never even opened some of it.

Alan:

It was weird: when local news anchors go to work every morning, they have makeup people and wardrobe people. We didn't have jackshit. Part of it was MTV trying to save money, but they were also trying to keep us humble.

Mark:

I sucked at putting on makeup. I didn't have a light touch—you could tell I was wearing cosmetics. J. J. *really* sucked at it. We both sweated a lot on camera, because it was hot under the lights. So the sweat would run down our faces and it looked like we had creases on our foreheads. I also looked like I had little slit eyes, because I wasn't putting eyeliner on correctly. It was a mess. We looked like we should have been on public access cable in Mississippi. Eventually, I got better at it—but not much.

We gauged Nina's moods by how much rouge she had on. If she was really rouging those cheeks, we knew she was stressed about something.

Nina:

That's just bizarre. I don't even remember going to the studio and being upset, with the exception of when my dad died. And certainly the director or the cameraman never said, "You've got too much makeup on." Honest to God, I don't even know where people would get that from. Maybe I came across more moody than I thought.

Alan:

I tried to do as little makeup as possible: I just powdered and put on some concealer.

Nina:

Alan used to have his eyelashes dyed.

Alan:

It was pragmatic, so I wouldn't have to put on eyeliner.

Mark:

I hated the process of putting on makeup. I decided I would dye my eyelashes too, so I could skip that step. Then I got used to being able to put a little makeup on and being able to go out at night looking better than usual! I didn't look like a guy in Mötley Crüe, but I definitely came to rely on it.

Nina:

Later on, we had a makeup artist for guests, but in the early days, there was nobody. So when Steven Tyler came in for an interview, I helped him with his makeup. He thought my eyes were pinned, and he asked me if I was as high as he was. I said no. That was right before he got clean.

Alan:

After the first year, MTV did pay for our haircuts. We went to Il Maquillage, this hoity-toity salon on the Upper East Side. It was predominantly a rich women's place—Bob Pittman's wife went there, so we did too. They started putting highlights in my hair. I had a mullet. The desire was to have it look nice and clean-cut at the ears, but longer in back. I went on a personal appearance, and a kid came up and said, "Hey, man, I had my hair done just like you." He turned around, and I didn't think his hair looked like mine—but he did have a mullet. Where did the mullet start? Was it with bands like the Romantics and the Hooters? I don't think I was copying any of those bands, but I know I didn't create the mullet.

Nina:

I'm one of those girls who cannot set her own hair to save her life. When I moved to New York, I hooked up with this hairdresser Edward Tricomi, who's very well known now. He saw my hair and said, "Oh, it's so '70s—I'm going to update it." The next thing I knew, he had chopped off half of it and I was worrying I was going to lose my job. Looking in the mirror, I almost passed out—I thought they might fire me, because they loved my hair. I'm not the type of person who faints, but I was gasping, "Bring me tea."

The people at MTV didn't complain—they just said, "We wish that you would've told us first." So my hair was kind of asymmetrical and it was really blond—it just kept getting lighter. I met a lot of girls who were trying to copy my hair, and sometimes guys. I met a guy, years later, who looked very Nuno Bettencourt: He had gorgeous straight hair down to his waist. And he told me that when he was growing up in Pennsylvania, he thought my hair was the coolest, and he got a perm. With his beautiful hair! Mine wasn't a perm, it was naturally wavy—but I might have been responsible for a whole nation of teenagers getting bad perms.

Martha:

My short haircut in the '80s was completely an accident. If my hair is the wrong length, it will stick out perpendicular to my head, and no amount of blow-drying will fix it. Early on, I got a haircut at that evil length and did not like it at all: The only thing I could do was make it shorter. So for a long time, I had that short hair, and even became known for it. It was ironic, because when I was a kid, my mother insisted on my getting a pixie haircut, and I *hated* that pixie. I used to wear tights on my head, pretending I had long hair. And there I was on MTV with that pixie cut again.

Mark:

In the '70s, I had a Jew-fro. I kept that the first couple of years at MTV, and it became my defining thing. I was okay with it: If Mike Nesmith had the hat on *The Monkees,* I had the hair on MTV. It also contributed, apparently, to a lot of people thinking that I was on *Welcome Back, Kotter.* I'd be walking down the street, and people would shout, "Epstein! Yo, I love you, man."

After a couple of years, the word came down from on high that Bob Pittman hated my hair and wanted me to get a haircut. John Sykes told me, and my first thought was, "Fuck you! What is this, high school?" At the time, I was friendly with Ian Hunter, from Mott the Hoople. He invited Carol and me over to his house one Boxing Day. And he had very similar hair to mine, so I asked him about it. He went to José Eber, who had a salon in Beverly Hills and cut people like Farrah Fawcett and Elizabeth Taylor. Ian was raving about José, so the next day I said to Sykes, "You want me to get my hair cut? That's who I want to do it."

José wasn't coming to New York, so they had to fly me out there, first class, and they put me up at the Beverly Hills Hotel. On the day I was supposed to fly west, I lost my wallet. It wasn't quite so stringent back then in terms of needing an ID to get on the plane, but you needed a driver's license to rent a car. I told Sykes that I would have to postpone the trip a week or so, until I got a new license. He said, "Pittman will kill me. No, no, no, you have to go." So they hired me a stretch limo.

I was terrified about the haircut—I knew people would be looking at it every day on TV. So I figured I'd take my time; I wanted José to do whatever he thought was cool, but I wanted to make sure it worked for me. The result was that I sat in his chair for six hours. I was calling John Sykes hourly to give him updates. If it was today, I'd take a picture with my phone and send it to him, but without that technology, I had to try to describe it to him. And he would ask, "Well, does it look different?"

While we were arguing about it on the phone, Cher came in. I said, "Cher, what do you think? This is my new—"

Cher snapped, "I don't give a shit! Get the fuck out of here—this is my appointment."

That stretch limo waited for me the whole six hours. Afterward, I called Corbin Bernsen. He was a friend of mine from New York—we worked out together. He had just started doing *L.A. Law*. So I kept the limo, and then I picked up Corbin and our friend Cameron Crowe, and we all went out drinking together. I never heard anything about the hair when I got back, so I guess they were happy with it. They spent enough on it, with the first-class ticket, the Beverly Hills Hotel, and the limo for forty-eight hours straight. I called it the ten-thousand-dollar haircut.

17

And Now You Find Yourself in '82

Early MTV Videos-a-Go-Go

Mark:

In some ways, it was a blessing that MTV didn't have that many videos in the early days. If we had any more Rod Stewart or Meat Loaf videos, maybe we wouldn't have played so much alternative music.

Alan:

U2 had a song called "I Will Follow" that Mark rightly spotted as a hit when they were totally unknown. I watched Bono with his white frilly shirt, ruffled cuffs, and huge mullet; I focused on the shirt more than the pleading voice. My response was, "Really? I don't see it." I would have made a lousy A&R man. But I got tapped to do the U2 interview. They came on the set, and I said, "With me today, the Edge and Bone-o." They laughed, and the Edge kept elbowing Bono: "Bone-o, Bone-o, Bone-o."

It was a very comfortable interview, despite that flub. Bono was as earnest then as he is now, but he was obviously serious about his craft. The Edge was rather quiet. They seemed less frivolous than a lot of the other groups that came through the studio. MTV didn't have a nihilistic rock edge—we had more of an irreverent new-wave edge.

Martha:

If you ask who summed up the '80s better, U2 or A Flock of Seagulls, I'd have to say A Flock of Seagulls.

Nina:

Just before MTV launched, Peter, a friend of mine, took me to the photo session for the cover of Stevie Nicks's *Bella Donna* album. Peter was a video producer, and he was very well connected: I only realized later that it was because he was also a coke dealer. Stevie was all decked out in that flowing white outfit, but she didn't have the cockatoo on her arm yet. She was a bit catty with me. The first thing she did was to comment on my hair: "If it was a little longer, it would be just like mine." She had to establish her dominance.

I was doing a lot of things that happened to be Stevie-esque, without trying to copy her: My hair, the type of clothes I like, my harp. I love Stevie, but I never copied anybody—even when my mom would try to sell me on an outfit by saying, "Everybody's wearing this." Years later, I spoke with Stevie again. We laughed about our first meeting, and she turned me on to the person who did her hair.

Mark:

I loved the Thompson Twins, who I thought were unlike a lot of the trendy bands of the time, in their music if not their wardrobe. They were all about beats and percussion; I've always been surprised they don't get sampled more. I don't think their arrangements are locked into that '80s sound, and they hold up really well—especially some of the lesser-known songs, like "Into the Gap." Tom Bailey, the lead singer, is an artsy guy, but in the coolest possible way.

Nina:

Peter was also really good friends with Ron Wood, the guitarist in the Faces and the Rolling Stones. Sometimes I'd have dinner with Peter, because I didn't know a lot of people in New York, and he'd take me by Ronnie's place—he was living with Jo, who became his second wife. Ronnie was fond of me, in part because I could drink with the best of them, and I liked him a lot. He was a good-time guy, just a giant kid.

The early '80s were not too cool for the Stones—Mick and Keith weren't getting along. Ronnie was at loose ends, so Peter talked him into doing a one-man show at Town Hall—the idea was that he would sit in a chair and narrate a slide show of his life. Ronnie knew me, and also knew and liked J. J., so we got recruited to host. I was in head-to-toe spandex—one of the few times I ever wore it—plus thigh-high boots.

The show was a disaster. Peter was completely wasted on God knows what. He dropped the slides on the floor, scattering them every-where. He was freaking out, but he was not together enough to be able to sort them out. Ronnie was sucking down Jack Daniel's, plus what-ever else Peter was giving him. By the time we got onstage to introduce the show, the crowd had been waiting a long time. They were heckling us; I wasn't even sure what they were saying, but I shouted back at them. Finally, we got offstage and they brought Ronnie on—and he was so drunk he couldn't talk, plus the slides were all out of order. It was a total mess, and we were just lucky the show wasn't filmed.

After the show, somehow word got to Ronnie that Keith Richards wanted to see him. Keith was staying at the Plaza Hotel, so we headed up there—it was Ronnie, Peter, me, J. J., and maybe one other person. Ronnie knocked on Keith's door, and he was still loaded. Keith opened the door, and he was so pissed at Ronnie, he practically lifted him up by the collar. Word had gotten back to Keith about what a mess the show was, and he was livid: You didn't damage the name of the Stones like that. J. J. looked at me, and we both knew this was not going to be our chance to hang out with Keith. We turned on our heels and walked out of the Plaza.

Mark:

I saw Jim Steinman onstage playing with Meat Loaf. He wasn't the front man, but he had the spotlight on him. He wore these enormous gloves, with tassels hanging off them; I wondered how he could pos-sibly play piano in those gloves. Meat Loaf was awful live—he couldn't carry a tune in a bucket. MTV ended up giving heavy airplay to a video from that tour, a version of "Paradise by the Dashboard Light" that had Karla DeVito on the female vocals, which Ellen Foley had done in the studio.

Carol and I had dinner with Steinman around the time he put out his solo record *Bad for Good*. He had a dry sense of humor, but he seemed bitter that everybody gave the credit to Meat Loaf for *Bat out of Hell*, when it was all him except for the singing—and Meat Loaf wasn't that great a singer. At dinner, Steinman ordered the whole menu. He literally ordered everything on the menu—he was that rich, and that into the rock 'n' roll lifestyle. He didn't want to have to decide; he liked being able to sample from lots of different plates.

Martha:

The Who did a press conference to announce their last-ever tour—the first time they ever did a farewell tour. Everybody at MTV was panicking because we wanted Roger Daltrey on the air, but J. J. was on vacation, and he was the one who had the relationship with the band. I went down to the restaurant where the press conference was—they were hoping that if Daltrey saw me, he would feel bad and do the interview. Somehow I convinced him, and he took a cab to the studio.

We placed Daltrey's chair as close to the front door as was physically possible—he barely had to take two steps. We were terrified that he would change his mind. J. J. was out of town and Mark wasn't there, so it had to be me. I was nervous because I wasn't one of the big boys, but psyched to get the chance, like an understudy who finally gets to go onstage.

Mark:

I liked Duran Duran, but I didn't listen to them at home, which I always thought was the acid test. I did play a lot of Bryan Adams at home. I was a huge fan—I thought he was a great songwriter. Around the time of "Cuts Like a Knife," I interviewed Bryan and he invited me to his show at the Bottom Line. I decided to bring him a bottle of champagne. "Thanks for champers!" he said. Bryan's opening act that night was Stevie Ray Vaughan, who was getting known for playing on David Bowie's *Let's Dance* album but turning down the tour that followed. The situation that night was uncomfortable, because everybody was talking about the opening act.

Nina:

I went to an AC/DC video shoot, down in Alphabet City at a condemned theater space. I didn't interview the guys in the band, but I noticed how they were smaller than I was—which was something, because I was tiny—and they were running around manically. It was like something out of *The Wizard of Oz:* tough little drunk Munchkins with Australian accents. I was told that the production company spent more on beer during that shoot than they did on the actual production of the video.

Mark:

MTV sent me out on the road to cover the Genesis tour for their *Abacab* record; I filed a report from the first gig, which was somewhere in the Midwest, maybe Indiana. I stayed in the same hotel as the band, and bonded with Phil Collins. We had a couple of days before the tour started where we basically hung out by the pool. He was a fan of MTV. We had some great conversations about soul music—although he had seen me on TV quite a bit, it was a shock to him that I had grown up listening to Motown and Stax-Volt. Phil was the sweetest guy in the world; I was shocked and flattered beyond belief when he invited me to his wedding.

Nina:

I really liked Cy Curnin, the lead singer of the Fixx. He was an intelligent guy, very well read. I think the band could've been even bigger than they were—they ran into some problems with their management and got stalled. They had hits, but they really weren't handled right. After the band broke up, Cy became a haberdasher. He promised to send me a hat, but he forgot, and now he doesn't do it anymore.

Their video for "Stand or Fall" was one of my early favorites, because it had a beautiful white horse in the woods. All videos should have white horses—and unicorns and fairy dust. Martha used to laugh at me because one of my favorite videos was Fleetwood Mac's "Gypsy." I would jump in and live in that video if I could: not the black-and-white section at the speakeasy, but the color section in the magical forest. Martha used to say, "Oh, you and your airy-fairy video."

Martha:

I briefly went out with Adrian Wright of the Human League, while the band was touring behind *Dare*. We had only two dates, but for one of them I went to see the band play in Toronto, and for the other, I took him to my grandparents' house, up in Troy, New York, just outside of Albany. I have no idea why I did that: It seems crazy. I was into the fact that my grandparents were super-cool—I went to visit them a lot—so maybe I thought it would be fun to bring him along.

Adrian ended up sleeping downstairs in my grandfather's woodshop. My grandparents probably thought, "What the heck? Why is this British guy in a motorcycle jacket sleeping in our basement?"

Nina:

The Stray Cats had to go to England to get acknowledged—but they were three kids from Long Island. I thought they were good, but a rockabilly act like that never would have gotten played on the radio if they hadn't done so well on MTV. One time, I was trying to interview them, and they kept running around the set, like a bunch of kids on the playground. Eventually I had to tell them, "Sit down, we got to do the interview." I liked them, but I used to call them my little bunch of monkeys.

Mark:

I thought Men at Work got short shrift—people treated them like the poor man's Police. It's unfortunate that they're remembered for "Down Under," which is a fine song, but not their best. I've gotten to know

Colin Hay much better in the post-MTV years—he's a cool storyteller with a sharp sense of humor, which comes through in the songs. A few years ago, I told Colin my favorite Men at Work song is "Overkill," and he said, "That's the thinking man's favorite Men at Work song." Thank you—that's me.

I did have my difficulties dealing with Colin's lazy eye. That goddamn eyeball.

Martha:

We did a MTV concert with Foreigner, and they were great guys. But "Urgent" has always made me laugh, because it was so totally written by a guy. Believe me, no girl is calling and saying "it's urgent" in the middle of the night, unless she's a groupie. During MTV's heyday, I guffawed when people complained that the music or the videos were sexist: "Oh, you people have to get a clue. You can't worry about this stuff." Now that I have a teenage daughter, I've got a long list of songs that make me cringe. "(She's) Sexy + 17" by the Stray Cats. "Hot Girls in Love" by Loverboy. "Super Freak" by Rick James. "Come on Eileen," not only because of the title, but because of the lyrics about taking off that red dress. I used to listen to that song over and over. I'd put it on my turntable and hit repeat. Now, my attitude is "Eileen, you keep that pretty red dress on!"

I was watching a John Parr video recently, "Naughty Naughty"— he's in a motel room and all these girls are groping him, and I was thinking, My God, what a horrible message this is. Why didn't I see that at the time? I have to admit, now I see where Tipper Gore and the PMRC were coming from.

Mark:

The Kinks had a big comeback on MTV. Who would have thought that a British Invasion dude like Ray Davies would segue into that? But he embraced videos and loved them.

During the time that he was together with Chrissie Hynde of the Pretenders, Ray lived in my building on Seventy-second Street. I saw him occasionally in the lobby. I really wanted him to come in for an interview at MTV; I made a request through an executive at Arista Re-cords, but I also slipped a note under his door. Ray agreed to do it, and I met him downstairs so we could ride down to the studio together. He was rushing: "Come on, hurry up, let's get a cab."

I said, "Okay, but we have a little time to get down there."

"No, no. I told Chrissie I was just going out for cigarettes. We're supposed to be on vacation—she'd fucking kill me if she knew I was doing an interview."

I wasn't surprised that relationship didn't last.

18

I know There's something Going on

Alan and Martha's Dangerous Game

Alan:

Early on, one of the producers said to me, "You know, Alan, I wondered if you'd keep that wedding ring off when you're on the air. The girls out there, they just want to have their fantasies." That was fine—I figured "VJ Alan Hunter" was a character, and I'd always taken my ring off onstage.

Jan wasn't happy about that. We debated it at home and she said, "You're married! Why shouldn't you wear your ring?"

I kind of agreed with her, but I said, "I didn't think you were going to be that upset with it, because this is just a role I'm playing."

"You need to stop acting like you're single and stop creating this fantasy world for the fans."

There was a tense situation for the first few months: I'd go to work and they'd say, "Take the ring off," and then I'd go home and she'd say, "Put it on!" I hated being in the middle, but ultimately I had to say that I was married and I wasn't going to pose. Every day, they would tell me, "Be natural and be yourself." Well, I'm married, and the audience is just going to have to deal with it.

Martha:

My shift intersected with Alan's, which meant we could do a toss, which was the transition from one VJ to the next. It was the best part of the day, because I could interact with somebody else. We had a very quick, sparky rapport, like Gracie and George Burns, or maybe Regis and Kathy Lee.

Alan:

And flirtatious, but just as part of that rapport when we were doing the crossovers on camera. You do what you can to create vibe and atmosphere.

Martha:

Well, here's the truth. I think our rapport was very flirtatious because I was being very flirtatious. When I first met Alan, he reminded me of my older brothers—I always saw them as perfect all-American heroes. I'd never met a guy who was so like them, and I couldn't believe he was married.

Alan:

The camera heightens everything that's going on. I knew Martha was flirting, and I was volleying back her serve.

Martha:

Flirting can be a default conversational setting between a man and a woman.

Alan:

The higher-ups would have loved for Martha and I to be an item.

Martha:

I didn't have a game plan. I was unaware that I was playing with fire.

Alan:

The VJs had offices up on Sixth Avenue, where the MTV corporate headquarters were. It was pretty token, but we had desks. We could tape our segments and then run up to the office and sit at our little desks, with pens and paper from the supply closet. It always felt like I was playing "office."

One day, Martha and I were in the conference room, watching some of our air checks on VHS. We hadn't seen a lot of them, and wanted to know how we were coming across. We were sitting on the conference table, next to each other, almost like a high-school boyfriend and girlfriend with our legs swinging back and forth. And then Jan came flying through the door.

Maybe she called and told me she was coming to the office, and I forgot. But when she came in, she flipped. She wasn't hysterical, but she let it be known she wasn't happy.

Martha:

That night, Jan called me at home. She said, "I want you to stop flirting with my husband."

I said, "No, Jan, you're all wrong. It's just fun, it's nothing like that." I denied it 100 percent. But my heart stopped, because I was busted. *Busted!*

Alan:

I wasn't looking to cheat, and at the same time I thought Martha was awful cute. I was complicit too—I was reciprocating the flirtation. That whole brouhaha was an early moment when I realized I had to grow up a bit.

Martha:

I was twenty-two, and Alan was twenty-four. So at an early age, Jan taught me a lesson that I've never forgotten: *Respect the sisterhood.* Never ever flirt with another woman's guy. There's a million fish in the sea: You don't need hers. To this day, if I run into a married couple at the grocery store, I immediately make eye contact with the wife. I don't care if I'm better friends with the husband—I talk to the wife.

Alan:

I had no idea Jan was going to call Martha. That whole thing was so embarrassing—I loved Jan, but didn't appreciate her making those assumptions, or acting out like that in front of Martha, who was my new friend and cohort in the best thing that had ever happened in my life.

Martha:

Jan sent me flowers later on, apologizing for her "green-eyed monster," but really, she was right and I was wrong. We wound up being good friends, which speaks volumes about her character.

Alan:

I resented having to be self-conscious about working with Martha, but our on-camera interactions changed after that.

Martha:

I became very formal when we did the toss after that. "Hello, Alan! Top of the morning to you! How is your *wife?* Tell me *everything* about your wife."

19

Things can only get Better

Cable TV's Potholes and Pitfalls

Mark:

Supposedly, MTV launched in two million households. That was what they told us, but they were feeding us the same crap they told everybody else. From what I understand, we were actually under a million. I never doubted MTV was going to work, but there were plenty of people above me who weren't so sure. It didn't feel like we were struggling, but we really were.

Alan:

Cable penetration was all-important. People saw the famous "I Want My MTV" ads, with Mick Jagger and David Bowie telling people to call up their local cable company and ask them to add MTV to the lineup. Behind the scenes, they sent the VJs out to glad-hand everybody in the cable industry. I would go to cable conventions and shake a lot of hands and sit in booths with guys who wore Members Only jackets. It was a weird low-rent world. Sometimes I'd sign pictures for guys who provided infrastructure: the actual cable.

"What do you do, Bob?"

"I build the Ditch Witch that digs the ditches for the cable to go into."

"All right. You want an autograph?"

"It's not for me—it's for my daughter."

Mark:

We called the cable operators the "pole climbers." We had to hang with them—not just selling MTV, but convincing them that MTV would sell cable.

Martha:

The VJs went from town to town, taking pictures with cable operators everywhere from Amarillo, Texas, to Fargo, North Dakota, trying to convert them to our cause. It felt like we were the Jehovah's Witnesses of rock 'n' roll.

Alan:

Cable was a male-dominated field, and I could see the disappointment in the men's eyes when they realized that I was the VJ who got sent, not Nina or Martha. I started a lot of those visits by saying, "I'm sorry Martha couldn't make it."

I don't think they ever sent us out to woo a cable operator that wasn't on board already. Some of the trips were to make sure they didn't drop us. I'd fly into a town and get picked up at the airport. Sometimes it was a limo, sometimes it was a limo that had seen better days, and sometimes it was a Camaro with Jenny Sue the manager and Bob the CEO. We were unbelievable rock stars for these people— MTV was so important for them selling their packages to customers. I was never jaded about it.

Mark:

We used to have VJ meetings with Bob Pittman every few weeks. But as the head of the company, he got too swamped, so we didn't meet with him anymore—and nobody else was meeting with us. We just got memos with edicts from on high.

Early on, Mattel made a major ad buy for their Synsonics electronic drums. It was a toy/musical instrument, so we were all supposed to mess around with it in the studio and look like we were having a good time.

Martha:

That was a goofy idea. I thought, "I have to pretend to play a drum machine? Are you kidding?" It was embarrassing, but I sucked it up and gave it my best shot.

Alan:

J. J. was disdainful of it. He played with it a little and giggled. I had the most fun with it: It was a toy, and the more toys I had, the better I felt. If I had a prop on the set that would distract people from listening to what I was saying—or not saying—I was much more comfortable.

Mark:

J. J. and I were irate—we were doing regularly scheduled commercials for a product, and it felt like MTV was stiffing us. Extra fees for ads is how DJs supplement their income! I called up Pittman and in the nicest, most respectful way, said, "Look, I understand this is a buy, but I usually get paid to do these things."

Pittman was very even-keeled, not high-pressure. But he had the demeanor of a southern Jack Nicholson: *If you don't do what I want you to do, I'm going to cut your nuts off.* He said, "Well, Mark, if you don't want to do it, I think we can probably find somebody who does."

"Okay, I understand, Bob, thank you."

Alan:

To me, it was all part of the job. But J. J. and Mark always held the flag high for journalistic credibility. Their credibility was more at stake than mine, at least in the music arena.

Mark:

I probably wouldn't have said anything if I had known how much we were struggling for advertising. Because we weren't getting MTV in Manhattan, we didn't really know what was going on.

At about twenty minutes past the hour, there was a local availability: That's a spot where the local cable affiliate can sell commercials themselves. That hourly spot was part of why cable companies would pick us up. And if they didn't show anything there, we would broadcast this stock NASA footage—just an astronaut floating in space, set to music. We sold a few national spots, but not a lot, and the affiliates sold hardly any local spots. People used to write to us about how great they thought that video of the guy floating in space was.

Alan:

Even though we weren't selling ads, we were showing that we could sell a lot of records. Stray Cats were a band that nobody knew in the heartland, but through sheer force of video exposure, they were selling a lot of records in towns that had MTV. Suddenly, Duran Duran were selling a lot of records in Iowa.

One day we had a meeting with Les Garland in the studio's conference room, which also served as our kitchenette. We sat around the table with the producers, and he told us, "There's this Australian band called INXS. We're going to do a huge experiment—the record company is going to spend a lot of money and we're going to see if we can break this band in America." Basically, MTV was trying to prove to the music industry that they could single-handedly put a band on the map.

Nina:

That was the first time we made a concerted effort to push a band. Luckily, they were worth pushing!

Alan:

We had "The One Thing" in heavy rotation and we had promo copy we would read afterward. Half a year later, mission accomplished: INXS were a huge hit in the United States and their album *Shabooh Shoobah* sold a ton of copies. I was amazed that the plan rolled out exactly the way it was supposed to. I thought it was cool; I didn't know or care about payola in the music business, and I didn't think this smacked of any kind of shady backroom deal. As far as I was concerned, we were just making some smart alliances.

> *J. J. Jackson, filming a VJ spot in 1982 that went unaired but made its way to an internal MTV outtakes reel:*
>
> *"That's the Finn brothers, a great band from New Zealand: Split Enz, 'Six Months in a Leaky Boat.' In New York tonight in midtown Manhattan, there's a party to celebrate MTV coming to the city. We want to send our regards to all of you at the party: Everyone from Manhattan Cable, and everyone who has come to celebrate with us. And we hope you're all having a wonderful time at the party—because none of us were invited to the goddamn party! And we're a little upset about it! We've been breaking our balls for a year, and none of us are invited! But you have a good time tonight at that party while we're just raunching it out. We'll be here until eleven o'clock. Hey, bring us some cake, a little champagne. . . ." The segment concludes with J. J. singing "There's No Business Like Show Business."*

Martha:

After a year, MTV finally came to Manhattan cable. I was very excited that I could wake up, go downstairs, and watch it. In reality, that meant climbing down the ladder from my loft bed and turning on my illegal cable. But finally, MTV was on my television set. I was flipping out: *"My God, this is incredible, it's really here."* It was very exciting. It felt like we were affecting the world, because our friends would say, "Wow, this really exists."

Alan:

I would roll in from a night on the town and turn on MTV. There's Phil Collins, "In the Air Tonight," and then runaway camera happens—oh, that's kind of magic. That's something I don't usually see on TV at three in the morning. Working in the studio, I hadn't been thinking about the audience beyond the TV camera—it was hard to grasp that there were dorm rooms full of college kids, partying to MTV, watching everything we beamed out.

Martha:

I found myself watching the channel for hours, because there was a major disconnect between what we were doing in the studio and what was broadcast. At home, I could see not only the videos, but all the cool animation and interstitial spots. Like the rest of America, I was obsessed. I would have a car downstairs, waiting to take me to MTV, but I'd keep it waiting too long . . . because I was watching MTV.

Alan:

All the time, people would come up to each of us and tell that VJ that he or she played the best music on MTV. That wasn't entirely accurate, because we didn't pick the videos, and at that time, MTV didn't do "day-parting," where you play different music at different times of day. We all had the same random mix. But what we talked about affected how people felt about what they were watching.

Mark got people throwing up the horns and saying, "Yo, Mark!" with a Jersey accent. My demographic skewed toward women: housewives who liked Howard Jones and did aerobics to my show. The female viewers saw me as the cute little boy next door, and they just wanted to hold on to me and mother me. And the rockers wanted to sleep with Nina and Martha. Nina got the most heavy metal fans.

We were only a small part of MTV; we did one-minute segments four times an hour, and the rest of it was videos and interstitial segments and commercials. MTV really was the epicenter of hip. It was on the leading edge, at the beginning of every new trend. The network was always morphing before the viewers had a chance to catch up. For at least six or seven years, it was never behind the audience. We were just the faces of the whole channel—but we definitely thought we were the most important part of the package.

ı spend my cash on Looking flash and crabbing your attention

Fashion in the 1980s

Nina:

Quarterly, MTV would give us five hundred dollars for on-air clothes. I'd go shopping down in the Village and SoHo.

Martha:

This was before the era of celebrity stylists. People would wear gowns at the Oscars, but if you look through *People* magazine in the '80s, you'll see photo shoots with stars like Geena Davis who are just wearing mall outfits.

Alan:

When I got that first five hundred dollars for clothes, before the channel launched, I went to Macy's and bought five pairs of the same drawstring pants: vibrant orange and pink and blue. Neon colors were the deal then. And big sweaters with swirling multicolors—the trend was looking like a pack of crayons had melted all over you.

And parachute pants, and big shoulders, and flaps of clothing with buttons.

Mark:

I really got into buying clothes. I'd go to Charivari, on Seventy-second and Columbus. I loved that place—they had a cool collection of styles, ranging from casual to dressy, all with a pulled-together look. I bought more than one New Year's outfit there.

Alan:

I thought Mark was a dopey dresser at the beginning. He would wear these cream-colored Hush Puppies. Then again, I was Mr. Tennis Shoes and Suspenders.

Mark:

The other jocks used to make fun of me because I had this giant puffy Norma Kamali down-filled coat. It was black and shin-length. It was designed to be born worn by a guy or a girl, but the girls' coats were usually white or bright iridescent colors. Not a lot of guys were wearing Norma Kamali at that time.

Martha:

To me, cutting-edge fashion was a Pee-wee Herman T-shirt.

Mark:

J. J. would wear his marine lapel pin on the air, or corduroy jackets. Or sometimes, a turtleneck sweater and a jacket like Hugh Hefner. The executives had issues with his wardrobe choices.

Alan:

I was also Mr. Padded Shoulders. David Byrne's suit in "Once in a Lifetime"—I was into that all day long.

Mark:

We used to go to the Parachute store downtown in SoHo. I had a Parachute jacket—it was a black canvas thing with a big collar and zippers. I was so excited when I met the guy who ran the showroom for Go Silk. I stocked up on shirts, pants, suits—whatever I could get. I loved their clothes, Jagger had been wearing their suits—and what the fuck, they were free!

Alan:

We weren't copying any of the bands, but we were going to Parachute around the same time as Duran Duran. We were wearing clothes that were ahead of the time, so I guess we were trendsetters.

Mark:

When I went back home to Philly, I felt out of place, in the best possible way. It's a working-class town, and people didn't wear clothes like that.

Alan:

The ubiquity of rock-star fashion on MTV allowed people not only to dream about it, but to dress like that. Go to the mall and get a Madonna-style outfit, or get your scissors and chop up your sweatshirt. Put the bandanna on like Mike Reno from Loverboy. That was one of the great things about MTV—everybody could join the party.

Martha:

Fashion in the '80s was about throwing convention out the window, in favor of asymmetrical hair and neon colors. It was a time of big dichotomies: chunky socks with high heels. Sweatshirts with pearls— I worked that a lot. We could wear two *different* earrings! We were rebels!

Nina:

I had this one outfit with jagged edges and tights, and it happened to be green. It was a little Peter Pannish, but Pat Benatar wore that stuff too. I mean, it's not like I made it at home. And I was really skinny, so I could wear that stuff—I was five foot four and a half, and I weighed ninety-five pounds, tops. Mark told me that outfit made me look like Miss Pippi, the host of a children's TV show in Pennsylvania. He gave me some career advice: Don't wear it.

Mark:

The character was actually named Pixanne—she had a kids' show in Philadelphia when I was growing up. She dressed up like Peter Pan, with green tights, a green skirt and top, and a little hat with a feather. She was cute and warm and completely nonsexual, and yet I always wanted to go on her show and hug her.

Martha:

After a while, they would send a stylist out with us when we went shopping. One stylist took me to Fifty-seventh Street to buy a cashmere sweater. I was saying, "We're going to blow all my money on this one sweater. Are you sure this is a good idea?" And she insisted. J. J. gave me the purple cashmere sweater she'd convinced him to buy—for years, I wore it as a dress.

Nina:

Having the "video vixen" reputation helped me get a little more high-fashion stuff. Norma Kamali and Betsey Johnson sent me clothes, and a lot of up-and-coming designers sent me pieces as well.

Mark:

The labels would send us lots of band T-shirts—obviously, they were hoping we'd wear them on the air. I collected them: I had drawers and drawers full of them. And I was working out, lifting heavy weights, so sometimes I would cut off the collar and the sleeves.

All five of us got sent replicas of the red leather jacket Michael Jackson wore in "Beat It." I have no idea what happened to mine.

Martha:

That makes me feel so much better—I don't have mine either.

Alan:

I have mine!

Mark:

Of course Al the pack rat still has his. J. J. used to wear his on the air.

Martha:

I saw an old photo where I was wearing a short-sleeved button-down shirt, tucked into a pair of khaki pants. I looked like a Yalie. It seemed fine at the time, but looking back, the preppy look was not sexy.

I interviewed Lenny Dykstra and Roger McDowell of the New York Mets, wearing a jean jacket and jeans. I looked like the batboy, but Lenny Dykstra flirted with me anyway.

Mark:

All the executives at MTV wanted to sleep with Martha—which I think means they were all perverts. She looked like she was twelve.

Martha:

If I could have dressed like Vanity, I would have. One of the reasons why I always drove in the cute lane instead of the sexy lane is that I have a physical deal. I was in Keds 90 percent of the time because I can't actually wear any kind of heels. My right side is smaller than the left side of my body and doesn't really work as well. My mother says the doctors told her that I had cerebral palsy when I was born, but she never told me that was the diagnosis when I was a kid. I don't know if that's actually the case, but whatever it was, when I was growing up I had to wear a big brace on my right leg to stretch it out.

Alan:

And men would come by with leeches and stretch her out on a rack.

Martha:

Now they would do physical therapy. Back then, they didn't do that. But that's why I can't wear heels—I don't have good enough balance. My life would probably be different if I could have. I look back, and clearly I was not embracing any kind of sex appeal. I'll never know for sure whether it's because of my physical condition or because I was sabotaging myself.

she's precocious and she knows just what it takes to make a pro blush

Martha Quinn, America's Sweetheart

Martha:

After Tony, I got serious very quickly—with a guy who'd worked with Tony. I wanted so badly to be in that secure, mature relationship I'd always dreamed of, the kind Al and Jan had. I moved in with this guy, but then it didn't feel right: I'd gone too far, too fast. I wanted to go back to my old apartment. I called the management at One Astor Place, where I had been living before, and got another apartment in the same building. I felt so bad, I paid rent on that empty apartment for seven months before I found the nerve to tell my boyfriend I wanted to move out.

When I moved back to Astor Place, I didn't have any furniture, so I bought a table from Conran's. It was a picnic table with a striped umbrella, and I kept the umbrella up—I felt very *New York* magazine.

Mark:

I never saw Martha's apartment. It was weird—none of us went to each other's apartments.

Martha:

I never had visitors because my apartment was such a mess. Always. My next-door neighbor, who became my friend, once came over to ask if she could borrow a cup of sugar or something. I said, "Yes, I'll bring it over"—but I wouldn't let her inside.

Alan:

A few months after MTV launched, Julian Goldberg, our executive producer, told me and Martha that the two of us were going to be the most popular VJs at MTV. That wasn't something I expected, or banked on.

Martha:

He probably said that to everyone.

Alan:

We had no ratings or Nielsen coverage back then, but somebody was keeping track of popularity. They were doing it through fan mail, they were doing it by polling their record-company buddies. I don't know what the metrics were, but we were definitely being judged.

Mark:

Martha was perky, she was plucky. She had that smile and those teeth, and she was cute in a nonthreatening way. Pretty soon, she was America's Sweetheart.

Martha:

Originally, I was on in the mornings and then they bumped me to the afternoons. I got J. J.'s shift and that's when Nina got overnights.

Alan:

I was on the graveyard shift and I went to mornings. That was the first time we realized they were paying attention.

Martha:

The afternoon drive-time shift was prestigious because everybody was coming from radio, when the biggest audiences come during the daily commutes. Those times didn't really make sense on TV, because nobody was watching us in their car. What made it a plum shift was that I was on after school got out.

When I took over J. J.'s shift, I felt terrible. I didn't want to be in a position where I was making J. J. look bad or feel bad. Also, most of my other friends were still going to NYU or working in entry-level positions; I didn't know how to talk about this amazing job. I went to Thanksgiving at my grandparents' house in Troy, and when all my cousins asked about MTV, I kept downplaying it. My mom pulled me aside and said, "You've got to stop doing this. Everyone's excited about you working at MTV and you're making them feel stupid for asking."

Alan:

It can seem pretentious to accept compliments from fans—self-deprecation and humility feel noble, but really, they're cumbersome. Fans just want you to own your status. I think the rest of us have no problem saying that Martha was the darling of the channel.

Mark:

She was definitely the fair-haired child with management.

Martha:

Early on, Billy Joel was dropping by the MTV studios, and Les Garland thought it would be good for the channel to manufacture gossip: He asked me to go out with Billy Joel on some public dates. I was like,

"Uhhh, but I have a boyfriend." Everyone at the channel told me I should do it anyway. I was saying, "Um, really? I don't think so."

Part of me thought this would be the first offer in a long series of staged romances with rock stars. As it turned out, that was the only time it ever came up. In hindsight, I should have said, "Hell yeah!" and told my boyfriend, "This is business—I'm going out with Billy Joel tonight!"

Five entertaining things about Billy Joel's "Pressure" video, which seemed spooky and portentous in 1982 and is pants-wettingly funny now:

1. *Billy writhes around in his leather jacket, attempting to simulate electroshock.*
2. *A car splashes water on Billy's shoes—replayed repeatedly in slo-mo, as if it's a presidential assassination.*
3. *Billy gets pulled into a white shag rug that appears to be made of quicksand.*
4. *A little kid gets sucked into a TV set, Poltergeist style—accompanied, for some reason, by a wide array of vegetables.*
5. *Billy appears on a game show, introduced by this on-screen text: "William Joel / Age: 29 / Occupation: Computer Software / Intersts [sic]: fast bikes, cooking, water sports, satellite." His actual age at the time of the video: 33.*

Martha:

I had a crush on Mark. One year for his birthday, I made him a tape where I sang a whole song to the tune of the Beatles' "Yesterday." It had lines like "But if you only knew the times I hid my eyes for fear you'd see my crush on you-ooo."

Mark:

How did I let America's Sweetheart slip through my fingers? The answer is that at the beginning, Martha seemed like a kid to me. I had nothing to say to her; she was like a little girl. So I had no interest. Later on, I think she got hotter. About a year in, maybe a year and a half, she started to dress cute, in short skirts. She started taking birth-control pills and her boobs got bigger. The entire crew noticed that! I went back and forth on Martha.

Martha:

Paul Stanley of Kiss, and his manager, Howard Marks, called me in for a meeting: They wanted to manage me. They said they'd put me in really cool outfits. I couldn't imagine what that meant—leather miniskirts? In hindsight, maybe that wouldn't have been so terrible. But in the folly-of-youth department, I thought it was an odd offer, and I declined.

Sometime later, I went on a date with Paul. We went to Bowlmor, a bowling alley on University Place in Greenwich Village. Paul brought his own shoes, his own ball in a personalized bag, the whole works. I thought, "Whoa—this is kind of intense. He's *really* into bowling." First frame, I rolled a strike. Paul did not. Then he got down on the floor and started analyzing the pitch of the lane. He wasn't happy. He went up to the manager and says, "There's something wrong with this lane. We need a different lane." I couldn't handle it. That was the only time we went out.

22

They Told Him Don't You Ever Come 'Round Here

The Irresistible Rise of Michael Jackson

Mark:

Before *Let's Dance* came out, David Bowie did a press junket in a hotel room. It was one of those deals where interviewers file in one at a time. I had interviewed him before, on the radio, but I'm sure he didn't remember me.

I said, "I have some tough questions for you, David—I hope you're ready."

And he said, "Ha, great, because at the end I'd like to ask you some punishing questions as well."

That comment just blew by me.

At the end of the interview, he started asking me why there was such a dearth of black music on MTV.

I said, not trying to toe the corporate line but honestly, "Listen, if this was a radio station, we'd be a rock station. It wouldn't make sense for us to play stuff that isn't in our format."

The conversation got around to Bowie saying, "Don't you think there are black kids in the audience who would like to see some of these videos?"

I said, "Well, I guess so, but this is what we do, and we have to think about the audience that has cable." A lot of times we were finding that cable's heaviest subscribers were in rural areas where they couldn't get any television reception at all, out in Oklahoma or whatever—not usually your biggest fans of urban music.

Bowie was hammering me, and I was trying to defend the network—but it was an awkward position, and I was looking around for some help. Gale Sparrow in the talent department was there, as was John Sykes, one of our big executives, but nobody was stepping forward. Ultimately, they cut that part of the interview out. I think they did air it years later, which is okay with me.

What irritated me was that I felt like a pawn. I had no say over what MTV played—I wasn't an executive. And Bowie knew what the situation was. He knew John Sykes, and he knew a lot of the other principals. He was just using me to bring this issue into the forefront. I felt like an idiot, and I felt used, and I felt insignificant to David Bowie—which I probably was, anyway.

It wasn't my finest moment. As I thought about it afterward, I worried that I looked stupid to Bowie, and to the people around me. And I wondered if there actually was an issue. J. J. and I talked about it. He was a rocker, but what he said to me—which I hadn't really thought about—was that we were playing white people who were basically doing black music. Even Bowie, to some extent. Why wouldn't we play black artists doing music in the same style?

Nina:

I did not believe that MTV was a racist channel at all. We played videos by Joan Armatrading, Jon Butcher, Garland Jefferies, and Phil Lynott with Thin Lizzy—but they were all in the rock genre.

Mark:

I didn't see the conflict so much as black performers saying, "Hey, that white band is doing the same kind of music as us, why shouldn't you play us?" I thought the point of view was more, "These bands are making all this money, we want some." I certainly know that's what the record labels were saying: There was a whole column of artists that we weren't touching, and they wanted us to play them because MTV was a very effective form of promotion. It radically affected record sales.

I grew up listening to black music and hanging with black people and going on black dance shows. But my naïve perspective was about making our format the best that it could be. I went home and listened to Prince, but for better or worse, I wasn't in a headspace of thinking, "Well, we should be playing black music too."

Martha:

I was in the music director's office when Michael Jackson's video for "Billie Jean" came in. I said, "Wow, this is amazing."

He chuckled and said, "Yeah, but we can't play this."

People said we didn't play the video because Michael Jackson was black—I just don't believe that. It was because we were rockers and it was pop.

Mark:

Bob Pittman's from Mississippi, but I don't believe he's a racist. I just don't. Les Garland and John Sykes and the other executives who came in over the years, I don't believe they're racist either. I think they were the victims of old-school thinking. They were believers in AOR radio: That stands for "Album-Oriented Rock," which was what the industry called the rock format.

CBS Records ultimately said, "You need to play 'Billie Jean' or we're going to pull all of our artists from the channel." And then they did.

MTV didn't play "Billie Jean" until March 2, 1983, after the Thriller *album and the "Billie Jean" single had already hit number one. The MTV executives have always insisted that they were blown away by "Billie Jean" and rushed it on the air. For example, Les Garland: "I was the first person at MTV to see it, and I'll never forget putting it in my three-quarter-inch machine, hitting the start button, hearing the bass beat to 'Billie Jean' start up and going, 'Holy shit . . . are you kidding me?' I called everybody in and said, 'You've got to see this. This is the best video of its time!' Pittman was on the West Coast. I phoned him*

*and said, 'Bob, wait until you see "Billie Jean." It's going to blow your
mind.' We put it on midweek. It wasn't even a Tuesday add."*

Mark:

I don't believe that for one minute. At this point, I don't even know
why they would deny that happened. I remember when CBS pulled
all their product—we had a production meeting where the word
came down that we wouldn't have all these artists anymore. I talked
to people who were doing the logs of what videos we played, and they
had to go through all of them to make sure there were no CBS artists
in there. It didn't last for a long time—it might have been less than a
week—but it was more than one day, and it definitely happened.

When MTV caved and finally agreed to play Michael Jackson,
CBS also forced us to play this Barbra Streisand video for "Emotion"
that had Roger Daltrey and Mikhail Baryshnikov in it. It was the worst
piece of shit ever, and the label basically said, "Yeah, you're playing this
too, bitches."

Martha:

We were ecstatic when "Billie Jean" got added—art trumped format.
What we didn't see at the time was how it was the foot in the door
to expanding the format. And then it became a constant exercise in
expanding it a little more: How about a game show? How about a
reality show?

Nina:

I think expanding was the right decision. How could you not play
Michael Jackson? You cannot think of MTV now without thinking of
it having Michael Jackson on it.

Martha:

It felt like we played that "Thriller" film every twenty minutes. But it
was more impactful at home than it was in the studio. For us, it was

just another segment. You'd say, "Wow, how about that Vincent Price rap," and then move right into "Well, anyway, this Saturday, we have a Triumph concert."

We had a *lot* of Michael Jackson coverage. When he got burned filming those Pepsi commercials, we got the news after hours, so the studio was closed—I went up to the MTV offices to film a news report. And when the commercial finally came out, we gave it a world premiere and played it over and over. I never met him—I wish I had. I used to daydream about the two of us on the cover of *People*: "MTV PIXIE MARTHA QUINN MARRIES MICHAEL JACKSON."

23

I Might Like You Better if We Slept Together

Celebrity Flirtations and Liaisons

Nina:

Robert Plant came to MTV, and of course, J. J. did the interview. I had just finished my show, and I was getting my stuff before I left the studio. As I headed out the door, J. J. motioned me over—he wanted to introduce me. Plant looked me over, acting like English rock-star royalty, and said, "Well, *hello*." He was leering at me, but I grew to like him.

Mark:

Nina and Martha got hit on a lot. They both went out with Roger Glover, the bassist for Deep Purple. On separate dates, he took each of them for a ride in his sports car. And they both deny anything happened.

Martha:

The two of us had no idea until many years later. Roger dipped into the well of Martha and Nina, apparently. Which sounds a lot worse than it was!

Nina:

I did Duran Duran's first MTV interview. Their career was just starting—they weren't huge yet. I wondered what they did to the boys in England, because all of them were extremely pretty, and with full lips. I went to see the band play at the Pier, and John Taylor asked me out. I had a personal rule against dating the people I was interviewing, but I would have broken it for him. He was my type, and tall. I'm sure nothing physical would have happened that night, because I just don't on the first date. I didn't go out with John, because my friend Ida kept saying I shouldn't. I thought she was being protective of me, but later I found out she had a major crush on him.

Martha:

For a while, Paul Shaffer and I palled around quite a bit. He even took me to a temple service, but we couldn't sit together—I sat upstairs with the women. After the service, we were hanging out on the sidewalk, talking to Mick Jones from Foreigner. Paul and I used to say it was the greatest thing to be young, free, and in New York City.

Nina:

I went out with Paul and Martha one time—I wasn't clear on whether they were an item, or if they were just friends. We went to the Hard Rock Café, because it was close to my house. Paul was a notorious drinker, and I could definitely drink too. I don't think Martha put away as much. We were trying to have a conversation, but it was very loud. Paul told me, "You would be perfect in Vegas." And at that time, I hated Vegas, so I got mad, and I told him, "That's a big insult!" I wasn't as mad as I sounded; I was screaming because he couldn't hear me over the music. He explained that he meant it as a compliment, and that he loved Las Vegas. At the end of the night, he and Martha walked me home, just down the block. Paul was a little loaded. "Ohhhh, I really like you," he said. And then he and Martha got in a cab.

Martha:

Paul and I had one horrible experience together, when we went to see *The Gods Must Be Crazy,* the South African movie about a tribe of Bushmen who find a Coke bottle. It was a comedy, but I was just devastated by it—I thought it was incredibly sad, and I was sobbing. I think I traumatized him so much, he stopped going to movies after that. I would watch *Late Night with David Letterman,* and periodically he'd say that: "Yeah, I don't go to the movies."

Eventually, Paul thought I was being a tease and that was the end of that.

Nina:

I'm so lame about even recognizing when somebody likes me. Sometimes I'd hear about it when a band came by the studio—the talent coordinator would tell me, "So-and-so's interested in you." I know that there was a certain element of musicians who wanted to befriend me, or whatever, because they were thinking that being at MTV, I could help their career.

Steven Tyler told me that he had wanted to ask me out. When I was putting makeup on him, I had no idea he had a crush on me, but much later, he told me that I had reminded him of one of his wives. He's somebody else who would have been worth breaking my rule for—although it probably would have been a mistake, since that was before he got clean and sober. But it was cool to know.

Martha:

I was an egomaniac with an inferiority complex. I managed to believe simultaneously that everybody loved me and that nobody loved me. I don't think I was especially conscious of being the object of desire, but that's because I went from one day to the next like a mole, with absolutely no perspective. It's also hard for me to believe now, because I look at old clips of myself where I look like a boy, and I don't see the sex appeal. Nina was way hotter than me.

When MTV hired Downtown Julie Brown a few years later, she

walked into the studio and she looked like she was stepping out of a video. When I walked in, I looked like I was stepping out of the back room of a radio station.

Nina:

John Cougar came down to the studio very early, when we were playing "Hurts So Good." I was standing at the table where we kept the bagels, and he literally picked me up, hoisting me up in the air for a minute. Then we did the interview—both standing on the ground—and the crew did not like him at all. They thought he was a loudmouth punk. I liked him as a musical artist, but I didn't have a crush on him or anything. After we finished shooting, he invited me to a party later that night.

That night, I went to see Billy Vera and the Beaters play at the Ritz. One of the Beaters, the keyboard player, had been married to the actress Amy Madigan; they had split up, and she was already dating Ed Harris at that point, but she and her ex-husband stayed on good terms. Amy went on to star in *Field of Dreams,* but I knew her because we took acting classes together in L.A. I didn't really know her ex, but I had gone to the show to meet him because I was friends with Amy.

I was sitting at a table with a bunch of other MTV people, and I was talking with one of our producers, Brian Diamond. I told him, "Oh, John Cougar invited me to a party later, at his manager's apartment." Shows at the Ritz didn't start until after eleven, and John said the party was starting at 2 A.M.

Brian said, "He's not inviting you to a party."

I said, "Yes, he is. He said it was a party."

"Trust me—he's not. You shouldn't go there alone."

So I took the guy I was meeting—Amy's ex-husband, the Beater—and we went up to the apartment on Central Park West. There was nobody there but John, a pal of his, and his manager. The manager also handled Barry Manilow, so the apartment was this huge, beautiful pad. He gave me a tour, and he walked me through the master bedroom and said, "This is where you and John will be staying." I could be pretty clueless, but at that point, it was clear that Brian was right, and I was glad I had brought the Beater along.

We all sat in the kitchen, talking and drinking. John's friend was a guy from Bloomington, Indiana, who lived in a trailer—I think he might have been the inspiration for "Jack and Diane." John was getting irritable because he was figuring out it wasn't going to happen between me and him, and he was a cocky guy to begin with. John and the Beater ended up in this huge argument about everything: politics, religion, stupid stuff. John was ready to punch him out, which worked out well for me, because it distracted him. But even if the Beater hadn't been there, I would have gotten out of that situation—I always found a way. I've walked for miles down country roads in the middle of the night after a guy I didn't like tried to put the moves on me.

Years later, I interviewed John on his tour bus and he admitted he had been trying to pick me up. I mentioned the Beater, and he got mad all over again: "Yeah, who was that asshole?"

Mark:

I always loved Nancy Wilson from Heart, but I wouldn't have crossed that line by making a pass at her. It would have been totally inappropriate to hit on somebody I was interviewing. But if somebody else crossed that line toward me, that's something else again.

Lou Ann Barton was from Texas, and she was produced by Jerry Wexler, the legendary cofounder of Atlantic Records. She was a bluesy barroom singer with cool songs. I went to Wexler's apartment to listen to her album *Old Enough*. Wexler said to me, "Mark, you gotta hear this—it'll put your dick in the dirt." We played her video a bit, and when Lou Ann came in to the MTV studio for an interview, she was hugely hitting on me. Afterward, she wanted to go and have drinks. I was tempted, but I went home to Carol.

Alan:

After I finished with my morning shift at MTV, I would often meet my brother for breakfast at the Applejack Diner. And Diane Lane, the actress, always seemed to be there. We'd say hello and talk for a little while. She was single, she was totally my type, and I had a huge crush on her. I like to think that if I had been a single man, she would have been interested too.

Mark:

I went to the premiere of *Purple Rain* in Hollywood. The after-party was around the corner, at this old theater called the Palace. I was dancing with Apollonia all night, and I wanted her, but I was too intimidated to make a move. I was pretty well known by this point, but still riddled with insecurity. That was her moment, and she was unbelievably beautiful. I also assumed that she was dating Prince, although they didn't arrive together. Everybody figured that anyone he produced, he was also fucking. Susanna Hoffs of the Bangles denied it; I don't know about any of the others.

David Lee Roth knew Apollonia from before her time with Prince. He told me, "Her name's *Patty*, man. I used to go out with her."

Martha:

MTV made a deal where they would send tapes over to a Japanese TV network, which would play like one hour a week of MTV, and I went over to launch that. I did the entire trip without eating any sushi, because I thought I wouldn't like it. I wasn't a vegetarian yet, so I spent a week in Japan eating beef. And the week after I came home, I went to the Japanese restaurant near my apartment and tried sushi, and it was really good. Why didn't I have sushi in Japan? What's wrong with me?

I rode the bullet train, and I got to introduce Toto to the audience at the Budokan Arena, which was kind of amazing. Afterward, we all went out to dinner and I hit it off with Steve Porcaro, Toto's keyboardist. We talked for a long time, and the next day all of us went shopping for pearls—they knew a guy with really good pearls, apparently. Steve bought me a pair of pearl earrings: I felt like I was living the glamorous life. Back in the States, Steve lived in L.A., but we dated for about six months anyway. He wrote me a song called "Astor Place."

I used to tell Steve I hated "penis plants"—which is what I called red anthuriums, because of the way their stamens stick out. Every time I'd see one, I'd say, "Who would get those penis plants?" Steve was a sweet guy, but eventually the long-distance thing got old and we drifted apart. I don't think of it as an acrimonious breakup—we're still friendly today—but something must have been going on, because Steve sent me an entire bouquet of penis plants, with a card that said, "Fuck you." (Later he told me he had asked the florist for dead flowers, but there weren't any in the shop!) I wish I still had that card, but it went into the same incinerator as the crocheted blanket!

24

YOU MUST BE MY LUCKY STAR

Madonna Louise Veronica Ciccone

Alan:

Mark, Nina, and I were hanging out in the greenroom. A producer came in: Madonna was playing a show at the Limelight that night, and he needed someone to interview her. Nina had something else to do, Mark as well. I wasn't busy, so I got the nod. Madonna wasn't huge at the time—I felt like I was more of a celebrity than she was—and we were always balancing what activity we would enjoy on a given night with the work of doing an interview.

I arrived at the Limelight and had a quick chat with Madonna in a room behind the stage. Our interview wasn't very long, or incisive. She was serious, though—she was focused as shit. In the middle of the backstage chaos, she told me about her album—not one extraneous word, tough but polite.

This was before Madonna was groomed for stardom. She was fleshy, and her baubles looked like something she might have bought at a downtown trinket store herself. She looked self-made, not handled, but she had the air of somebody who knew that stardom was inevitable. The subtext of her attitude was "Alan, you have no idea how big I'm going to be. You'll rue how you weren't more respectful today." She was right; I don't think I even stayed around for her show.

Mark:

When Madonna came into the studio, I did the interview. I was a huge fan of hers from the very beginning—that's why I got to do it, because nobody else really gave a shit. She wasn't a great singer, and I didn't even think she was a great dancer, but confidence poured off her records, combined with sex, and that just got me. The *Like a Virgin* album hadn't come out yet, and although she was happening for us on that first record, she wasn't the star yet that she would later become.

I questioned her about the BOY TOY belt she used to wear: "So what does that mean, 'Boy Toy'?" And she said, "What do *you* think it means?" I should've stepped up at that moment, but I didn't, and I've regretted it for years. What I should've said was, "Well, I think it means that you're a toy for boys and that you love having wild sex," which is what we all thought, right? Instead, I said, "Oh, that's really good, Madonna, you're just turning the question around on me," and we moved on. I didn't follow up the way I should have.

Mark Goodman, wearing a gray jacket, interviews Madonna, who has a Tintin quiff of hair protruding from her headband, circa 1984:

MARK GOODMAN: *"Do you have fashion influences, let's say, I don't know, maybe Vivienne Westwood?"*

MADONNA: *"Um, yeah, well, she's one of my favorite designers, actually."*

MARK GOODMAN: *"Is she really?"*

MADONNA: *"World's End is a great store in England, great clothing shop. Whenever I go to England, that's where I buy all my clothes."*

MARK GOODMAN: *"Are you the designer of your look, your hairstyle, the clothing?"*

MADONNA: *"Oh, yeah. Do you think someone else could come up with this?" (She laughs coquettishly.)*

Mark:

A couple of years later, I interviewed her again, in Miami. When we first sat down, I said, "I'm Mark Goodman, I interviewed you at MTV before you were *Madonna*." She said, "Mark, I was always *Madonna*." Okay, point taken.

I was a little braver at that point. I was talking to her road manager and some of her dancers, and asking questions like, "What's she like, really? She's a ballbuster, isn't she?" They were all saying, "No, no, no, she's great! We love her!" I knew she was incredibly tough—I had been watching rehearsals for her tour, and she was a dictator—but nobody would come clean.

Nina:

I judged a Madonna look-alike contest at Macy's. They had a whole department of these clothes, during her street-urchin period with the boots and the bow and the streaked hair—not the pointy bra yet. So there were dozens of teenage and pre-teenage girls dressed up like Madonna, and that was surreal. The other judge was Andy Warhol, and he didn't speak very much: just a couple of words, and he was always staring.

> *From* The Andy Warhol Diaries *(June 6, 1985):*
>
> *"Went over to Macy's to judge the Madonna look-alike contest. They expected 200 girls but there were only 100. They'd spent a fortune, these girls, on the clothes and jewelry. It was over pretty fast, by 5:10, and it'd started at 4:30. . . . Went to Radio City Music Hall for Madonna's concert (cab $6). And the show was so great. Just so simple and sexy and Madonna is so pretty. Now she's thinner and just so great."*

Martha:

I never met Madonna, although I got the celebrity nod from her once on Fifty-seventh Street when we were walking in opposite directions. She got lambasted recently because it was reported that her camp made the people who worked at the Toronto Film Festival look away when she was walking down the hallway. And she denied it: *Oh, I would never make people turn away from me, that's outlandish, who would say that?* Well, maybe it didn't happen then, but I saw that very thing happen backstage at Live Aid: Madonna and Sean Penn were heading to the stage, surrounded by a phalanx of people, and their bodyguards told people they had to turn away. So I know for a fact she would do that.

Mark:

I don't think most musicians think of themselves in opposition: When I was a kid, people talked about the Beatles versus the Dave Clark Five, but they were just two superstar acts. I never understood the whole Madonna versus Cyndi Lauper thing, because they were completely different. Cyndi had a much better singing voice than Madonna. There was no comparison.

Madonna says she made MTV. And she's probably half-right.

εverч Time ι think of чou, ι alwaчs catch mч breath

Romance and Regret with John Waite

Nina:

A friend of mine from Cleveland flew in to visit, and I took her to Madison Square Garden to see Pat Benatar. We went backstage afterward for the party—there was always a party afterward—and this guy with red hair came up to me. We had a spark of recognition—we were both very hyper. He said, with an English accent, "Do I know you?"

I said, "No, I don't think so." He scribbled down his name and number. The next day, I looked at this little piece of paper, and it looked like it said "Joe Dante." Eventually, I figured out it was John Waite. I had seen him on *The Midnight Special,* singing with the Babys. My friend Robin kept saying I should call him; I never did, but I ran into him on Halloween in a restaurant in Greenwich Village. We drank like crazy and wandered around the Village—and New York on Halloween, it's just whacked out. I picked up a pay phone, and it had shaving cream all over it.

John and I had a really intense connection. It felt poetic, like we had known each other in a past life. He was doing his first solo album, *Ignition,* at the House of Music in West Orange, New Jersey, and he invited me to visit. That was why he had been at the Pat Benatar show—her husband and guitarist, Neil Giraldo, was producing the album. And Timmy Pierce, this guitarist who had played with Danny, was playing on that session with John, which was weird.

John and I didn't see each other much, but we talked on the phone a lot. He was going through a bad period—at first I thought it was just career-related, but he was prone to depression. At one point, he was even going to give up singing. I gave him a lot of encouragement. We weren't often in the same city, but one night he was in New York and we went out to a saloon. John drew a picture-perfect version of Rodin's *The Kiss* and gave it to me. He was wearing a light aqua scarf, some type of Indian print—he ripped it in two and I kept half. We sent little gifts back and forth, and met up now and then. John epitomized the tortured poet artist, the romantic figure that's my big weakness. He was a walking Byronic archetype, down to his look and his cologne. I absolutely loved the guy.

A couple of years later, my friend Ida invited me to a party. She said, almost in passing, "Oh, John may show up with his new wife."

My stomach tied itself into knots. All I could say was, "What?" Apparently, he went back to England and got married. Even though John and I weren't officially a couple, I thought we had a deep connection—I was totally thrown.

By this time, he was making his second album, *No Brakes.* They were recording in New York. He phoned me up at my apartment; it sounded like he was crying. He was calling from the studio, and he asked me to come down. I told him I couldn't—I wasn't the sort of person who was going to be with a married man.

A few weeks later, John called again. He said, "I have a song. I was thinking of you when I wrote it, and I want you to hear it." So we met, not too far from my place, on West Fifty-seventh Street, in Little Steven's apartment. I don't know why we were there—I didn't even know they were friends. Neutral territory, I guess.

John played me the song, and it was "Missing You." I didn't tell many people that he said he had been thinking of me when he wrote it. I did play the song for J. J., who knew that I cared a lot about John. J. J. thought John was a fabulous singer—which is true—and when he heard it, he said, "That's going to be a number one hit." Which it ended up being. John gave me a gold record, which I still have.

Sometimes I had to introduce the "Missing You" video on MTV. I never told the story, but now and then, I'd say something like "A song close to my heart." There are lyrics in it, like "a telegraph to your soul," that I know came from our conversations. When we were apart, I used to tell John that he should look up at the moon: I would send my wishes for him up to the moon so they would come down to wherever he was. I was a sappy romantic—but that whole experience with him dumbfounded me.

For a while, we stayed in contact, and wrote each other cards now and then. A few years ago, Ida told me she had spoken with somebody else who said that John had told her that "Missing You" was written about her. Apparently, they had been having an affair at that time. I made the mistake of telling Mark, who asked John about the song during an interview: "Was it really written about Nina?"

John answered, "It was written about her and a bunch of other women."

"I don't think she knows that," Mark said.

"Oh, yes, she does."

No, I didn't. I guess he said that to all the girls.

If we had actually gotten together, who knows whether it would have worked. But to this day, if I see John, my heart starts pounding. I can't help it.

26

That's My Soul Up There

MTV Hits the Road

Alan:

MTV sponsored the Police's Synchronicity tour, which meant each of us went out on the road for several of their dates to introduce the band. I was the MC in Birmingham, Alabama; that was a very satisfying night, standing in front of my hometown at the BJCC Arena. I was also onstage at JFK Stadium in Philadelphia, introducing them to seventy-five thousand people, which was a rush. It was less nerve-racking than doing an introduction in a small club, actually.

Martha:

I introduced the Police at Shea Stadium, and somebody in the crowd threw a tennis ball at me. It only hit me on the leg, but I was really shaken up. I felt like I was out there by myself. I think it's trickier for a young woman to be out on her own, blazing a trail, than it is for a young man. Sometimes I wished I had someone looking out for my back.

Alan:

I found it odd that we didn't ever interact with the Police. I'd fly into town and sit in the greenroom in the arena. At one venue, I asked their tour manager, "Hey, what are the guys doing?"

"Oh, they're getting ready. They go on in about fifteen minutes. You need anything?"

I didn't ask to go hang with them—I didn't want to beg—but I did wonder, "Why can't I go in there and say howdy? I'm not the local DJ—I'm one of five VJs, and MTV's promoting the tour." It felt out of sync with our popularity, and I felt dissed, but I didn't have the balls to ask to say hello. I do have a photo of me and Sting—but only because I hung around the studio when Mark was interviewing him and stepped into the picture once the interview was over.

Martha:

For some reason, the Police wanted only the younger VJs to come out and introduce shows: me and Alan and Nina. I thought that was insulting to J. J. and Mark.

Mark:

I wasn't even aware that was going on.

Alan:

The Police kept asking for Martha to come out—I think all three of them were hoping to score with her.

Martha:

Believe me, those guys did not feel that way. In fact, they did something really rude—although at the time, I thought it was my fault. I was interviewing them after one of their shows, and one of them said, "Well, this is kind of a bad time to talk to us. You know, we just got offstage."

I wish I had said, "Dude, I didn't set this up. This time wasn't my idea—talk to Miles." That was Miles Copeland, their manager—drummer Stewart Copeland's brother. What I actually did was look off camera, making eye contact with a producer to find out what I should do. And the Police started throwing drinks at each other, and then they got up and left.

At the time, I felt horrible, thinking I had let down the company: I couldn't control the situation and I didn't get the interview they wanted. I wouldn't have blamed them if they had fired me. Now I look back and think, "I was just a kid. It was crappy of them to do that."

Alan:

MTV also sponsored Yes, when they were promoting *90125*—the 9012Live tour. I was a huge Yes fan back in the "Roundabout" days—they played the first concert I ever went to. I had despaired over how they would translate their sound to the '80s. My brother had been a big fan of acoustic singer-songwriters like Kenny Loggins, and there was very little acoustic guitar in the '80s—it was mostly synths. So I had seen how a whole category of musicians could get squeezed out, "Footloose" and "Danger Zone" notwithstanding. But then Yes put out "Owner of a Lonely Heart," which was genius. It incorporated elements of their prog-rock heyday, but the rest of it was straight Art of Noise. I saw the video and said, "Oh, they're going to survive. I'm proud of my boys."

Nina:

We did the Big Bam Boom tour with Hall and Oates. One city, I hung out after the show with G. E. Smith, the band's guitarist, drinking and telling stories in his hotel room. Nothing else went on—I always feel like I have to say that when I hang out with a guy, because everyone assumes that only one thing can happen between a man and a woman.

Alan:

I introduced Hall and Oates one night, but they didn't run on right away. So I returned to the side of the stage. I was real close to the stairway that led to the dressing room. John Oates came by at a moment when I was holding up my hand—and I whacked him right in the face. He said, "Goddamn it, what the fuck?" The stage manager was trying to figure out what was going on—it was really dark, and nobody could see anything. Oates walked onstage, rubbing his head. When the lights went up, everybody looked at the stage manager, figuring it was his fault, because he was standing around there. I just tried to disappear.

Martha:

I had to introduce Hall and Oates, and I had a huge case of stage fright. I didn't know what to say, and I was worried that people were going to boo me.

G. E. Smith told me, "Just go out and have fun. Don't worry about it—you can say anything."

I went out and started talking to the crowd, and after a while, G. E. came up to his microphone and said, "Hey, Martha?"

"Yeah?"

"There's a phone call for you."

"G. E., I can't take a phone call right now—I'm talking to these people!"

He smiled and gave me a look: *See? You can say whatever you want.* Later that night, G. E. tried to convince me to sleep ("Just sleeeep") in his room at the hotel we were all staying at, but I wasn't *that* stupid. I declined.

Lineup on the first day of the 1982 US Festival (September 3):
Gang of Four
The Ramones
The English Beat
Oingo Boingo
The B-52s
Talking Heads
The Police

Lineup on the first day of the 1983 US Festival (May 28):
Divinyls (eight years before "I Touch Myself"!)
INXS
Wall of Voodoo

Oingo Boingo
The English Beat
Missing Persons
A Flock of Seagulls
Stray Cats
Men at Work
The Clash (the last show they ever did with Mick Jones)

Mark:

I got tapped to do the '83 US Festival. J. J. had done it the year before, when it was a smaller affair. I think he felt miffed that they didn't send him out again when it became a bigger deal.

The '83 US Festival was basically a three-day festival. The metal day was the highest attendance: That was Woodstock numbers, like five hundred thousand people. It was all in San Bernardino, California, which was hot and dusty and nasty—they were hosing the crowd down. We drove in the night before and hit the ground running: We had three days of nonstop coverage. It was a madhouse, but I don't believe anything really bad happened: Nobody OD'd, nobody got trampled.

Outside of New Year's Eve, it was the first time MTV had done a live broadcast. We filed multiple reports and did several live updates a day. I don't remember sleeping. I was constantly exhausted and smoking a lot of pot. I wasn't doing any coke—maybe I should have been. And I was very glad to be "talent," because other people on the crew not only had to follow me around, they also had to go back to our trailer, where we had an edit suite, and put together finished pieces.

That weekend was the first time I met U2. I spoke with Bono, who was a serious guy, even back then. You could tell that he was taken with the United States—they came to conquer. Bono was pissed off at the Clash, who were being total dicks at the festival. Bill Graham was running the show, and he was a notorious stickler for staying on schedule. Everything was on time until the Clash, who showed up an hour late for their set. Bono felt the Clash were poseurs. Talking about them, he told me, "We didn't come here to hide behind our haircuts."

We were planning to do a live hit just before Ozzy Osbourne's set, with me onstage, bringing him on. I was waiting by the side of the stage, looking at a crowd of five hundred thousand people, and waiting for the signal to go, because we were going to be live—no tape delay. I got the word, walked out onstage, and did my usual thing to whip the crowd into a frenzy—which was pretty easy, since it was metal day. I went through my big rabble-rousing, make-'em-nuts speech, and then I said, "All right, everybody, Ozzy Osbourne!" I looked around, and no Ozzy. I walked off and found out they held him back because we were too early to hit the satellite for the live feed. They told me I had to do the introduction one more time. And again, there were half a million people.

So I walked out, and said, "Take two!" *Live television, everybody.* But the metalheads were good. They got into the same frenzy again—they had commitment.

I also interviewed Ozzy in his trailer. I wanted to smoke pot with him, but Sharon, his wife and manager, was really terrifying. She was in rare form that day, having a huge argument with Bill Graham, and I didn't want her to focus on me instead. Ozzy was nearly incomprehensible, but also funny and lovable, like a whacked-out uncle. In the middle of our interview, there was a power failure, and every light in the trailer went out. Sitting in total darkness but not missing a beat, Ozzy shouted, "Keep pedaling, Sharon!"

27

I've seen you on the Beach and I've seen you on TV

The Cultural Impact of MTV

Martha:

I was young enough when MTV launched that I thought the Police were great—but I was an adult, so they couldn't be my first teenage love the way that the Beatles had been, or James Taylor. I still acted like a kid sometimes, but there was a crucial gap of a few years between me and the teenagers who were watching MTV. When people ask me how much I loved Duran Duran, I'm not quite there with them. When MTV started, I was already a college graduate, a half-step out of the demo.

Alan:

What I miss most about MTV was the innocence of '80s music. I'll hear something like "The Safety Dance" now, and I'll say, "You know, that's a crappy song, but it sure was fun." We presented this vision of American culture, which was tolerant of sincerity and tongue-in-cheek self-deprecation at the same time: We could play Bruce Springsteen and Culture Club right next to each other. It wasn't an era of body piercing yet, but we had flashy clothing and crazy hair. The message was acceptance, which was counter to the politics of the day.

Mark:

Even when MTV played the exact same songs as a top 40 station, it had a different visceral impact. Seeing different skin colors and different musical tribes right next to each other was powerfully inclusive, even if you muted your TV set.

> *The ideal party in an early MTV video had as varied a guest list as possible. For example, the video for "Heart and Soul," by Huey Lewis and the News, takes place at a loft party. There's some diversity in ethnicity and age, but the real range comes in the types of characters we see: a shirtless guy in glittering shoulder pads and headband, a black dandy under a parasol, a midget in a gaucho hat, a new-wave guy in visor sunglasses, a bearded dude with a top hat and monocle, a punk rocker who looks like Ron Howard despite the Mohawk and leather jacket, a harlequin in white face paint, and a belly dancer. The News themselves include a preppy, a cowboy, and a vampire.*

Martha:

When I started working at MTV, I weighed 110 pounds, which may not sound like a lot, but I'm only five foot two. I was still a bit chunky from all that college food—ice cream and bagels every meal—so I started jogging and going to aerobics classes. But workout culture was new, especially in the music world. I hate when I see period pieces set in the old rock world, and the guys have shaved chests or are buff. Like *Almost Famous*—Cameron Crowe should know better. Go watch *The Song Remains the Same* and see what Led Zeppelin looked like: They might have been super-thin, but the only six-packs were on the tour bus.

Nina:

MTV's a big part of the reason that all changed. Musicians got more visually conscious. Or self-conscious.

Alan:

The biggest metamorphosis was Bruce Springsteen. I grew up with him being a geeky, skinny guy, with his jeans falling off his ass. Then the "Dancing in the Dark" video came out, and wow, he had muscles. I think he watched some videos and said, "Oh, I gotta look good in these things if I want to compete."

Mark:

I voted for Reagan in 1980. I wasn't traditionally Republican, and I wasn't sure what type of politician he might end up being, but I appreciated the fact that he was able to galvanize the country, which I thought was important. I did not vote for him for a second term—by that time, I realized what an idiot he was. Trickle-down economics sounded so right, but was so wrong.

Alan:

I voted for Reagan over Carter, but I soured on him, because when he came on board, he slashed the NEA, and arts funding dried up. Before I moved to New York, I had an NEA grant to do theater, and Reagan ended that. Now I think the country could really use somebody like Reagan, but at the time, I took it personally.

Nina:

I didn't track on politics at the time, but when I heard Reagan speak, I thought it was ironic that everybody called him "The Great Communicator." I just heard a phony actor. Studying acting, you learn when somebody's speaking from their soul—the Method calls it being connected. I never felt that Reagan was connected at all, which is why I did not like listening to the man speak.

Alan:

The ethos of the '80s was very conservative—Middle America voted for a Republican president, and he supported austerity measures and the religious right. And then this irreverent entity called MTV came along and stuck its finger into the conservative eye. There were plenty of right-wingers shutting off the cable after they discovered that MTV was flashing tits and ass in their religious faces all day long. But that conflict just created a pent-up demand for MTV, especially if kids had to go to a friend's house to watch it. People needed a 24/7 bubble called MTV so they could forget about whatever bullshit was going on with politics. MTV and the Moral Majority needed each other to thrive.

Mark:

I thought MTV would stick around, but I never imagined it would have the cultural impact that it did. I think that shocked everybody at the channel, all the way up to Bob Pittman.

Martha:

We could see MTV's influence everywhere. Even commercials got edited differently after we launched. *Miami Vice* was commissioned with the two words "MTV cops."

Mark:

I don't think there will ever be another equivalent to MTV in the music business, just like there will never be another Beatles. Even if the world's greatest band came along today, there wouldn't be the same pandemonium. People love their iPods, but they don't relate to them the same way they did to MTV.

Alan:

MTV was all about change; we trained the audience to expect it. If a graphic felt stale after six months, MTV changed it, and if they needed to hire a new team to do that, they would. They went through a lot of creative people to make that visual environment happen, and they gave them a lot of freedom.

Mark:

We're the reason you have no attention span. And you can pin reality TV on us too. You're welcome.

ı want to ʙe the one to walk ın the sun

The Most Unusual Miss Cyndi Lauper

Nina:

Soon after I moved to New York, I went to the Ritz to see Blue Angel, the band that Cyndi Lauper was in before she went solo. And she was so good, she freaked me out. I got on a pay phone and called Danny in California, saying, "You would not believe this girl!"

Martha:

Cyndi had this Betty Boop speaking voice. Then she would open her mouth to sing, and it would be this staggering sound.

Mark:

Cyndi and I got along very well in the early days. I interviewed her right as her record was coming out. I was aware of Blue Angel, and we talked a little bit about that. I probably should have asked more questions about how she was working with the Hooters, since they were my pals from Philadelphia. She was goofy and funny.

Alan:

She's So Unusual was a quintessential MTV album—Cyndi was clearly thinking about her look, and it was a big part of her appeal. Girls loved dressing like her: She was the bubbly, colorful fashion icon of the '80s. She had tons of personality, and she had a cute little giggle. She personified the fun of MTV.

Mark:

I wouldn't say this about everybody that MTV played, but I think Cyndi would have made it without videos. She had such an amazing voice, and the production sounded great on the radio. But the visual element was so strong, and so integral to people getting her—I think Cyndi and us together made it way more of a cultural phenomenon, way faster.

Alan:

Cyndi cast Captain Lou Albano, the wrestling manager, in her video for "Girls Just Wanna Have Fun"—he played her father. And then, in the most unusual move that any of us could remember, she and Albano teamed up to do a "Rock 'n' Wrestling" campaign for a whole year. I think it was the brainchild of her boyfriend/manager, David Wolff. The idea was that she would be "managed" by Captain Lou Albano, and they were going to fight against the forces of "Rowdy" Roddy Piper and other wrestlers.

So we did a lot of remote "Rock 'n' Wrestling" shoots and some big events. There was a documentary with a wrestling announcer, and we hosted a two-hour special. Cyndi would go into the ring, taunting females and then wrestling them. Vince McMahon, the head of the World Wrestling Federation, had cut some sort of deal with MTV.

Mark:

I interviewed Cyndi in the MTV offices and tried to get some sense of what the hell she was doing with all that Captain Lou stuff. I thought it was a huge mistake for her. I suspect it was simple on her end: She was a wrestling fan and she really liked Captain Lou as a person. I kept beating on that door, and she pulled back into her Cyndi Lauper character. Suddenly she was ditzier than before, and the New York accent was thicker.

Alan:

We kicked off "Rock 'n' Wrestling" with a press conference: Cyndi, Captain Lou, and "Rowdy" Roddy Piper. I was the host. It was all very mock-serious. It was live to tape, so we had to get it right the first time. The plan was that Roddy and Lou would get into a "fight" and I would be the mediator. Before we started, everybody discussed the choreography. "You cold-cock me with a ramma-jamma"—whatever the lingo was—"and then you pull my hair, and Cyndi's going to hit you with a chair."

"Alan, I'm going to take you by the scruff of the neck, and I'll pull you here." Roddy Piper was an extremely nice guy, while Lou was crazy, but they both were pros.

Showtime: I introduced everybody and made my serious announcement. Lou Albano and Roddy Piper got into a fake back-and-forth argument. I tried to intervene, like a referee would: "Gentlemen, gentlemen, we must keep sanity here."

Roddy shouted, "Shut up, pipsqueak! Hunter, you pipsqueak!" He came around the front of the press conference table and taunted me: "You little VJ pipsqueak!" He grabbed me, lifted me over the apron of the table, and threw me down. It looked out of control, but the wrestling guys knew what the parameters were. The segment ended, I managed to say, "We'll be right back," and we went to commercial break.

I was dusting myself off, and Roddy immediately asked, "Hey, you all right, little buddy? Sorry about that, man, but that was great!" Everybody was high-fiving each other. It looked real—not real anger, maybe, but physically real. That was my initiation with these crazy people.

I had grown up with local small-town wrestling, but I didn't realize until I started working on all these "Rock 'n' Wrestling" events that these people were unbalanced. The blood was real—they showed me how they hid their razor blades.

I got to know Cyndi pretty well that year. She was like Jane Wiedlin of the Go-Go's—they both have ditzy on-air personas. Cyndi didn't change dramatically when the cameras were off—she always had the thick accent, for example—but she definitely was a real person off camera, and a sweetheart.

After one of her concerts, I was backstage, chatting with her lawyer, Elliot Hoffman. I told him, "I can't use my boss's lawyer anymore—I need my own guy." He agreed to represent me, and I stayed with him from then on. He made better deals for me, and helped me get an agent at ICM. Elliot was an eccentric New York figure: Around fifty-eight years old, he sported a handlebar mustache and rode a motorcycle to work in a pinstriped suit. He also had a role in Cyndi's "Girls Just Wanna Have Fun" video, as the eccentric older dance partner. Everybody loved Elliot—he was a mentor to me. He handled the Who and Barbra Streisand, so I wasn't one of his higher-paying clients, but he liked the world of MTV.

Nina:

My dad and my grandfather had recently passed, so I had my mom visit me in New York. I thought she'd enjoy a fancy New York City party; we got dolled up and I took her to Tavern on the Green, where video director Bob Giraldi was throwing an elaborate bash. My mom turned out to be the belle of the ball. All sorts of people came to visit me at our table and ended up being enchanted with my mom. She was reliving the Roaring '20s, dancing and generally having a swell time, as opposed to her daughter, who was being her customary wallflower self. I didn't mind—the less party chitchat, the better. At one point, my mom chastised me for gluing myself to the table. I believe her exact words were "Why are you being such a flat tire?"

This guy Quentin came up to the table, and gave us his verbal résumé—he was a big-time producer of music videos, including all of Cyndi Lauper's stuff—and then asked if I wanted to go to lunch with him sometime. I was coy about answering, as I wasn't blown away by him, but we did exchange telephone numbers. Well, he was just my *mom's* style. As soon as he left the table, she began to say, "You should go out with him. He's so nice, and he looks like Tom Selleck." Which he didn't, although he did have a mustache.

Even after my mom went home to Massachusetts, she kept asking if I had "called that nice young man." I didn't, but Quentin called me, and we had lunch. He turned out to be an interesting guy—he had just done a documentary in India about tigers. We started dating. Quentin was about ten years older than me; maybe with the loss of my father and grandfather, I was looking for an older man.

I went to visit him on the set of Cyndi's "Time After Time" video, which was shooting down in New Jersey. Quentin said I should borrow his car and meet him there. So I drove his Saab down to this little town in Jersey and pulled into a parking lot off the main street. Word had gotten out that the Cyndi shoot was happening, so there were lots of fans there. They saw me in the car and swarmed the parking lot—and because I had never driven the Saab before, I could not figure out how to get out of it. I was locked in the car, with fans surrounding the car and climbing over it, like it was Beatlemania. I was having a complete panic attack. Finally, one of the fans pointed at the fancy lock control and I managed to get myself out.

Quentin and I stayed together for almost two years. I liked him, but I didn't love him. This sounds cold, but maybe it was a relationship of convenience. I guess I needed a relationship of some sort, just for the companionship. But I didn't know he was going to turn out to be a schmuck.

One time, I went to L.A. on vacation, and I cut it short to go with Quentin to his high-school reunion in Darien, Connecticut. We were sitting at a table with his high-school friends, and this woman walked up with her daughter, who wanted to get into making videos. He ended up talking to the daughter the whole night, while I thought, "I flew back for this?" At the end of the reunion, Quentin said he'd give the daughter a ride home. Somehow, I ended up sitting in the backseat.

So he hired this Darien girl, fresh out of high school, to be a video assistant at his production company. I was friendly with two girls who worked with him, Andrea and Susie. One day Andrea called me up and said, "I can't take this anymore." Quentin worked out of his apartment—not only was the Darien girl working there, she was staying there with him. I broke up with him, and then I found out he had been hitting on some of my girlfriends. He was the mayor of Schmucksville.

Quentin showed up at the MTV New Year's Eve show that year with the Darien girl. Martha and I were sitting on a couch, getting ready to do our shot, and he got right in my eyeline. Martha was so upset, she said she was going to throw her champagne glass at him.

Later on, I interviewed Cyndi Lauper. As we were getting miked up, she whispered, "You know, I went out with Quentin too." She made this horrible little snorting sound and said, "Isn't he disgusting?" We were dying of laughter, like two little girls going, "Ew, ew, ew."

29

you play the guitar on the MTV

Heavy Metal Thunder

Mark:

Metal fit right into the MTV rotation. We didn't play the more extreme stuff like Megadeth, but we played a lot of bands on the border between metal and harder rock: Deep Purple, Rainbow, Quiet Riot. That symbiosis allowed for the rise of hair metal. Basically, the channel would rather play any piece-of-shit metal band than a black act. Early on, we played a lot of Judas Priest: "You've Got Another Thing Comin'" was one of my favorite videos back then. The best part was a guy walking across a bridge at what appeared to be some sort of oil refinery. And as he makes his way across this scaffolding—*blam!* His head blows off. Very funny.

Martha:

When Mötley Crüe came into the studio, we were terrified. We hadn't dealt with Sunset Strip bands in any way. We were worried that they would kick over the furniture, spit on us, or throw Jack Daniel's bottles at the cameras, but they were fantastic. They were excited to be at MTV.

Martha Quinn, in a short leopard-print skirt and a big red necklace, talks with Vince Neil and Nikki Sixx (both wearing leather jackets, with big scarves and big hair), discussing that night's installment of the Friday Night Video Fights, *a show where viewers got to vote for one of two hit videos. (The show was taped in advance, with two alternate endings filmed, one for each victor):*

MARTHA QUINN: *"Tonight's an exciting night for us here at MTV, and for you guys, I'm hoping as well, because we have your video, 'Looks That Kill,' going up against ZZ Top, 'TV Dinners'—have you seen 'TV Dinners'?"*

VINCE NEIL: *"Oh yeah, great."*

NIKKI SIXX: *"I like that little alien."*

MARTHA QUINN: *"I know, he crawls over that guy eating potato chips. Well, you can use this opportunity to look in the camera and do a little campaigning and convince the American audience why they should call up and vote for Mötley Crüe tonight."*

VINCE NEIL: *(Pointing into camera)* *"You better call. Or we're gonna come lookin' for ya."*

NIKKI SIXX: *"We'll find ya."*

VINCE NEIL: *"We will."*

NIKKI SIXX: *"Vote for us. Because we're the bad boys of rock."*

MARTHA QUINN: *(laughing)* *"I'm scared."*

VINCE NEIL: *"C'mon, call. Pick it up. No, pick it up. Pick it up. Now dial that number."* (He makes a circular dialing motion.) *"Now you got it. Okay, perfect, thank you."*

Mark:

They had Dee Snider, lead singer of Twisted Sister, come into the studio to surprise me for my birthday. I was in the middle of a segment—suddenly they started playing the Beatles' "Birthday," and out walked Dee. He said, "Hold it, hold it. All right, Mark, it's your birthday. Congratulations. And in honor of your birthday, we've got Mr. and Mrs. Goodman from Tuba City, Wyoming. Come on out. Oh, they couldn't make it? Okay, let's move on." He was doing the full-on Dee

Snider show, and I was just trying to roll with it. "This is your life, Mark Goodman. We're going to show you some—what? We don't have any pictures? Okay, then."

Alan:

Kiss came to MTV for their big unveiling: the boys without makeup. J. J. hosted the special, but we were all down in the studio watching. It was very dramatic. The camera went down the line, like we were looking for the winner on a game show.

A standing J. J. Jackson interviews the seated members of Kiss: In September 1983, that means Paul Stanley, Gene Simmons, Eric Carr, and Vinnie Vincent. With their makeup off, seated behind a table with name cards in front of them, the quartet look like middle managers in the Kiss Corporation. Gene Simmons explains that people already identified him without his makeup: "It happens often enough, we get into, I don't know, Madison, Wisconsin, or something, and people in-variably come up and say, 'Aren't you Gene Simmons?' It could be the ten-foot sign that says, 'Hi, I'm Gene Simmons.'" Simmons then makes an uncharacteristically discreet allusion to his fondness for groupies, who have also seen him without his makeup: "And we've made a lot of friends over the years."

Nina:

I was very much against anything to do with the devil. I wasn't brought up especially religiously—my dad was a Methodist Sunday-school teacher, but he wasn't strict. I just didn't want anything to do with the forces of darkness. I wouldn't listen to AC/DC's "Highway to Hell"—and I would never make the devil-horns symbol that Ronnie James Dio claimed he invented, holding up the index finger and pin-kie. Actually, I still don't do that today. My grandmother was Italian, and in the old country, you made that gesture when you were cursing somebody.

When I had to interview Dio, I swore he had something to do with Satan, and I stayed as far away from him as I could. In my head, there was an odor coming off of him. Not sulfur—I thought it was the musky scent of evil, but it was probably just his giraffe-skin boots.

Normally when I'm done with an interview, if I feel close to the person then we hug, and if not, it's a handshake. Not Dio—I wouldn't touch him. As soon as it was over, I ran down the hall, heading into a producer's office. I even thought he looked like the devil.

Years later, I saw Dio again—of all places, we ran into each other early in the morning in the garden department of Home Depot. I didn't smell Satan on him that time; as far as I could tell in the midst of all the flowers, he was fresh out of the shower.

Mark:

Randy Rhoads, who was the guitarist in Ozzy Osbourne's band, died in a plane crash in March 1982—the pilot was fucking around, trying to buzz Ozzy's tour bus. When the news broke, they called me back to the MTV studios, and the news department quickly wrote a couple of segments. After we were done, they had to messenger the tapes out to the broadcast center in Smithtown, Long Island, to get them on the air as soon as possible.

We did a few replacement segments like that early on: Another one was when John Belushi died. When I shot the Rhoads segments, it was very late in the day—a lot of people had already gone home. I needed to stay serious, because of the gravity of the news. It was, after all, really sad. But Michael Pelech was not helping: He stood behind the camera, making crashing airplane sound effects.

you may find yourself in a beautiful house with a beautiful wife

Mark and Carol

Nina:

I had nothing against Carol, but I didn't think she liked me, or the rest of the VJs. I don't know if it's because she resented not being a VJ herself. And Mark was a different guy when he was around her. He's always been a big brother to me—over the years, he's been selflessly supportive. When I was scared of getting a computer, he was the one who told me, "You're a smart girl, you can do this." But when Carol was around, it seemed like the VJs would be together, and then Mark and Carol would be in a separate group on the other side of the room. I didn't feel any kindness coming from her.

Mark:

Carol was aloof and a little icy, which led to some people thinking she was snooty or elitist. I was very sociable, while she was the opposite. She was also judgmental: Sometimes I could laugh at her condescending assessments of people, and I might even have agreed with her at times, but I wanted to be less like that, not more.

She was also more conservative than I realized: I thought because she lived in the rock world, she would be more of a drinker and a partier. Because I didn't want to come off as a lout, I had to be more conservative than I would have preferred, in all aspects of our life. All those issues were real, but the problems in the relationship were more about me than her.

I had no understanding of the gears in my head. One time, before we were married, Carol came home from work and we had a fight. I don't even know what it was about, but the most heinous insults were coming out of my mouth. I was calling her all these terrible names and saying the most hurtful, ugly shit. I was dumbfounded and flipped out. Not just by the fact that I was having a fight with her, but by the discovery that there was this demon inside of me.

There was a blizzard that night, but I had to leave the apartment. I got on a train at ten P.M., and went down to Philly. I stayed with my sister that night—I was too freaked out to call Carol. Right after that, I started seeing a shrink; a couple of years later, Carol and I started couples therapy.

I wasn't committed to the relationship the way I should have been, but I couldn't figure that out. If I had been more together, I would have said, "My God, Carol, look at what I'm doing. I'm miserable, you're miserable. I don't want to do this to you—let's cut it short." But it took me a long time to get to that. I loved Carol, but I was lost and hurting.

I started cheating about a year into our marriage. The first time was with this Asian girl who worked in the office. I don't even remember her name. It happened on the spur of the moment: We had drinks after work, and then we went back to her apartment. It was a one-off thing, and I felt awful about it, so I put it aside and tried to pretend it hadn't happened. But a voice inside me was telling me that I'd opened a door that should have stayed closed and locked.

As MTV became more popular, all these girls started approaching me—girls who, under normal circumstances, I never would have been able to talk to. I would have been too afraid or shy. It happened the most when I was traveling. Whether we were in a club or a backstage party, there would inevitably be some hot girl who was friends with the promoter. I would always have to get hammered if I wanted to hook up with somebody. I felt bad about it while I was doing it—but it took me years to realize that what I was doing to make myself feel better was actually making me feel much worse.

One time, I went to Pittsburgh for a segment. I met someone after the event—we went back to the hotel bar, and she stayed with me that night. We slept in a little late the next morning, so we both came out of the hotel at the same time. All the marketing people from MTV were waiting for me in the lobby so we could get the car to the airport, and they saw me come out with this girl. They laughed about it a little, but one of them, this girl Karen, said to me, "What are you doing? I understand the position you're in, but that's not really cool, is it?"

I made light of it, and everybody dropped it. Cheating became known as what happened when Mark went on the road, just the thing I did. So in addition to the fact that I was being unfaithful, I made it even more messy and stupid by involving these third parties. When Carol came to MTV events, it was unfair to my coworkers that I put them in that position, and unfair to her that I put her in that light.

I don't have an addictive personality, and yet this was unstoppable for me. It fed the *love me, love me, love me* part of my personality and helped me get through the parts of my marriage that felt empty and fake. When I was having sex, I went somewhere else in my mind—that was a relief from the problems that I felt like I was facing every day.

I looked forward to my infidelities; I craved them. They were all wrapped up with my whole MTV experience. I'd fly first class, stay in beautiful hotels, and meet gorgeous women whose lives were far more mundane than mine. I would be their momentary escape. They didn't realize (and to a great extent, neither did I) that they were my escape too.

After a while, it started to happen in New York. I had an ongoing thing with an intern: I would get us a hotel room for two hours or so. The taboo attracted me and just fucked up my opinion of myself even more. That was when I started to be more conscious of how much I hated myself for doing this. I realized I was not able to maintain a real adult relationship.

I also had a long affair with somebody I met at the gym. This was the Vertical Club—at the time, the coolest gym to go to. It was a lot of money—to join was five or six hundred dollars, and then a huge monthly thing. But they had state-of-the-art machines and lots of trainers around who really worked with you. I'd work out so hard, I'd go into the bathroom and throw up. There were lots of soap actors and models—a never-ending parade of gorgeous women. I'd be on the StairMaster next to Brooke Shields, chatting her up. It was a social scene as well, which was new in gyms.

One night I met Melanie at the free weights. She was in perfect shape, with a stunning body. Full lips, long straight blond hair, a huge toothy smile, and a laugh that was loud but not at all obnoxious. She seemed to know exactly who she was, and what she looked like, and was not shy about it. She was smart, aware, and young—about twenty-three. I felt amazed, and then lucky, that she dug me. I started hanging around with her way too much. We'd go out to dinner sometimes—I don't think anybody ever spotted us, but it was so cavalier to risk hurting Carol, just for my own need to boost my ego.

Melanie was basically living with her boyfriend, but she still had her own apartment, so we went there pretty regularly in the afternoons, or after the gym. There was a song on 'Til Tuesday's second record, "Coming Up Close," that I used to play like crazy at her place. It was never a hit, but it really articulated how I was feeling in that moment with her: "Everything feels like welcome home." In my own apartment, I was feeling so not at home.

I knew it wasn't just fucking, so I felt even worse about it. It went on for over a year—then one day, out of the blue, Melanie called me crying. She got caught by her boyfriend. I was really bummed out, and we agreed to meet at a restaurant. Melanie was a completely different person that night: She was crying, and she felt terrible that she had hurt this guy so bad. That meal was much shorter than I imagined it would be. I thought I could change her mind, but at the end, I stood on the sidewalk in front of the restaurant, watching her walk away. I couldn't believe she didn't even turn to look back at me. I was really self-centered about it: I was just thinking about how the relationship was my safe harbor, and I was upset that I was losing that. I didn't even consider how it would have worked out if Carol had found out and the situation was reversed.

As the years pass, I've come to understand how I wound up being that guy, but I'm not sure I've forgiven myself for the damage I did.

That aspect of my time at MTV is something I think about often, and regret totally. I can only hope that I will be forgiven by the people involved. It's hard for people to understand: If you are deeply insecure and then you end up, by luck, doing what I do and having some success at it, it really requires a lot of strength to fight that insecurity. I didn't have what it took to stay in my marriage.

31

My Beacon's Been Moved under Moon and Star

MTV Heads Uptown

Alan:

After a couple of years, they finally got rid of the coed dressing room—they built out this space upstairs in the Teletronics building into two dressing rooms, one for the guys and one for the girls. Robin Williams came by—he was promoting *Moscow on the Hudson,* starring him and Maria Conchita Alonso, who, coincidentally, was dating Les Garland around that time. Robin was really coked up. He came upstairs and saw our grungy little attic dressing rooms. I thought it was a little embarrassing, but he didn't seem to mind—you don't when your top priority is a glass table to do another line.

By 1984, MTV was a pretty big deal, and we were still working out of this shithole in Hell's Kitchen. It was becoming incongruent. So we were euphoric when they told us that we were moving to a new studio. An executive came down to Teletronics and showed us the architectural drawings. It was an indication that MTV was here to stay.

The day we moved studios, from Teletronics at Thirty-third Street and Tenth Avenue to Unitel at Fifty-second Street and Sixth Avenue, I got tapped to visit the set of the video for the Cars' "Hello Again." It was at the Bebop Café and it was directed by Andy Warhol.

Andy Warhol on the cameo he made in the "Hello Again" video, in his Diaries, *the entry for Thursday, March 29, 1984:*

"I had to be a bartender and wear a tux. The crowd of extras looked like the old Factory days—Benjamin in drag, and a bald-headed mime in a Pierrot outfit, and John Sex with his snake. And then there was Dianne Brill with her big tits and hourglass figure. The Cars were cute. They finally got to my part at 8:00 and I had to sing a song but I couldn't remember the words. And I had to mix a drink while I was doing it, and with my contacts on I couldn't see the Coke button on the soda dispenser. And that meant being face to face with the Cars for a while, and it was hard to talk to them. I didn't know what to say."

Alan:

I had met Andy Warhol before—the first time was when Duran Duran made an appearance on MTV and brought him along to the studio. They did the same thing with Keith Haring. But Andy was at the center of pop culture. Once I was walking down the street in SoHo with some friends, and Andy was walking in the other direction; he recognized me and said hello. We started yapping, and he pulled out a little Kodak Instamatic camera, and took a picture of me while we were talking. Apparently, he did this to everybody.

I said, "Should I smile?"

He said, "No, no, it's good." And he just kept talking, keeping the eye contact.

At the Cars video shoot, I interviewed the guys in the band, and then Andy. During a break, the tape kept rolling, and I said, "By the way, I got one of your prints the other day at a flea market. I paid ten bucks for it, but if I could get your autograph, maybe it would be worth a hundred." I laughed, and he giggled.

Andy signed it, saying, "That's great, that's great." He was weird, but fun. Everything was "great" with him.

Martha:

That night, we had a party at a bar in Hell's Kitchen. We were saying goodbye to the crew. We couldn't bring those people with us, and that was so wrenching—they were an essential part of what we had created together.

Alan:

They were all working for Teletronics, not us. Also, they were union—we were never allowed to move chairs and props at Teletronics—and Unitel wasn't. After working together so long, the Teletronics crew felt like family. So we all went out drinking at a bar in Hell's Kitchen. I sat on a stool while everybody in the crew rotated around me, offering me shots of tequila. The only thing I had eaten all day was a doughnut, and I got totally plowed. Everybody was asking what was wrong—I never got drunk in public.

I wandered outside into the snow, and Jan had to follow me out. I walked down this deserted street, in a snowstorm, with no clue where I was. She snatched me up, put me in a cab to take me home, and I puked all over the cab. At home, I sat in the bathtub, trying to sober up. Even feeling like death, I thought that I had a pretty charmed life. But I didn't drink tequila for a long time after that.

Mark:

The studio at Unitel was much bigger. At Teletronics, there were only four or five spots that were prelit for us to go to, but the new one had tons—suddenly, there were fifty places we could shoot. We had a diner booth with one of those mini-jukeboxes, which is where I interviewed Madonna. On the other side of the diner, there was a counter with stools—I interviewed Brian De Palma there. We could walk through a door into another room, where I interviewed Frankie Goes to Hollywood. We could start on a metal balcony and walk down the staircase. It was a big change.

Alan:

It was an amazing 360-degree playground of a set—at the time, it was unlike any other set on TV. I was like a monkey on a jungle gym: "Oh boy, I can jump off that platform and slide down that pole."

Mark:

Once again, we had a bay window looking out into nothing. I don't know why they didn't put a skyline out there, like on Letterman's set, or some twinkling lights at nighttime. Something!

Alan:

The camera guys at Unitel were younger, not as experienced as the crew we had been working with. They were thrilled to be working for MTV, and they were very reverent, saying things like "Whatever you want, Mr. Hunter." I was confused by that—I was used to being slapped around verbally by the stagehands.

Martha:

We all got separate dressing rooms, and that was the beginning of the end for us as a VJ family. We were still close to each other, but proximity equals intimacy.

Alan:

There were four small dressing rooms and one big one. We drew straws to see who would get the big one, and Quinski got it. The smallest one of us got the biggest room. At the time, she was certainly the most popular of the VJs—it seemed like a karmic coincidence.

Nina:

We were all allowed to decorate our own dressing rooms. I got my inspiration from my trips to San Francisco and did my room in the Victorian "painted lady" style. I had white wicker furniture and a white Victorian rocking chair. The color scheme was white, but I had some pastels and a Monet print—one of his "Water Lilies" series. I loved my dressing room: I could just close my door and feel at home. I probably spent more time in that dressing room than in my apartment.

Mark's dressing room looked like a frat. J. J.'s was like Mark's: utilitarian. Alan's was painted all in primary colors, and it looked like the clothes he wore. And Martha's was a disaster. It looked like a tornado had hit it. I can't say what style it was, but I think she had a couch in there somewhere. It was funny, because her on-air persona seemed so together—you'd think everything would be in its place, in a notebook or a Trapper Keeper. I'm the one who looked like she should be passed out off camera after shooting heroin.

Martha:

We broadcast seven days a week but shot only five, so we always had two days where we did double shifts—we called them "forty-eights." But not until we got to Unitel did they finally ask, "Why are we recording Mark, Nina, J. J., Al, Martha, Mark, Nina, J. J. Al, Martha?" After three years, they figured out it made more sense to do Mark, Mark, Nina, Nina, J. J., J. J., Al, Al, Martha, Martha.

Mark:

Pretty much everything in television and radio was shot out of order— I don't know why we didn't do it that way earlier. Maybe it was the radio sensibility, or wanting us around to do the throw to the next person. After a while, it became clear that it didn't matter that much if we did that or not.

Poor J. J.—somehow, he invariably ended up first. And he was the one who was out all night at clubs.

Alan:

We were right across the street from the CBS headquarters, where Dan Rather did the evening news. We had literally moved uptown. Going to Unitel was the end of just fucking around for our own amusement. There was a lot more corporate oversight, and a lot more management by memo. You could tell the network was starting to generate money—they were moving into corporate lockdown mode.

About a week after we moved to Unitel, I got called into the office of John Sykes. He put in the tape of me interviewing Andy Warhol, and played the part where I told him that I bought a picture of his for ten dollars, and if he signed it, then it would be worth a hundred.

John said, "Alan, we can't be offending major celebrities and stars like this."

I said, "Dude, that was funny. *He* thought it was funny."

He said, "Well, I don't think it was funny. You've got to watch that."

It seemed arbitrary and overblown. He didn't ever call me up for other stuff, or to tell me I did a good job on something—but out of nowhere, I got called up for this picayune thing. It was a weird, but telling, slap on the wrist.

Nina:

When we moved to the new studio, they wanted to polish us. They hired a communications coach for the five of us, Lillian Wilder. She was a professional—she had taught big network guys like Dan Rather. I don't like people giving notes on my air checks—my confidence isn't really an oak tree, and I get flustered. But I liked going to Lillian. She critiqued me, but she would also point out my strengths, and she was always teaching me something.

Alan:

Lillian's job was to make us better communicators. As much as I bitched and moaned about having to go to school for a job I'd been doing for three years, she helped me and the others a lot. If nothing else, I got my shit together on the air to avoid her brutal critiques. Things were getting more professional—we had a front desk, real dressing rooms, and a wardrobe area, but we still had to press our own clothes and do our own makeup. Sometimes I wouldn't bother with makeup, especially if I had just been on vacation and had a little bit of a tan. That was just me saying, "Fuck it—I don't need makeup. It's MTV."

Mark:

I pushed for them to send copies of the videos to the stage. Often, we'd be doing segments with new videos, and not only would we not have seen the video, we wouldn't know the song, and wouldn't even have any idea whether it was happy or sad. We had to react as though we had just watched the video, and it was nuts. So I came up with the genius idea of actually getting to see the videos in advance. They started sending down three-quarter-inch tapes every week with the new videos in the rotation. I created a library in our greenroom, with a card file, so we could jot down some notes about the video, especially the intro images and the final frames, so we'd have something to play off when we were on camera, either throwing to the video or coming out of it. It was just an alphabetical card file—no Dewey decimal system.

Alan:

We started to lead our separate lives in Manhattan. We didn't see as much of each other, and we didn't hang around waiting for the next shift—we'd just come in ten minutes before our shift started, which meant minimal crossover. Occasionally we'd ask, "So what'd you do this weekend?" In the old days, we would have known. We still ran into each other at clubs, but we didn't travel in a VJ pack anymore.

I had a better handle on the VJ job, and was more comfortable on the air. What I wanted from the producer was shorthand factual info: Prep me briefly me on the segment, and I was good to go. By this point, I was living the life I was talking to the audience about: "I went to see Tina Turner at the Ritz the other night, and you can catch her in your town. . . ." It usually took me an hour to prep, but depending on the previous night's escapades, there were times when I went in cold and took my chances with the teleprompter. I was good at cold reads.

Mark and I started to get competitive, seeing who could get a shift done fastest. I basked in the glory of a high five from the crew: "Hunter wins!" I'd go back to the dressing room and be out of there in forty-two minutes. But eventually I felt guilty: My main gig was to speak to people who really wanted to hear what I had to say. And I had reached a point where my only concern was speeding through it so I could get the hell out of the studio.

32

Jokerman Dance to the Nightingale Tune

Paul McCartney and Bob Dylan

Martha:

I got assigned the Paul McCartney interview, and I was beyond excited—I was shaking. Nobody could have been a bigger Beatles fan than me. I was a member of the official Beatles fan club; I couldn't wait to get those brown paper envelopes airmailed from England with xeroxed newsletters in them. I even went to Beatlefest conventions. But then the Police needed me to introduce them somewhere at the same time, so the producers gave the interview to Mark. I was shattered. The interview ultimately got rescheduled, but they didn't give it back to me. I don't even know if it was up to Mark or not.

Mark:

It wasn't.

Martha:

I died a million deaths.

Mark:

The Paul McCartney interview was for a special edition of an interview show I hosted called *Liner Notes*. I flew to London to do it—my first time in England—and brought Carol along. Paul was promoting his film *Give My Regards to Broad Street,* and he was still mixing the sound. He invited me into the control booth. George Martin was sitting in the booth, and we watched Paul in the studio, playing his violin bass; it was this surreal, amazing moment. We weren't even shooting—Paul was just being gracious. Paul was beyond cordial, actually. He bent over backward to make me feel comfortable. He was very aware of how people reacted to him, and sympathetic about that.

He laid down a bit of bass and came into the control booth. They were about to play back the movie to see how it worked when synched, so there was a freeze-frame of him up on the screen. I said something inane, "Wow, that looks just like you."

He said, "Oh, that's not me. I'm dead, y'know."

Paul was a savvy guy—he knew what MTV was and he knew if he made me feel good, then I was going to say positive things on national TV in the United States. But then again, he was fucking Paul Mc-Cartney! He didn't have to suck up to me—I was going to rave about him anyway! I walked away from that interview thinking he was operating on five more levels than I was, and had a much larger view of the conversation than I did. I was down in my trench, dealing with a dickhead director, who wanted all the questions written out in a script and didn't even want me on camera. I wanted to talk a bit more about John Lennon, and the director wouldn't let me.

Paul was in command of the whole situation. Who's done more interviews than him? If he didn't want to talk about something, he could move on, and you almost wouldn't notice. We were supposed to have fifteen minutes for the interview. That time went by quickly—I hadn't covered half of what I wanted to talk about when Paul's publicist started waving at me from behind the camera. I told Paul that they were asking me to stop. He gave me that impish McCartney grin and said, "Let's not!" I flipped—Paul Fucking McCartney wanted to talk more with me! We went on for another forty-five minutes.

After the interview, Paul asked me about what else I was going to do in London, and if Carol and I would be going out to dinner; she had come along to the studio. He mentioned a place, and then said, "Oh, actually, that's a little pricey."

If Paul McCartney thought it was pricey, how much could it be?

Then he suggested Stringfellows, which later became known as a trendy dance club, but at that time was more of a restaurant. And he got on the phone and called Stringfellows: "Hi, this is Paul McCartney, and my friend Mark Goodman is coming in with his wife for dinner tonight." Paul McCartney made me a dinner reservation!

Martha:

A few months later, MTV was setting up an interview with Bob Dylan, who was touring behind his *Infidels* record. Bob requested that I do the interview, and Mark freaked out. He said, "You have no right to do that interview—you don't know anything about Bob Dylan. I remember when you got here: All you knew about was Earth, Wind & Fire. I should do it."

Mark:

I was so pissed. I felt like we were always battling to establish credibility with the rock community. And we were sending this inexperienced girl to talk to the voice of my generation? I couldn't understand that thought process when MTV had me and J. J. available. Ideally me, of course.

Martha:

Mark's theory was that because I was friendly with Dylan's publicist, I got him to feed me the interview—which wasn't true. Mark yelled at me in our dressing rooms, just eviscerating me. He said that he was going to find out the truth: "When I find out, I'm not going to tell anyone in the office, but I'm going to tell *you*."

I responded, "Mark, I would have killed to interview Paul McCartney, but I wouldn't have killed you."

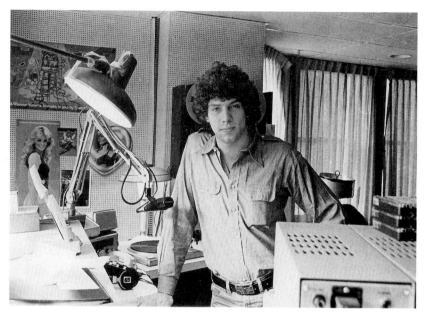

Mark in the WMMR studios in Philadelphia: "Here I am, looking really pompous about playing Meat Loaf." (© Scott Weiner)

Nina with her harp: "Taken by my manager, Danny, in the front garden of his parents' house, in Russell Township, Ohio." (© Danny Sheridan)

Alan with his high-school girlfriend (and head cheerleader): "Mary, on a Spartans football game day, telling me sweetly that if we don't win, there'll be no nookie afterward." (courtesy Alan Hunter)

Martha's theatrical headshot from her junior year at NYU: "You can tell I cut my own bangs!" (courtesy John Hart Studio, NYC)

Mark hosts MTV's first live call-in show, with Hall and Oates—it was plagued with technical disasters. "This must be before it started—everyone looks happy." (© Ebet Roberts)

Nina: "John Mellencamp has come a long way since his Cougar days of snatching me off my feet." (© Gary Gershoff)

Alan versus Joe Jackson: "He wasn't actually squaring off with me— he thought being a rock star in videos was silly and pretentious, but he did want to promote his music." (© Gary Gershoff)

Martha serving as an appetizer for Ozzy Osbourne: "Ozzy discovered that my head was considerably larger than a bat's." (courtesy Mark Weiss / WEISSguygallery.com)

J. J. with the Eurythmics—his favorite musical acts were rock bands with bold front men, but he also enjoyed new wave and the New Romantics. (courtesy MTV)

Nina interviews Bryan Adams: "He was the boy who'd stick your pigtails in ink. To this day, he can tease me into blushing." (© Gary Gershoff)

Mark's contentious meeting with David Bowie: "After this interview, I called him Bowie the Ambusher." (© Gary Gershoff)

Alan with Jon Bon Jovi and Tico Torres of Bon Jovi, at Club Hedonism in Negril, Jamaica. "Jon Bon and I were looking at the fabulous sunset. Tico was thinking about how much MTV wasn't paying him to go on this trip for a week." (courtesy Doug Herzog)

Martha in the embrace of David Lee Roth: "Seriously—a Boy Scout shirt? Can I please turn back the hands of time, just this once?" (courtesy Mark Weiss / WEISSguygallery.com)

J. J., Alan, Nina, and Mark welcome Zippy the Chimp to the MTV studio. Nina: "Of all the celebrities who visited our set, Zippy was my favorite, hands down. It was love at first banana!" (© Gary Gershoff)

Alan with Mick Jagger at Live Aid: "I was saying to myself, 'I can't believe I'm talking to Mick Jagger.'" (courtesy Doug Herzog)

Martha backstage at Slane Castle in Ireland, with Bono and Bob Dylan: "Bono was twenty-four and had just met Bob for the first time—U2 were at Slane Castle because they had just finished recording *The Unforgettable Fire* there." (© Ken Regan/Camera 5)

Mark interviews Madonna: "I was trying to figure out how I could clandestinely chain myself to her wrist." (courtesy Mark Weiss / WEISSguygallery.com)

Nina: "Once a cheerleader, always a cheerleader. Go Team MTV!"
(courtesy Mark Weiss / WEISSguygallery.com)

Martha on the CBS sitcom
E/R with Elliott Gould and
George Clooney (not to be
confused with Clooney's
later hit, *ER*): "I'm looking
at George—'Hey, you make
house calls?'" (courtesy
Embassy Television)

The VJs hang out
in Sherman Oaks,
California, in 1988.
Martha: "The number
one question I get is 'Are
you guys really friends?'
The answer is yes!"
(courtesy Alan Hunter)

The VJs in 2011,
celebrating the
thirtieth anniversary
of MTV. (courtesy
SiriusXM)

Mark:

That's a good line. I don't remember Martha saying it.

Martha:

Really? That sucks. It was one of the greatest things I've ever said in my life. It was a big moment of maturity for me: I stood my ground with Mark, and I had a good point.

Mark:

I was a dick. I don't remember yelling at Martha, but I'm so sorry. I love Martha and I think she's blossomed into the person that she wanted to be back then. I never meant to hurt her feelings, but I was just a jerk back then. So I apologize.

> *The camera rolls on Martha Quinn, in a baggy black sweater, interviewing Bob Dylan, who has shown up in a zebra-print shirt—but first, she applies eyeliner to him. Dylan tells Quinn that his favorite videos are Cyndi Lauper's "Girls Just Wanna Have Fun" and the Police video "where they're jumping around in the studio and they're all wearing hats" ("Every Little Thing She Does Is Magic"). They discuss Manny Roth, proprietor of Café Wha?, where Dylan played some of his first gigs. Manny is also the uncle of David Lee Roth, making him the secret connection between Dylan and MTV.*
>
> MARTHA QUINN: *"What kind of audiences have been coming to the shows?"*
> BOB DYLAN: *"Mostly foreign audiences. In France, we had mostly French audiences. In Spain, we had a lot of Spanish audiences. In Germany, there were German audiences."*
> MARTHA QUINN: *(deadpan) "What about Italy?"*

Martha:

I flew to England and interviewed Dylan backstage at Wembley Arena. I was nervous, but I knew I had good questions. The interview went great. When it was over, one of Dylan's assistants came up to me and said, "Bob wants to know if you can go to Ireland."

What?

"Do you want to come on our plane to Ireland with us?" I jumped in a cab, raced back to my hotel, threw all my stuff in a bag, grabbed my passport, and zoomed back to Wembley. I missed the whole concert but drove right to the airport, where I boarded Bob's private jet to Ireland.

I wasn't sure why Bob brought me along—he didn't seem interested in me. But the next day, when we all got on the bus to go to the concert he was playing at Slane Castle, he was sitting with some girl that he had pulled out of the audience from the London show. I thought, "Oh, I get it. It's like the Rolling Thunder Revue and I'm one of the players in the Bob Dylan parade." That's a legendary place of honor—I was flattered.

The show was incredible—backstage, Bono, Van Morrison, and I were hanging out. Afterward, I was on Bob's tour bus with the band and his family, heading back to the hotel, and the bus hit a motorcyclist. I don't think the guy was killed, but it was pretty gruesome. I was sitting next to Dylan's daughter, who was a little kid at the time. I grabbed her and covered her eyes, because I didn't know if there were body parts outside.

Someone called for a cab to take the Dylan kids back to the hotel. Dylan's oldest son, Jesse, indicated that I should leave with them. I said, "No, no, it's just you guys," but he insisted. We made our way back to the hotel, and everybody was freaking out. I had a brilliant idea: I ordered brandy for everybody. "Here, kids, have some brandy!" I didn't know what I was doing.

The next day, I took a cab to the airport with Ian McLagan, the piano player from the Faces. I went to France, where I met a girlfriend of mine from Ossining High School. We stayed in Paris for a week, staying in a youth hostel on the Left Bank. I was having these worldly experiences, but I was also still very close to being a kid.

That may have been the craziest trip of my life. On the way back home, I had a one-night layover in London. Walking around, I ran into Valerie Bertinelli, who had been married to Eddie Van Halen for a couple of years; the band was doing a European tour. I spent the day shopping with her and Alex Van Halen's wife: The two of them were buying all these expensive things that I couldn't afford. When Valerie pulled out her credit card, it was a gold card—and gold cards were *très chic* back then—with the name VALERIE VAN HALEN. That was the raddest thing ever.

In the evening, they all went out, and invited me along. Eddie Van Halen joined us, as did Neal Schon from Journey! Everyone was sweet, but I felt like a total third wheel. I couldn't shake the feeling of *who am I to hang out with these superstars?* J. J. wouldn't have felt that way, but I did. We went to some happening club and couldn't get in. We were standing on the street, so Neal started talking to this huge bouncer: "This is Eddie Van Halen, you know, from *Van Halen*. Dude, he played the solo on 'Beat It.'" And that got us in!

Back in New York, I dated Jesse Dylan for a little while. He really looked out for me, but I wasn't at an age where I could appreciate such devotion.

Nina:

Jesse called me one time, because Hurricane Gloria was coming in. It was a major storm, and they were evacuating a lot of the Eastern Seaboard. Jesse was worried about Martha, so he contacted me. I told him that I didn't know where she was, but I was sure she was fine.

Martha:

A few months after Jesse and I broke up, my neighbor at One Astor Place told me she had seen him walking down the street, holding some girl's hand. I called him up and went totally insane, throwing my phone across the room like I was the Incredible Hulk. Gawd, what a drama queen.

33

The Kids in America

MTV Contests' Winners and Losers

From the promo for the "Paint the Mutha Pink" contest:

VOICE-OVER GUY: *"It's our little dream house—the MTV Party House! You win it, you own it! Like it or not! It's smack in the middle of the heartland: Bloomington, Indiana, hometown of John Cougar Mellencamp! And, oh yeah, you have to paint it pink. You can be the grand-prize winner and owner of the first rock 'n' roll estate. And we'll even throw in a housewarming party! Just call up twenty-five of the wrong people and we'll fly everybody in for the weekend. John Cougar Mellencamp is your barbecue chairman. And later that night—"*

JOHN COUGAR MELLENCAMP, SHIRT LARGELY UNBUTTONED: *"The house band's going to be me, and I'm going to be playing in your brand-new living room!"*

VOICE-OVER GUY: *"Even later, there's a private screening of Universal's new movie,* Streets of Fire. *We never know when to stop! You'll also get a Jeep CJ—we'll paint it MTV pink! A complete stereo system from Pioneer, and a garage full of Hawaiian Punch fruit punch! Here's how to enter and win! Just send an average American postcard to the MTV Party House, P.O. Box 1280, Radio City Station, New York, New York, 10101. One thousand runners-up win a John Cougar Mellencamp album,* Uh-Huh. *So pack your bags—you're moving!"*

JOHN COUGAR MELLENCAMP, WITH PAINTBRUSH IN HAND: *"I give you the deed, and the keys, and then we paint the mother pink."*

Alan:

I did the "Paint the Mutha Pink" contest with John Cougar Mellencamp. Martha went out a month later when the girl got the house, but I did pre-interviews in Bloomington, Indiana. We were riding around Bloomington, trying to put together some stories, and running out of daylight. As we drove down a road, I spotted a couple of horses in somebody's backyard. I jumped out and interviewed one of them, the other horse nervously prancing close by. And then in the middle of my "interview," the mare opened up her legs and started prepping for nookie. Not being a farm-raised boy, I had never witnessed such an act. I was only five feet away from this breathtaking event—I continued to interview her, thinking we'd air it somehow, when the lady of the farmhouse came out the back door screaming at these two lovers, barking at them to stop. The MTV audience saw the foreplay but mercifully, nothing after.

As for Mellencamp, he was a sweetheart. He had an attitude, but he appreciated what MTV did for him.

Martha:

I flew out to Indiana, and went to John's house, which was very nice, in a woodsy area. We went swimming in his private lake, with a dock in the middle. He had the second Mrs. Cougar Mellencamp hanging around, Victoria Granucci, and I couldn't get over how gorgeous she was. Then we went and painted this house pink.

Alan:

MTV had bought the house cheap. We gave the house away to the poor winner, and it turned out it was on top of a toxic waste dump. John was furious.

Mark:

They literally had to tear the house down and buy another one across town and paint *that* mother pink.

Alan:

I don't know if anyone said, "How are we going to vet this shit out in the future so this doesn't happen again?" Obviously, they should have.

Nina:

We did a lot of "One Night Stand" contests. People sent in their postcards, and we'd pick one at random. The winner would fly with a VJ on our quote-unquote MTV Learjet to see a concert. They'd see the show, go backstage, and come home on the same night. Once, at the Rhinebeck, New York, airport, the winner and I were posing for pictures in front of the Learjet, which had the big MTV logo on the tail. And as they took the picture, the logo fell off. It was just taped up there.

Alan:

One of the early One Night Stands was with Journey. We went to pick the winner up somewhere in the Midwest—Iowa, maybe? I flew out there on a commercial jet, and met up with the winner and three of her friends. Four really sweet people, but very heartland. She kept telling me that she just couldn't believe she'd won, and kept hugging and pawing me. Her friends were dying to ask me a thousand questions. They'd have their chance, because we all piled into a Learjet for the four-hour return flight to John F. Kennedy airport: The Journey concert was in Long Island. For four goddamn hours, I was the entertainment. There was a lot of "Wow, man, I can't believe it's you" and "Whoa, can we take a picture?" I was trapped in this plane with four very enthusiastic fans. And then "Have you ever met Duran Duran?" and "What's Martha Quinn like?" By the time our wheels touched the tarmac at Kennedy, my face and my brain were dead.

Nina:

It's funny that Alan, of all people, would run out of stuff to say. He never does, and sometimes you wish he would.

Martha:

I did the One Night Stand with Fleetwood Mac. I was eating dinner with Fleetwood Mac and whoever the winner was, and Lindsey Buckingham said to me, "Hey, if you ever come to California"—saying I should give him a call. I swear I did this: I put up my hand and said, "Oh, I'll find you." First of all, that was so rude. Second of all, how was I going to find him? Was I omniscient? For years, I've wanted to apologize to him, but I never saw him again.

Mark:

I went to New Orleans for the One Night Stand with the Rolling Stones. I was running around the French Quarter, drinking pretty heavily. The humidity was disgusting, and the poverty was overwhelming; every twenty feet in the Quarter, there was a group of little black kids who would dance, do crazy stuff, anything so you would give them money.

The winners were happy, but I felt bad for them. It was a whirlwind: You were in the rock 'n' roll fast lane for twenty-four hours. But we had dinner, we went to the show, we went home. We didn't get to go backstage or meet anybody. I could understand we wouldn't get to see Mick or Keith, but c'mon, we're MTV. How come we didn't get to say hello to Charlie Watts or Bill Wyman—one of the loser Stones? A lot of what we did was about access—be a roadie with Van Halen!—and with the Stones, we had no access. And in my typical fashion, I was moaning about it: How come I have to do the crappy one?

Nina:

I flew to Winnipeg to do the One Night Stand with Men at Work. I was excited—I love flying—but I wasn't feeling good. At the concert,

I was seeing purple polka dots. On the way back, I started running a fever; somehow, I contracted bronchitis and laryngitis at the same time. But it was a treat for me, even though I was sick, because I had never been in a Learjet. I love speed: fast planes, fast cars, fast motorcycles, fast boats, fast horses. I had been reading books about planes, so I was very happy to be in this Learjet, because they're little souped-up sports-car airplanes.

Mark:

Learjets are Volkswagens with wings. Fun, but it's terrifying being in a plane that small, where you can't even stand up.

Alan:

The five of us started jockeying not to be sent out to do contests, except for Martha, who loved it all. Mark was the biggest curmudgeon.

Mark:

We had this campaign going to get more people to enter all of our contests: The promos would show various winners and say, "People really win on MTV." But a lot of people who won, well, they weren't cool like the people in the videos, or even like the people you'd see now on reality TV. They were just regular people: a little overweight, not the best dressers, and a lot of the girls had "mall bangs." So the behind-the-scenes phrase at MTV was "Losers really win on MTV."

Martha:

I never got tapped to do that many contests—I don't know why, it was always fun. I went to Mount Clemens, Michigan, with J. J. to do the first MTV House Party in May 1982. The winner was this sweet fifteen-year-old kid, Rob Kettenburg. We gave him a party for thirty of his friends with Huey Lewis playing, a wide-screen TV, and a year's supply of Pepsi. I sat on his hearth, talking to him. I'm sure he was psyched, but he didn't seem overwhelmed; I think he was rolling with the whole situation. At that point in time, MTV wasn't what it later became. Even Huey Lewis wasn't that big a deal in 1982—it was before the *Sports* album, so his big hits were "Do You Believe in Love" and "Workin' for a Livin'." I wasn't thinking, "Oh my God! Huey Lewis is here!"

Mark:

The craziest promo I did was "Asia in Asia," where you went to see the band Asia play at the Budokan arena in Japan. It was a very, very long flight to Tokyo, and I was sitting next to the winner, this girl from somewhere in the middle of America, who I hooked up with in the bathroom. When I traveled around the country and went to shows, sometimes I would see a good-looking girl, and I could see she was the prettiest girl at her high school, and there was something really charming about that—an innocence that wasn't there with girls from New York or L.A. This girl was like that: She was cute, she was funny. I got to know her for a couple of hours, and I'm sure a lot of alcohol was involved. We were in first class, so we got free drinks and felt like we were getting crazy, like the rock stars. I said, "Why don't you go back in the bathroom, and I'll meet you back there."

We casually slipped into the bathroom—at least, I think we were casual—and started to grope and unbutton and unzip. We tried to have sex, but our balance sucked, and we kept bonking our heads on mirrors and getting leg cramps. It was kind of fun, but incredibly uncomfortable. The mile-high club is great in theory, but not in practice.

That was just the beginning of the insanity. We stayed at the Akasaka Prince hotel, which was beautiful. But nobody in Tokyo spoke English, and all the signs were in Japanese, so I felt even more disconnected, like I had wandered into a scene from *Lost in Translation*. I was there with the MTV crew and executives—the A&R guy from the label knew a geisha house in the Kawasaki district. They said it was the one that the mayor of Tokyo would go to. I wanted to go—not necessarily because I wanted to get laid, but because I wanted to have the experience of a geisha house. And at the end, an executive put the whole thing on his card, which was a great joy to me. MTV picked up the tab for my first hooker!

We were there for five or six days, running around to different neighborhoods and being a foot and a half taller than everybody else walking on the street. The trip was one of the high points of my life. It was crazy to see what the concert hall at Budokan was selling: You could buy octopus from a vending machine.

The band was fighting with John Wetton, the lead singer. Carl Palmer was the drummer, so for this one show, they brought in Greg Lake to do vocals—they had been in Emerson, Lake and Palmer together. The concert was broadcast live, and I had a little thing that I needed to say onstage: "I'm Mark Goodman and right now you are all live on MTV in America." Somebody translated it into Japanese for me and wrote it out phonetically. I wanted to say something else, but the translator convinced me it wouldn't translate, so he wrote something that would make sense to a Japanese audience: "Are you ready to rock? Let's rock! Asia!"

When I delivered my spiel onstage, the audience was looking at me like I couldn't speak. *Is this guy all right? Does he have a speech impediment?* But they cheered at the appropriate moment—apparently "let's rock" is a universal sentiment.

Nina:

One time we had Zippy the Chimp come in the studio to pick the winning postcard. Zippy had been on *The Ed Sullivan Show* and was a big star down in South America. I love animals, so I wanted to work with Zippy. Alan got to do the segment—I was really envious.

Alan:

I think it was a contest where we gave away a Pac-Man machine. The tension was thick because, legally, this was a real drawing, so we could do it only once. No retakes. The lawyers in the studio were hovering nervously. I was introduced to the famous Zippy by his handler, like Zippy was a little kid who could understand that my name was Alan. Then he said, "Just get to know Zippy a little bit," and walked off. Zippy was larger than I expected—he came up to my chin—and he wanted to play, but his favorite game was to jump on somebody and do back flips. The handler hadn't told me this, and this crazy monkey kept trying to communicate that he wanted me to grab his arms and flip him over. What the fuck?

I looked around for the trainer, but he was hobnobbing with the VIPs on the other side of the studio. It was like being at a party at the neighbor's house where the dog starts humping your leg. Zippy kept jumping on me—I bent over awkwardly to catch him and I jacked my back. We finally started the drawing, with me in no small amount of pain, and Zippy kept messing with the barrel full of postcards. The lawyers were about to lose their minds, and I jumped in to save the event: "Gimme the dang card, Zippy." I've had a bad back ever since then, because of Zippy the Fucking Chimp.

ı Always Feel Like somebody's Watching Me

Celebrity and Its Consequences

Martha:

Anytime MTV got mentioned in the outside world, we would go bonkers. The lyrics of the first Asia record name-checked us: "The evening comes, we sit and watch the VJs." We were ecstatic about that. And then, when Dire Straits released "Money for Nothing," all about MTV, we were out of our gourds.

Mark:

I bumped into Mark Knopfler's manager at a concert; he said Dire Straits had just recorded a song about MTV. I was shocked, but excited and proud. "What's it called?" I asked.

"Money for Nothing."

I was not happy. I believed in what we were doing, and felt like I was part of something that was important in the growth of music. It hurt my feelings that the only people who loved us were the audience members. The national music critics really disliked us, and apparently by this time, the musicians had a love/hate relationship with MTV.

Alan:

We had this weird middle-ground celebrity. We weren't superstars, and we didn't have the money or the trappings or the safety that came along with that, but we were in everybody's life all the time.

Mark:

People would tell me, "I lost my virginity with you playing on the TV, and you were a great night-light. I don't know what you were saying, because the volume was down." Okay, I'll take it. Apparently, I looked sincere.

Nina:

Being celebrities snuck up on all of us. It wasn't something I thought about, but I got used to getting invitations everywhere. I was so busy working, I didn't have time to go to most of them. I admit it was nice to get a better table at a restaurant.

Alan:

Nina is one of those beautiful women who sits in the corner like royalty and waits for everyone to come around. She always ended up with the best seat at concerts—everyone catered to her, with Nina acting innocent: "Oh, am I in the best seat? How'd that happen?"

Nina:

I was lucky that during our time in the public eye, it wasn't like it is today with all the cameras and TMZ. I wouldn't have survived that.

Mojo Nixon and Skid Roper released a rockabilly song called "Stuffin' Martha's Muffin," which combined a lewd expression of desire for Martha Quinn with an anti-MTV rant: "Music television / Should be covered in jism." Despite this deeply held belief, Nixon later recorded PSAs for MTV and hosted their pregame show for the 1988 Super Bowl.

Martha:

At the beginning, I was bummed about that song. Rosanna Arquette got "Rosanna," and I got "Stuffin' Martha's Muffin"? But I was a little flattered, too. When *Saturday Night Live* parodied Nina, we were all so jealous—I thought, "Damn, she's lucky."

Nina:

Julia Louis-Dreyfus put on a blonde wig and did an impression of me. I didn't see it live—somebody brought in a tape. Her big schtick was that she kept saying things were *"hottttt, hotttt."* My first thought was that I didn't say "hot"! And I didn't realize I bopped my head all the time, but I actually did do that. I had no idea until she did her bit, though—nobody ever said anything to me. Why didn't someone stop me?

I was a little taken aback by the sketch, and I had to be convinced it was a compliment. Then I realized you've really made it when somebody imitates you. I thought she was really funny, and she's an amazingly talented comedic actress. If I ever meet her, I'd like to thank her.

> *From the* Saturday Night Live *of April 7, 1984 (Michael Douglas hosting, Deniece Williams performing), Julia Louis-Dreyfus as Nina Blackwood, delivering the music news:*
>
> *"Following the success of our 'Lost Weekend with Van Halen' contest, MTV has plans for a 'Lost Weekend with ZZ Top'—all right!—where some lucky viewer gets to spend two wild days vacationing in one of the band's beards."*

Nina:

Years later, I was hired to do some TV rock 'n' roll show, and they wanted me to say *"hotttt."* They had it on the cue cards, and the director was saying, "Just say it the way you used to say it." I told him, "That was Julia, not me!"

Mark:

Rich Hall did me on *SNL* one night. Not well, in my opinion. He was wearing an army jacket—not my style.

Alan:

I thought I was going to strike up a friendship with Kevin Bacon after he did a guest VJ spot; he hung around the studio after his taping. We connected with some similar life stories, but mostly, we talked about our hair—really—and what kind of mousse we used.

He said, "My hair is really flat."

I said, "I know what you mean, man."

"I use this foam stuff."

"Really? I need to use that too."

Slow day for both of us, I guess.

Nina:

A pal of mine, Jon Bendis, was friends with Cubby Broccoli, who produced all the James Bond movies. Jon said he wanted to introduce me to Cubby: "We're going to be doing a new James Bond film and you'd be a great Bond girl."

We went over to a gorgeous brownstone on the east side of Manhattan. Somebody told me that it cost a million dollars to build—in the 1800s. We waited for Cubby for a long time, and when he showed up, we just talked; I didn't have to read a script or anything. But I didn't get to be a Bond girl—whatever he was looking for, I wasn't it. I was fine with that; I was no Ursula Andress or Halle Berry. If I had gotten the part, I suppose my Bond girl name would have been "Nina Givewood."

Alan:

Peter Wolf, the lead singer of the J. Geils Band, did a guest VJ spot. Afterward, he followed me into my humble dressing room and started giving me tips on how to handle the MTV executives. He didn't have an axe to grind, but you could tell he didn't think much of authority. He told me, "Man, I really appreciate what you do—you don't realize that we're watching." He used to be a DJ himself, so maybe he was coming at it from that angle.

I asked him what it had been like being married to Faye Dunaway—they were together in the '70s. I thought that had been the oddest pairing ever, although I didn't say that. He said, "Man, she was *tall.*"

Nina:

My team in L.A. (my agents, Vicki Light and Eric Gold, and my manager, Danny) started to field some nice offers. Danny lined up a distribution deal for a Nina Blackwood poster: That would have been good money and exposure, but MTV nixed the idea. Universal TV approached Vicki about doing a sitcom—I nixed that one, because it would have meant leaving MTV. Agents are about getting you jobs, and mine were growing frustrated turning down all these moneymakers. My team constantly warned me about the possibility of being typecast.

Then an offer came up that even I couldn't refuse. Merv Griffin Productions was putting together a music TV show called *Hollywood Palace*—named after a landmark theater owned by Merv—and wanted me to host. I would be able to shoot MTV during the week, and then fly out to L.A. on weekends to tape the weekly show. Danny contacted Les Garland and got the okay to shoot the pilot.

The night of the taping was a dream: Searchlights in front of the theater and my name on the marquee. I sat in my dressing room, surrounded by flowers (courtesy of Merv), and thought, "Judy Garland might have sat in this very spot!" What I didn't know while I was shooting the pilot: Danny and my agents were taking calls from MTV, who had decided that they didn't want me to do the show.

When I got back to New York, I was called into a meeting with all the executives. They gave me an ultimatum: It was MTV or *Hollywood Palace*. I asked Bob Pittman, "Can you please open that window so I can jump out?" I don't like reneging on contracts, but I chose to stay at MTV. Merv could have sued us all, but he was decent about it. In hindsight, staying probably wasn't the best career decision, but I felt like MTV was my family.

what a pity you don't understand

The VJs Versus MTV Management

Mark:

Ken Ceizler became the executive producer, taking over for Julian Goldberg. We all liked Kenny. He had a quick sense of humor and knew what his job was supposed to be.

Martha:

He's still our friend today.

Mark:

But at work, Ken was just a bastard. He had his own way of doing things and he did not care what you thought. You didn't argue with him, because you weren't going to win. He was the one who gave me a hard time with the Paul McCartney interview, telling me that I couldn't ask him questions about John Lennon. And he acted the same way with Bruce Springsteen. I got an interview with Bruce, which was a very big deal. Carol was friendly with him—she helped me bring that one in.

Kenny micromanaged me on all the questions I was going to ask, and then made the decision that I wouldn't be on camera for the interview: just Springsteen sitting against a cinder-block wall, backstage at the Brendan Byrne Arena in New Jersey. I was furious: "Are you fucking kidding me? I'm the reason you *have* this interview." The whole MTV thing was kind of peripheral to Bruce—he wouldn't even have appeared in his own videos if his relatives hadn't talked him into it.

So I wasn't appearing on camera, my questions had all been reworded and reworked and reordered, and I wasn't supposed to ask follow-up questions. I said, "Well, Kenny, why don't you sit down and do the interview? What's the point of my being there?" I was furious. That interview was a big deal for me, but he wanted it that way and that was the way I had to do it.

Alan:

The summer of 1984, they told us, "By the way, we're going to have a Video Music Awards show, and it's going to be at Radio City Music Hall." We all thought, *"My God! That's fabulous!"* It was a huge indication that MTV had arrived. We assumed that the VJs would be hosting the show, but then we found out it was going to be Bette Midler and Dan Aykroyd. That's neat—we've got major stars hosting our little awards show. Okay, what's our role? In preproduction, they handed us the scripts.

Martha:

We all flipped through, looking for our spots.

Alan:

We quickly discovered that there wasn't a lot to use the yellow highlighter on. I think I had exactly one solo segment, up in the balcony, throwing to a commercial. Together onstage, we introduced one segment and introduced one award.

Nina:

We felt shortchanged. I don't know what the thinking was, but we were the faces of the channel the rest of the year—and then on this night, we weren't cool enough. We sat in the audience, watching something that we weren't really part of.

Mark:

When we found out how little we had to do with the show, it was a huge slap in the face. It underscored how the executives didn't think we were credible. J. J. was particularly upset about it. It felt like we were being dragged down.

I think the overall attitude toward the VJs was formed by the way Bob Pittman regarded talent: Keep them down, because it'll keep our costs down. He couldn't see the wisdom of giving us things to do that would enhance our reputations. He made a point of saying to me, "MTV will be the star, and because of that, you'll be a star too."

Still, they hired J. J. and me. There were plenty of people who knew as much or more than either of us, but they weren't TV friendly. Like the old saying goes, they had faces made for radio. The five of us original VJs are forever intertwined, and the whole is greater than the parts. Some days I'm fine with that, and other days it frustrates me.

> *The inaugural Video Music Awards took place on September 14, 1984. Major awards (in the shape of the MTV "moonman" astronaut) included:*
>
> *Best Video (The Cars, "You Might Think")*
> *Best Male Video (David Bowie, "China Girl")*
> *Best Female Video (Cyndi Lauper, "Girls Just Wanna Have Fun")*
> *Best Concept Video (Herbie Hancock, "Rockit")*
> *Best New Artist (Eurythmics, "Sweet Dreams (Are Made of This)"*
> *Artists performing on the show were David Bowie ("Blue Jean"),*
>   *Huey Lewis and the News ("I Want a New Drug"), Madonna*
>   *("Like a Virgin"), Ray Parker Jr. ("Ghostbusters"), Rod Stewart*
>   *("Infatuation"), Tina Turner ("What's Love Got to Do with It"),*
>   *and ZZ Top ("Sharp Dressed Man").*

Alan:

The afternoon of the show, Madonna was rehearsing her performance of "Like a Virgin" while a bunch of us—me, a producer, some executives—milled around in the Music Hall, about halfway up an aisle. She started off her routine on top of a big wedding cake, and she was blocking her moves on and around the cake. She strutted around, and then started rolling on the ground, and her wedding dress was definitely giving her trouble. It got bunched up, or snagged on something, and her boob popped out. Madonna was totally casual about the public reveal—she stuffed herself back in and kept going. All of us got really quiet and looked at each other, clearly thinking, "Did I just see what I think I saw?" I wanted to start giggling like a schoolkid, but I kept it together, because we were just fifty feet away.

Her performance that night had no mishaps, but we all had our hopes.

ı saıd to the man, "are you tryıng to tempt me?"

White Lines

Mark:

In high school, I hadn't done cocaine—I had only read about it. I asked Thierry, my meth connection who ended up getting deported, "What's coke like?"

He said, "Well, Mark, it's like shitty speed." I tried it, but I wasn't into it because back then, I preferred meth and acid.

Alan:

Two days before Jan and I got married, I visited my brother Randy in his Birmingham apartment, drinking beer with him and a buddy of his. Randy said, "Well, little brother, you want to do some cocaine?" I did my first bump and waited for the ceiling to lift off, only to experience a really clean high. The first hit is always the best. I didn't do another line until I had been at MTV for a year or so. I could afford it then, and it was part of the New York scene.

Mark:

Coke was a social thing for me. It was what happened when you went out, the way that people used to pass a joint around. People still passed joints around, but in the '80s, they also did blow. It was cool to be out late, and to say, "Hey, do you want to go do a bump?" I was always shy, so it gave me a way to talk to people. If you had great blow, it gave you credibility.

Nina:

I hate that drug with a passion. I tried it when I still lived in Ohio—just once. I was so hyper to begin with, I couldn't breathe. I went home: My heart was pounding and I couldn't swallow. I called the hospital; they told me to drink milk, which helped.

People say, "I bet you saw a lot of things." Yeah, I did. I saw cocaine ruin so many people. I believe it's even worse than heroin, because with heroin, people know they're getting into something heavy, but with cocaine, people think they're fine.

Alan:

Early on at MTV, we were pulling long shifts at the studio, and I knew Mark and J. J. were doing bumps in the dressing room. For them, it kept their energy up. I didn't do coke on the job because I was terrified of its effect—but I was pissed they didn't offer me any. Shortly thereafter, I mentioned it, and they were like, "You do coke?" They were appalled and pleased that little brother partook.

Mark:

I went to see Stevie Ray Vaughan when he was headlining at the Pier. He knew me, but not well. I saw him backstage, and asked him if he wanted to do a bump somewhere. He said, "Yeah, come back to my hotel." So I went back, and there were some other people in the room I didn't know. I'm sitting on one bed, and he's sitting on the chair, and he says, "Anytime, Mark. I brought you back here, what the fuck?"

I said, "Well, I didn't know if—"

"Yeah, it's cool, it's cool." I stayed there for a few hours, doing coke with him. He was a little more into it than I expected—I didn't know that he had this terrible problem. I was generally oblivious to other people's habits, not because I didn't know people could get addicted, but I never had that issue myself. I loved to do coke, but if I couldn't get some, it wasn't a big deal.

Alan:

One Tuesday night, there was a big party at the Palladium, and everybody was there: MTV staff, industry people, friends, musicians. I was hanging out with a couple of the MTV producers, and one of them said, "J. J.'s got coke."

I said, "Aw no, it's a school night, man."

"Well, we're not going clubbing. Just hanging here."

I got tapped to approach J. J.: "You got a little something?" He was a little irritated—when you're packing, you don't want people to bug you for it—but he handed me a teensy rolled-up old plastic bag. Enough for a few rounds, but not enough to get in trouble. I thought it was funny that he had this mini-packet in his pocket, and it made me wonder how many of them he had. Was he planning on doling them out to get people like me off his back?

I thanked him, and headed into the bathroom with three of my MTV friends. We all walked into the stall like a gaggle of geese. I reached in my pocket—and the bag had busted in my pocket. Everyone was saying, "Nooooo!" I turned my pocket inside out, and some of it spilled on the floor. One guy was using his finger to wipe it off the bathroom floor. We weren't strung out—we just really wanted that bump. I held out the pocket, and one by one, my pals hoovered my pocket, inhaling every residual bit of blow.

The three of them got their desperation hits, but I was left with an inside-out pocket and no ability to contort my body to reach it. It was the stupidest thing ever.

J. J. asked, "You guys do all right?"

I said, "Yeah, but do you have another one?"

His look in response—*oy!*

Mark:

I was in Champaign, Illinois, for the first Farm Aid. We went out to dinner the night before with John Fogerty, Carlene Carter, and a bunch of other folks. In the men's room, I offered Les Garland my vial. He did some and I did some.

Then I was standing at a urinal next to John Fogerty—both of us were peeing. I stretched out my arm to hand him the vial. He said, "I don't know what that is, but I don't want any of it." I felt like the biggest schmuck in the world.

Alan:

I was good about keeping school days sacrosanct—I didn't do cocaine on weekdays, just on the weekend. I've always had pretty good willpower, and the idea of not having my wits about me when I had to go in front of the camera scared the shit out of me. But once in a while on a Friday night, if Jan and I didn't have anything to do on Saturday, we'd get some coke, see a show, and go clubbing. Staying out until six-thirty in the morning was the norm. It didn't feel like a dark period—I was stepping out with my wife.

I fucked up once. I made the mistake of scoring a gram before the weekend. Thursday night, me and the honey were going to go out, have a lightweight club experience, and make an early night of it. But by midnight, the coke was burning a hole in my pocket, and we succumbed. Then it was two in the morning, and I knew I had the earliest shift on Friday, but we weren't heading home. Four A.M. turned into 5 A.M., and I was thinking, "Man, I have to be at the studio at eight-thirty." At 6 A.M., we were having breakfast at the Empire Diner, drinking as much liquid as possible, trying to come down.

I went home long enough to take a shower. I was still buzzing when I got into the studio at eight-thirty, and my excuse to the crew was "This cold is kicking my ass. I'm so miserable. Will y'all help me get through this?" They all knew exactly what was going on, and they were kind of bummed out—they were used to J. J. coming in from the clubs, but they didn't expect it from me. One of the stage managers said, "Al, we never see you get fucked up."

The reason for that is I don't operate well when I'm fucked up. Taping that day was an hour of hell. I sat there, looking at the television camera, knowing that a million people out there were watching me sniffle. "Oh God, okay. And that was the Rolling Stones, and coming up, U2. Can you give me another Kleenex?" I never even came close to doing that again.

Mark:

Les Garland called J. J. on the carpet for having a coke problem, and J. J. was not happy. He told me, "Garland was telling me with a straight face that I had to clean up my act." They lived in the same building on the Upper West Side, and J. J. had gone through some situations with him. J. J. said there was one night when Garland came home so fucked up, he couldn't get into his own apartment, and J. J. had to drag him in. So the hypocrisy pissed him off.

Alan:

MTV started doing spring break coverage, which meant doing live segments on the beach with lots of half-naked college kids, drunk off their asses. I can't think about those broadcasts without remembering the smell of stale beer and suntan lotion. The first one we ever did, MTV put me on a bus with some university students from Ohio all the way to Florida—my job was to be the court jester for that seventeen-hour ride. I messed with them all day and all night. When we finally got down to the beach, I was exhausted, but we had a couple of days off before we had to start filming.

I went out and partied with the producer and some camera guys. We hit the Fort Lauderdale clubs, accepting the gracious hospitality of the managers of each one. They wanted to be friendly, and that meant offering us some blow. I was cavalier about who I accepted lines from. In a sober corner of my brain, I knew the potential consequences of getting busted, but there were no MTV handlers keeping me out of trouble. For whatever reason, the channel didn't worry about that. Of course, TMZ and phone cameras didn't exist at that time.

Another night, I broke off from the crew and went looking for the busload of people I drove down with; I knew they were at a party somewhere. I walked up and down almost every floor of my hotel, only to realize that they were in a different hotel. So at three in the morning, I had a half gram of blow in my pocket and was in the sad situation of hunting for a party.

I walked past a door and heard a party going on. I looked at the door number, went up to my room, and called that room. When they answered, I said, "Hey, is Charlie there?" I didn't know a Charlie, I was just making up a name.

The guy on the phone said, "No, man, must be a different party." Then he asked, "Are you Alan Hunter?"

"Uh, yeah, I am."

"All right! Hey, everybody, it's Alan Hunter."

Then I said, "It sounds like you're having a little party down there." It was totally shameless, but I was desperate. They invited me to what turned out to be a very lame party. They couldn't believe I had come down to their party—at 6:30 A.M., back in my bed, I couldn't believe it either.

Mark:

Drugs thrashed my body; I have cirrhosis. Right now, I don't have too many symptoms that you can see from the outside, but I've been told that surgery is in my future. If I had never done drugs, I'd be a lot healthier today.

ı waɔ тнеrе тo маtсн мy ınтellect on natıonal тv

The Toughest Interviews

Mark:

Before MTV, I interviewed a lot of people on the radio; most of the time, it went pretty smoothly. The worst were probably Bob Geldof and Joe Jackson. Geldof was pissed off that America didn't recognize him, and Joe Jackson was just a pain in the ass. In general, interviews went better at MTV. After the first couple of years, musicians knew the power of the channel and its effect on sales, and that changed the timbre of the conversation: they'd pay attention and engage with you more. Many were fans of ours. There were exceptions, though.

Martha:

Early on, we learned that the bigger stars, the Mick Jaggers of the world, were totally nice and professional. The ones who were younger, or felt like they had more to prove—some of them were total jerks.

Nina:

I interviewed Bow Wow Wow, and the little brats didn't want to answer the questions. Liz Nealon, who was the producer of the segment, put the kibosh on that. The singer was fourteen years old, which was way too young to be giving us that much attitude.

Mark:

I loved the Frankie Goes to Hollywood album—this was before "Relax" got placed in *Body Double* and the single took off. I made sure that I got to interview them when they came to New York.

The band was basically two gay guys, Holly Johnson and Paul Rutherford. I thought they were lovers, but I didn't know for sure. They were pretty young, and it was their first time in the city, so they stayed out all night at the clubs and rolled into MTV for the interview in the morning. Fine, no problem.

I was asking them basic questions, introductory new-band stuff. Holly would say yes, and then whisper in Paul's ear for a while, and then they'd giggle. I laughed, trying to play along, but all I was getting were the one-word answers and the giggling and the whispering.

Finally I said, "Listen, you know what? America doesn't give a shit about you. I think your band's great, and I'd love to talk to you guys. So if you want to do this interview, great. If not, let's just stop right here."

Holly said, "Yeah, let's stop."

I had never stopped an interview before in my life. I couldn't believe I was doing it. Holly came back to the studio a couple of days later, apologized to me, and did the interview with somebody else. I don't think he wanted to apologize, but his manager probably said that they needed MTV on their side.

Martha:

I was scheduled to interview the Romantics—"Talking in Your Sleep" was rising up the charts. The night before, there was some party at a recording studio, maybe the Power Station. Nina and I went, and we ran into the band. It was friendly—we all had our picture taken together.

The next day they came in, and it was like a reunion—"Hey, how you guys doin'?" We started talking on camera, and randomly, one of them said, "Well, you know Wally, the guy you had sex with." I was frozen. There was a Wally in the band, but I had no idea why they would say something like that—nothing at all had happened between us. It was totally random. I was completely embarrassed, because this was happening in front of the crew I worked with every day.

I've played that moment back in my mind many times. In the replay, I stand up and announce, "You know what, gentlemen? This interview is over." And then I unclip my microphone, throw it down, and walk out, leaving them dumbfounded and ashamed. Instead, I sat there like a stone, and went back to reading my cards: "So who produced the record?" My internal monologue was "MTV is going to fire me if I don't get this interview. I have to keep going." At the time, I didn't realize that the interview was much more important to the Romantics than it was to MTV.

After that happened, I got a call from Les Garland that I really appreciated. He told me, "You don't have to take that. If that ever happens again, you can stop the interview."

Alan:

MTV sent me out to L.A. to interview Prince, and he canceled. I did get to hang out at the Greek with the Go-Go's and the Bangles and various Hollywood up-and-comers. I met Drew Barrymore that night—what a little charmer. Only later did everyone find out she was doing drugs at a very young age. I should have realized something was wrong with a thirteen-year-old at a club at one in the morning.

Martha:

We did a contest where the prize was a date with Prince to see his movie *Under the Cherry Moon,* plus he would play a concert in the winner's hometown—which turned out to be Sheridan, Wyoming. I covered the event, and before the concert, Prince came up behind me and said, "Oh, you seem tired." He didn't say anything else, but that might have been the most substantive conversation any VJ had with him during my time at MTV. Prince was another artist I had a huge crush on. I thought, *I'm perfect for you! I'm short!*

Alan:

I worked really hard to prepare for my Ozzy Osbourne interview—I was a big fan. But when he came on the set, his vibe was immediately crazy: lots of sniffles and tics and general weirdness. Sharon was diplomatic: "Oh, he's sick and he's taking some medicine for his virus." It might even have been true.

Ozzy sat down, and started saying, "This is all right, this is all right. I'm okay, are you all right?" I tried to calm him down, and then we started taping. I asked my first question, and he didn't even come close to answering it. It was just this fugue state of "Oh, oh, really, really, you know, no, it's right, I didn't do this." I tried another question, and he kept being unintelligible. He wasn't being an asshole—he was just incapacitated.

I looked over at the producer and said, "What are we going to do here?"

She said, "Okay, let's stop taping for a minute." We had to act like it wasn't his problem. The producer and I went to talk to Sharon. I said, "I really want to make this go well. What can we do?"

Sharon said, "I think he'll get better. He gets a little nervous—just keep going." While we talked, Ozzy just sat there, like a kid at the pediatrician's office when his mom and the doctor are discussing him.

We kept going, and it got a little better as he relaxed. I had a long list of questions I never got around to, because I followed the flow of his conversation, responding to whatever he could get out. Some poor editor had to hack the shit out of that interview. But I did ask him about biting the head off the bat—I kind of crawled up to that question. One of the nice things about MTV was that we could ask a clichéd question without too much embarrassment. Even if a story had been told in *Rolling Stone,* we could get them to repeat it—hey, we ain't ever told it on MTV before, right?

Nina:

Producers would feed us questions for interviews, and sometimes it would be basic stuff like "How'd you get your name?" To my surprise, sometimes we'd get great answers from those fundamental questions.

But when I interviewed Roger Waters, I was glad I had some material that went beyond that—I don't think it would have gone well if I had asked him how Pink Floyd got their name.

Martha:

I was flying on MGM Grand, which was an airline that went only between New York and L.A., with every seat first class. In the departure lounge, I spotted Eric Clapton—honestly, I knew it was him only because he was carrying a bag that had CLAPTON emblazoned on it. I'm normally hesitant to approach celebrities out in public, but he was sitting by himself, three feet away from me, looking bored, so I threw caution to the wind: "Oh, are you Eric Clapton?"

He conceded that he was, and I introduced myself. And then, because I couldn't help myself, and what the hell, I said, "Hey, can I ask you a question? Is it true that you played Dobro on Corey Hart's album and you're uncredited?"

"Uhhhhh, yeah." They had the same manager, or something like that.

I tried to keep the conversation going: "Oh, is it true you didn't start playing guitar until you were seventeen?"

He yelled, "I'm not going to do a *fookin' interview!*" And I just shrunk into nothingness. I was completely humiliated. The whole plane flight, I was afraid to get up and go to the bathroom, because I would have had to go past him, and I thought he might jump up and yell at me some more.

38

THere comes a Time when we Heed a certain call

"We Ruined Live Aid"

Mark:

I drank the Kool-Aid on Live Aid. I felt like we were helping something big, fighting hunger in Africa, and I was really proud to be part of it. We were there from start to finish.

Alan:

Live Aid was seventeen tough hours for me. I didn't have anything really insightful to say, about, for example, the reunion of Led Zeppelin. Even after four years on the job, the breadth of my music knowledge was limited. Give me Duran Duran or U2, maybe, but talking extemporaneously about Zeppelin was difficult.

Mark:

The American half of Live Aid was in Philadelphia—I was super-excited, because that's my hometown. I knew the promoter, I knew people working backstage. Nobody hit me up for tickets, but I think everyone I had ever met was at the show. JFK Stadium held a hundred thousand people.

Alan:

Our production crew wasn't feeding us note cards filled with research. Basically, they said, "Three, two, one, you're on, Al." Mark had the ability to contextualize what was going on, but we'd come out of something really monumental, and I felt like I should have something better to say about it than, "Man, that was great." But it was awesome to be sitting twenty yards left of the stage, witnessing one of the biggest musical events in history.

Nina:

Live Aid was a hot day and it was a lot of work, but it was cool to be part of something that important. I stayed on our platform pretty much the whole day. I didn't eat. I think I took a bathroom break a couple of times.

Martha:

I didn't pee once the entire day, from 6 A.M. to midnight. I was totally dehydrated, plus the porta-potties were disgusting.

Mark:

We were all cruising on adrenaline. And it was a thousand degrees that day, so we were sweating a lot. I wore shorts at Live Aid that have haunted me in pictures ever since. I've taken a fair amount of shit about them, but they were cool at the time. And I was working out, lifting heavy weights. I was in good shape and I knew it was going to be hot. I still have the T-shirt I wore that day: It was a paisley T-shirt that I had cut up.

Nina:

Martha got nervous on the day of the broadcast, so I had to step up a bit. It felt good being the one that they were relying on.

Martha:

I don't remember being nervous or overwhelmed that day. We'd done a bunch of live TV with the New Year's Eve shows, and I knew the bands inside and out. My only problem was that I was *over*confident. There were a few times during the day when I thought, "Maybe I should have prepared a little more."

> *Lineup at Live Aid, as seen on the MTV broadcast of July 13, 1985: Status Quo; Style Council; Boomtown Rats; Men at Work (in Australia, part of "Oz for Africa"); Ultravox; Spandau Ballet; Joan Baez; Elvis Costello; Nik Kershaw; the Four Tops; B. B. King (in Holland); Billy Ocean; Black Sabbath; Run-D.M.C.; Sting and Phil Collins; REO Speedwagon; Bryan Ferry (with David Gilmour); Crosby, Stills and Nash; Judas Priest; Paul Young (with Alison Moyet); Bryan Adams; U2; the Beach Boys; Dire Straits (with Sting); George Thorogood (with Albert Collins); Queen; Mick Jagger and David Bowie (video); Simple Minds; David Bowie (with Thomas Dolby on keyboards); the Pretenders; the Who; Santana; Sade; Elton John (with Kiki Dee and Wham!); Madonna; Paul McCartney; London finale ("Do They Know It's Christmas?"); Tom Petty and the Heartbreakers; Kenny Loggins; the Cars; Neil Young; the Power Station; Prince (video); the Thompson Twins (with Madonna, Nile Rodgers, and Steve Stevens); Eric Clapton and Phil Collins; Led Zeppelin (with Phil Collins); Crosby, Stills, Nash, and Young; Duran Duran; Patti LaBelle; Autograf (in Russia); Hall and Oates (with David Ruffin and Eddie Kendricks of the Temptations); Mick Jagger (with Tina Turner); Bob Dylan (with Keith Richards and Ron Wood); Philadelphia finale ("We Are the World"); Paul Young; Ashford and Simpson.*

Alan:

Roaming up and down that alleyway backstage, it was a smorgasbord of unbelievably iconic celebrities, all just sitting around, waiting to go onstage.

Mark:

Some people were there for a reason, because this was an important sociopolitical thing, and others were just hanging out to prove that they were groovy. I guess that's inevitable with the music business.

Alan:

I interviewed Mick Jagger. That dude is *short*.

Martha:

Back in the compound, I passed by Jack Nicholson—everybody still loves him today, but he was *major* then. He was with a posse, but I called out, "Hey, Jack." He nodded at me, and I said, "I'm Martha Quinn, from MTV."

His response was "I know who y'are." I was on cloud nine the rest of the day.

Alan:

I was walking around with a producer and a camera crew, and we had carte blanche to approach anybody. Crosby, Stills and Nash were hanging out in a little bungalow, sort of a picnic area, and the producer said, "Oh, we got to talk to them." And as we were approaching, the producer says, "Ask Crosby about his drug problems."

This was the heyday of Crosby going to rehab and jail. I said, "No, don't make me ask that. It's David Crosby, I can't." So I started talking to him about the album, and it was easygoing—they're fairly nice guys. Once again, the producer whispered in my ear: "Ask him about the drug problem." I capitulated, and said, "So how are you with the recent troubles?" And he said, with chilly eyes, "Well, I'm not going to go there, Alan." That pretty much shut down the interview.

Nina:

We had the worst seats in the house for actually seeing the show. We were over on the side, and there was a barricade between us and the stage. I did take one little break where I got to see Simple Minds play. Chrissie Hynde had broken up with Ray Davies and was with Jim Kerr at that point—I could see her watching him backstage, which was cool.

Mark:

I interviewed Chrissie Hynde backstage, and she was just bitchy. It was hot and sweaty—I think she was just responding to that.

Alan:

I bumped into Mark Gastineau, who played for the New York Jets. I didn't know much about football, but the producer clued me in, and we interviewed him. He was very funny, and at the end of the interview, he reached down, grabbed me by the ankles, and held me up like a prize fish. Steroids!

Mark:

All through the day, Martha kept talking on the air about how Bruce Springsteen was going to show up. There was this lighting rig, and she kept going on about how it was Bruce's lighting rig. What? There's no special lighting. She kept spewing this on the air: "Bruce is gonna play, he's gonna." And I was like, "Martha, come on, that is not happening."

Martha:

Someone in Bill Graham's office told me that Bruce might show up. It didn't happen. In retrospect, I'm sure he wishes he had done it.

Mark:

That was one of the glaring errors of that day. Bruce practically lived up the block. If Phil Collins could take the Concorde, Bruce Springsteen could have fucking driven down the New Jersey Turnpike.

MARK GOODMAN, LATE IN THE DAY OF THE LIVE AID BROADCAST, WEARING AN INCREDIBLY SHORT PAIR OF SHORTS AND DISCUSSING THE LED ZEPPELIN REUNION: *"You can't help but wonder what is going to become of these relationships once Live Aid passes."*

Sitting next to Mark: Ben Orr of the Cars, in a white dinner jacket, and Martha Quinn, wearing a dress printed with butterflies, a hat with Japanese characters (given to her by Steve Porcaro), and a bunch of laminated passes on a lanyard.

BEN ORR: *"Unbelievable. It wouldn't happen again in, I couldn't even imagine."*

MARTHA QUINN: *"Ben, altogether, how would you rate today's events as a rock 'n' roll concert?"*

BEN ORR: *"I'd give it a three."*

Mark:

Live Aid would have been huge no matter what, but MTV was really powerful at that moment, and the fact that we made such a massive commitment to it meant something. People told me that they were watching us all day long, in bars and all over the place. Dick Clark and ABC went on the air late in the day, but everybody was watching MTV that day. It felt like everything we had worked for over the last four years had come together.

At this moment of triumph, it was also the beginning of the end for the five of us. By the time of Live Aid, MTV was done with J. J. They sent him to Wembley, and they tried to pretend that was special, but we had no real crew there. So J. J.'s participation in our broadcast that day was almost nonexistent—when there was news at Wembley, the four of us in Philadelphia were delivering it. We all felt really bad about that. We knew the sun was setting on him, and he knew it too. He was a smart guy—he could read between the lines. Not that they were especially subtle about it.

J. J. was philosophical about it, and he resolved to have a great time. The satellite transmission got fucked up during the Who's set, so J. J. was the only one of us who got to see the whole thing. He was an Anglophile, and a huge fan of Queen, and a friend of Freddie Mercury's. A couple of years earlier, he had taken me to a Queen show at Madison Square Garden—at the after-show party, they had all these boys in loincloths, running around serving drinks. Queen's set at Live Aid was, by consensus, the best show they ever did.

Nina:

I thought J. J. had the best Live Aid gig of all of us—he was hanging with friends he had known for decades. When he came back, it sounded like he had a blast.

Martha:

Paul Shaffer saved the day when the satellite feed went out. The Who were doing "My Generation," Roger Daltrey sang, "Why don't you all ffff—" and then the screen went blank. Suddenly, Mark and I had to vamp, but we had no idea when the feed might come back, and we were freaking out. Paul was watching from the side of the stage—he was on hand to be the bandleader for the "We Are the World" finale—and ever the consummate pro, he *sprinted* over to Mark and me. He jumped in front of the camera and, reprising his Artie Fufkin character from *Spinal Tap,* apologized profusely for knocking out the plug.

Nina:

When Paul McCartney was playing "Let It Be," the director wanted the VJs to sway along with the song. I didn't sway, and I stayed off camera. But he cut from McCartney to the swaying VJs, and the critics just ripped us to shreds. It hurt, because we were really proud of the work we did that day.

Mark:

We ruined Live Aid. People were pissed off at us, and it just made no sense to us.

> USA Today: *"The MTV video jockeys should hang their heads."*
> The New York Times: *"Unhampered by even the vaguest notions of rock's history and heritage."*
> Rolling Stone: *"MTV made matters worse by constantly segueing from performers to close-up shots of swaying veejays."*

Alan:

That was the most criticized part of the whole day. Well, whose choice was that? That's not my fault—the director is cutting away to us swaying and singing. Sometimes as VJs, we got blamed for things we had nothing to do with—but sometimes we got credit for things we had nothing to do with either.

Mark:

We arrived very early and stayed very late. I put in eighteen or nineteen hours of nonstop work. As they were closing the day with "We Are the World" at JFK, the director pulled me aside and said they had decided to do a one-hour wrap-up show—and by the way, Mark, you'll be hosting it. I was a little worried about weird feelings from the other VJs—"How come Goodman's hosting?"—but okay. There was no teleprompter or anything. We just pulled information together, and I went for it. At the end of the day, the director told me, "Mark, your stock is really high right now." We all had our moments, but Live Aid is one of the days in my career I feel proudest of. That's why the beating we took in the press was especially hurtful.

Martha:

Mark was amazing all day long. I'll never forget his intro to Led Zeppelin: "This is rock 'n' roll . . . and they're *doing 'Stairway'!*" What a rock star.

Alan:

Afterward, I ended up in Paul Shaffer's hotel suite—tons of other people from the day were there. Yes, people brought coke. And there was a huge glass table.

39

LOVE IS A BATTLEFIELD

Martha Meets Stiv Bator

Martha:

The Lords of the New Church visited MTV for an interview. I met the lead singer, Stiv Bator, and thought he was funny and clever and cool. I heard Stiv say that he was staying at the Mayflower Hotel, so that night, I called the Mayflower and asked for his room.

The front desk connected me, and I said, "Hey Stiv, it's Martha Quinn, ummmm, we just met—"

"This is Steve, I'm his dad."

"Ooooh, hi, could you tell him I called?"

Stiv was leaving town, so we didn't get together, but a few months later, he came back to New York to do "Sun City," the Artists United Against Apartheid record with Little Steven, and he called me up.

Stiv Bator (sometimes Bators) was lead singer of the Dead Boys, a punk band famous for "Sonic Reducer." After they broke up, he moved to London and started the goth-flavored Lords of the New Church with members of the Damned and Sham 69. Bator's onstage trademark: pretending to strangle himself with the microphone cord, a stunt that went awry at a 1983 gig when some fans started pulling on it. Rushed to the hospital, Bator was clinically dead for two minutes. He later said, "I once died onstage. How do you top that, for Christ's sake?"

Alan:

Martha brought Stiv down to the studio, and I could see the electricity between the two of them. I asked if they were dating, and she said yes. I loved Stiv—he was a sweetheart. But it was an odd pairing, to have the girl next door, who I thought of as a sister, dating a full-on punk rocker.

Martha:

I saw the Lords all over the country, from Virginia Beach to Orange County, in weird little joints. That final tour was rough for the Lords—the crowds were thin. It was kind of heartbreaking.

Alan:

As time went on, Martha became more enigmatic for me. When she started dating Stiv, I was thinking, "Wow, what is her taste?" I assumed she liked blond-haired all-Americans, like me. But apparently she went for rockers and roadie types, which made her seem more grown up.

Martha:

There's something about bad boys that's compelling to good girls—just ask Sandra Bullock. People still ask me, "How could you have gone out with Stiv Bator?" But he was a special guy—in his own, unique, carve-an-X-on-his-chest kind of way. *Rolling Stone* named us the oddest couple of the year, right behind Melissa Gilbert and Billy Idol.

Once Stiv came to pick me up at my apartment, along with Michael Monroe from Hanoi Rocks. They had the fringed leather jackets and the cowboy boots and the feather earrings and the eight million jingly-jangly things. And the hair spray—even the punk rockers had big hair back then. The doorman, who was an old-school Irish fellow, buzzed my apartment and said, "There's two gentlemen here to pick you up." I came downstairs, and I could see the doorman was thinking, "You're seriously going out with these freakos?"

I schlepped Stiv up to Troy, where my grandparents lived. My mom had moved out of the house where I grew up, so my grandparents' house was my safe place. We were all sitting at the mahogany table where we had so many Thanksgiving dinners. Stiv was sitting there in his leopard-print shirt and red pleather pants, but he made my grandmother laugh hysterically. My dad, formerly a navy pilot, was . . . unsure about Stiv, but once Stiv started pulling out baseball trivia, even he was charmed.

When we were going out, it always took Stiv ages to get ready. I didn't wear much makeup—I just worked the Pat Benatar look. But Stiv would have the hair spray and the eyeliner and the lip gloss. And then he'd have to put on his bangles and bolos and belts and boots. I'd be ready in two seconds, and he'd still be getting his vinyl pants on. It made me a little crazy, but it was funny.

Mark:

One time, Stiv was supposed to be interviewed at MTV, and he showed up two hours late. He came sauntering down the hallway toward the studio. And our teeny, good-girl, all-American Martha—who I couldn't believe was going out with this guy who looked like a junkie in the first place—came bolting out of her dressing room. I don't know how she knew he was there. It was like she had radar.

Martha:

Our brilliant receptionist, Carmen Walker, called back to my dressing room when Stiv finally arrived. I'd been talking all day with Nick Turner, the Lords' drummer. He was the one in the band who had management savvy—later on, he worked for Miles Copeland—and he was freaking out too. Stiv was staying at my apartment, and not picking up the phone.

Mark:

Martha started laying into Stiv. "What do you think you're doing? You can't show up here two hours late. This is MTV—you have to be on time! Who do you think you are?"

He just took it: "Sorry, Martha, sorry, I couldn't help it. Sorry."

"That's not the way we do it around here!"

"Sorry, sorry." It was one of the funniest things I ever saw. He was the quintessential punk, and the ultimate squeaky-clean girl was tearing him a new asshole. It was the best moment ever.

Martha:

We had worked so hard setting up that interview. Stiv told me later that he had pretty much blown it off on purpose—he didn't want people to think he got on MTV just because he was my boyfriend. I understood that, but he should have just said no in the first place, instead of letting everyone do all that work. Stiv was a great guy, but he was also totally irresponsible. He was Axl before Axl, which was fine for a punk rock legend, but was tough on a girl from Ossining, New York.

Stiv and I didn't last that long. Partially that was because I lived in New York and he lived in London. He would do things like tell me he'd be in New York on Tuesday, and then not show up. There were no cell phones back then—I'd call his place in London, and if he didn't pick up, I'd have no idea where he was. And then I'd walk into my apartment on Friday, and he'd be there, waiting for me.

"You said you were going to be here on Tuesday—what the hell?"

He'd plead, "But I was trying to finalize my divorce."

I told Stiv, "I can't live like this. I know you think that I'm not going to break up with you, but I will." I was thinking farther down the road: What if we had a kid and he did that when it was their school play or a PTA meeting?

Anybody who knew Stiv will tell you he was the greatest guy. But those who were closest to him—his bandmates, his girlfriends—will also tell you it was too difficult to stay in a long-term relationship with him. Finally he showed up three hours late for something, and I told him that was the end.

In 1990, Bator was hit by a motor vehicle in Paris. He declined medical attention and died later the same day.

40

I Guess I Should Have Known by the Way You Parked Your Car Sideways That It Wouldn't Last

The Final Days of Nina and J. J.

Nina:

I wanted to move out of my little apartment and into a high-rise on the Upper East Side. Danny kept saying no, telling me that I should save my money. But then there was a stabbing across the street, and somebody used my lobby as a bathroom—even though there was a doorman—so finally I insisted. At the beginning of 1986, I moved into a place on Eighty-eighth and York, overlooking the East River.

Around that time, I went to a party at the House of Music recording studio in West Orange, New Jersey. I met this guy, Dennis, a tour manager who had just gotten off the road. He was a cool guy—we both loved rock 'n' roll, food, and German culture. I had finally gotten out of the relationship with Quentin the schmuck, so I wasn't looking to start up something new, but Dennis was really nice. When he called me up, I agreed to meet him at the China Club. On that first date, he noticed how quirky I was, and came up with a nickname for me that I loved: Henrietta Glockenspiel.

Dennis was smitten with me, but I was reluctant. I sat down with Ken Clark, who was the assistant to the VJs, in the lounge at the studio, asking him what I should do. "I'm just not ready for this, K. C.," I said.

"Well, get ready," he told me. "Because he really likes you." Before I knew it, Dennis was living in the high-rise with me.

Martha:

That spring, we heard that MTV wasn't going to be renewing the contracts of J. J. and Nina. I was devastated, of course—the VJs were like family to me—but not scared for myself. I knew I'd be staying at MTV forever.

Nina:

In 1985, the year before, I had been offered a job cohosting *Solid Gold* with Rick Dees, and I turned that down, because I wasn't ready to leave. But then things started changing at MTV. Our duties were lessening, and there was no upward mobility—they didn't want the VJs to be producers or do anything new.

Paramount came back again, and they offered me two jobs, doing *Solid Gold* and *Entertainment Tonight* simultaneously. I had a bunch of other offers, including a syndicated radio show that I took. Three jobs seemed like plenty, so I decided it was time to graduate from MTV and go back to L.A.

One evening, I went out to dinner with Dennis and told him what was going on, letting him know I was leaving town. It wasn't an ultimatum, but I wanted to know if he was interested in moving west with me. On the spot, he asked me to marry him. I didn't say yes right away. But when I thought about it, I felt like nobody would ever ask me again. The only other time somebody had proposed was in the seventh grade. I had loved John, but he had gotten married. So I decided, "Why not?"

We picked May 19, because I wanted a wreath of lilacs in my hair, and they're in bloom in May. I asked for one day off and didn't tell anybody. I was being very private—I didn't want anyone to think I was leaving MTV because I got married. We had a ceremony on Long Island with a justice of the peace, my maid of honor Ida, Dennis's best man, and the couple that introduced us. My mom wasn't even there—she was in the middle of some heavy-duty dental work. We had one night for our honeymoon, and then Dennis had to go out on the road with Patti LaBelle. I headed out shortly after him, to do Hands Across America in Little Rock, Arkansas. I was being a hand. Two hands, I guess.

Mark:

One day, Nina just showed up married. She had the shift after me, and I was doing the throw to her. She came out on the set, and I noticed she was wearing a wedding ring. And I didn't even know she was going out with anybody. I said, "What's this, Nina? Did you get married over the weekend? Ha ha!" She didn't say anything, and I realized it wasn't a joke. "What? You got married?! And you didn't tell us?" I was so shocked that my sister didn't tell me about this huge event in her life.

Martha and J. J. had noticed the ring in the dressing room a few minutes before me. We all felt it was bizarre.

Nina:

Some designer had sent us a bunch of bathing suits. We were looking through them, and Martha spotted the ring, and said, "What's that?"

Martha:

I saw that ring and felt like I was sucker-punched: "You bitch!" That sounds horrible, but I was *really* hurt. I didn't understand how she could do something like that. Okay, fine, she didn't invite us—but to not even tell us? That sucked.

Nina:

Martha told J. J., and he *blew up*. He took me in his dressing room, slammed the door, and bawled me out. "Why didn't you tell us? We're your family, Bean." He used to call me Nina Bean, or just Bean. I said, "I didn't tell anybody, except Ida. I didn't want people to get the wrong idea about my leaving." I just wanted to keep it private until I was leaving, but I never heard the end of it. All the other VJs were really mad at me.

Martha:

It rocked my world, but after I said my piece, I was over it.

Mark:

We had a farewell party for Nina and J. J. at some restaurant. I hired a stripper for each of them. J. J.'s was this athletic blond woman who did some high kicks and eventually stripped down to her underwear. J. J. leaned against the wall, enjoying the show. And for Nina, I hired a super-muscular black dude, who stripped down to a cup. Nina acted like a kindergarten kid: freaking out, running away from him, hiding her face.

Nina:

It was just gross. I ran into the bathroom—my favorite place to hide.

Mark:

I thought it would be funny, but it never dawned on me she would be *that* embarrassed. She knocked over a chair to get away from this guy—if she could have crawled into the wall, she would have.

> For his final segment, J. J. Jackson stood with his arm wrapped around a clearly distraught Martha Quinn, flanked by Alan Hunter and Mark Goodman. In front of them was a large cake in the shape of the numeral 5. J. J. said goodbye to his fellow VJs, and to the audience: "It's five years we've all been together, and Nina couldn't be here. She sent me a lovely note, saying why she couldn't be here. But it might be the last time you see the four of us together."

Nina:

I stayed in my dressing room because it was just so emotionally over-whelming.

Martha:

J. J. covered for Nina, but I was worried that he might be hurt that she didn't make it out for his last segment. In retrospect, he handled the situation beautifully.

Mark:

He was Mr. Aplomb. Nina could be a little melodramatic, but she was always a sweetheart. She wasn't great at articulating her emotions, so it all led to tears.

Nina:

Of all the VJs, J. J. was the only who really seemed to understand the extreme degree of my shyness. The others didn't pick up on that, or if they did, they never said anything. But J. J. knew that my being in the middle of things was not comfortable for me. He described me as "painfully shy," and he was right.

Mark:

No one has ever said anything to me about it, but when J. J. was let go, or when his contract wasn't renewed, I figured they felt he didn't fit with the channel anymore. But the guy he was when they let him go—he was that same guy when they hired him. He always had this elegance about him that was not "Hey, kids, rock 'n' roll." He was always connected, and the stars knew him. He was always a bit chubby and sweaty on camera. I think they just thought he was getting old.

Martha:

We got to say goodbye to J. J., but Nina just left without saying anything.

Nina:

Well, there was that farewell party, and Martha was there. But my last day turned out not to be very momentous. I had a lot of vacation time, so I didn't have an official last day—MTV said to just go ahead and leave. *Solid Gold* and *Entertainment Tonight* were champing at the bit for me to get out to L.A.—I didn't even have time to finish packing. After I started on those jobs, I had to come back to New York twice before all my stuff was packed for the move.

On my last day, I passed by Downtown Julie Brown in the hallway—they had hired her as a new VJ. We met very briefly, standing next to the wardrobe room. She was moving into my dressing room—either mine or J. J.'s.

I quickly settled back into the California life. J. J. had beaten me back to Los Angeles, but only by a few weeks. A few months after we left the channel, he and I went to the third Video Music Awards—that year, they were broadcasting the show from the Palladium in New York and the Universal Amphitheatre in L.A. We asked MTV for tickets, and they gave them to us: two seats in the Universal balcony, in the second-to-last row.

41

The kid is hot tonight

Alan Hunter Coast to Coast

Alan:

The Amnesty International tour was a year after Live Aid; we broadcast the final show from Giants Stadium. It felt like Live Aid Light, with the Police, U2, Peter Gabriel, Jackson Browne, and Little Steven, and it seemed like these types of mega-concerts were going to be all the rage from then on. But everything that happened at that show is a bit of a fog for me, because Jan was extremely pregnant with our first child. She had decided that she didn't want to crack Broadway; she was ready to be a mom. By the time of the Amnesty show, Jan was too pregnant to come waddling out to Giants Stadium, so I strapped a pager on my belt and spent the whole time worrying about her going into labor. I made it through, and our son, Dylan, was born three days later, on June 18, 1986. Somebody in MTV's PR department got *USA Today* to write about it; I framed the article and kept it in Dylan's bedroom: "MTV's First VJ Baby."

Mark:

Amuck in America was a thirty-day cross-country trip that had Alan and a hot model babe, Josie Bell, in a convertible, with a crew following them. They drove across the country and got in trouble everywhere. Alan was great for it, but it was a mess for him to do it—he had just had a baby, and it did not go down well with his wife. I was dying to do it, and it would have gotten me away from *my* wife, which is what I was looking to do as often as possible at that point. But I was the knowledge VJ and Al was the funny VJ.

Alan:

We were negotiating a new contract, and the bosses came to me and said, "Alan, we need you to go on the road for thirty days."

I said, "I can't—my son's just two months old." Before, I had always been a company man—that was the first time I had ever pushed back. They kept asking, and finally I negotiated that they would fly Jan out three times to visit me.

Bob Pittman and Tom Freston were the merry prankster executives behind this whole thing, and they put our producer buddy, Joe Davola, in charge on the road.

Mark:

Joe Davola was a really funny guy. He was involved in creating *Remote Control,* and he produced Arsenio Hall's show. They also named a character after him on *Seinfeld*—"Crazy Joe Davola."

Alan:

We were doing twelve segments a day. At the beginning, we put together these little comedy skits, and the word we got back was, "We don't want the skits—just turn the camera on." They wanted to run us ragged and see what would happen. We didn't know it, but we were inventing the next generation of reality TV. I was happy to be out of the studio, freed from the obligations of being a talking head and interviewing bands. I just wanted to talk to regular people and be funny.

On the third day, we went to Philadelphia, and ended up at a dance club that was having a wet T-shirt contest. I was on my knees with a pitcher of beer, spewing it all over these girls' T-shirts. It felt like an out-of-body experience—when the camera turned off, I was thinking, "I can't believe I just did that." But that was exactly what they wanted.

It was a bare-bones operation. We couldn't afford a big rock 'n' roll tour bus, so we had a small RV. It was six or seven crew guys, plus Josie and me. Josie was lovely. She and I got along really well—if I hadn't been a committed family guy, we would have hooked up, I think. We'd all haul our bags into the hotel at the end of the day, and then wake up at 8 A.M. and think about what we were going to do. The route across the country was roughly planned out, but we took a lot of detours.

It was probably the best time ever in my career, and the hardest-ever time in my personal life. I felt like the businessman who went on the road—I sold a lot of vacuum cleaners, but my family got left behind. There were no cell phones, and we were running and gunning the whole time, so I wasn't calling home very often. And poor Jan was watching the debauchery every day on MTV, with a three-month-old hanging onto her breast. I was finally hitting my stride at MTV, but Jan didn't like staying at her folks' house in Mississippi, watching me get crazy on TV.

I'd call from a pay phone on the side of Route 66, and I'd hear Dylan crying. "How's the baby?"

"He's fine. How are you?"

"Oh, I'm fine. It's hard out here, and I'm tired."

"Hold on, one of your segments is coming on. Oh, great. You're in a hot tub with Miss New Mexico. I'll talk to you later."

"No, baby, it's just TV!"

Amuck in America deteriorated pretty quickly—or maybe got better, depending on what side of the camera you were on. Somewhere in Texas, we pulled up to a diner and jumped out with our fake Uzi machine guns. We ran into the diner—no advance work, no warning, nothing. I jumped up on the countertop and said, "Everybody down!" People weren't quite so fearful about terrorists back then, but I was lucky not to have an off-duty cop put a cap in my ass.

Everyone in the crew ended up being on camera, so after a week or so, we had a production meeting where we tried to figure out how the logistics would work—someone had to remember to turn the camera on, even if he was filming himself. We'd roll all this footage and send it back to New York and hope they'd edit it in the right way. We started hearing that they were running large blocks of unedited video, not just the bits we intended for segments. We had to do what we called "black to black"—camera on, make a golden one-minute segment, camera off. That put more pressure on me to have my act together, or sometimes not have it together at all and just go for the gusto.

We had a day off in Birmingham, Alabama, my hometown, and we stayed at my parents' house—my mom and stepdad were out of town. The local newspaper reporter interviewed me as we were hanging out by the pool. She made it sound really glamorous, like I was hanging out with all my Hollywood pals, which was funny, because we were traveling from hotel to hotel, each of us schlepping two large orange-and-blue duffel bags: MTV had issued them to us at the beginning of the trip, with our names written on the side with Magic Marker, like we were going to camp. I still have those bags today.

With twelve segments a day, we had to be more efficient, even as we were unraveling. After a while, we decided we would start every day with a talk-show segment we called "Good Morning Amuck," complete with a theme song. We'd be sitting poolside at our hotel, semi-blitzed from the previous night. We'd recap what happened the day before, and sometimes introduce a special guest, like the janitor or a hotel security guard. Our crew would be sitting around, drinking coffee and eating doughnuts on camera. We could usually get two segments out of that—three if a Barney Fife security guard showed me his gun.

In Detroit, we visited Aretha Franklin's house. We didn't mess with her—we were reverent to the point of being meek. We looked pretty grungy, with shorts, tennies, and backward hats; I had even grown a road beard. We turned on our little handheld camera, rang the doorbell, and Aretha opened the door: "Oh, hi, I'm expecting you." MTV had played a lot of "Freeway of Love" and her cover of "Jumpin' Jack Flash," so she had every reason to be polite, but we stayed at her house for three or four hours, and she never seemed to get tired of us. Aretha serenaded us at her piano—and cooked us a big pot of chili!

After a while, Jan came out to visit, and it was a tough scene. She wanted to hand Dylan off to me and take a break, but I was going nonstop, sometimes twenty hours a day. Jan and Dylan weren't even allowed to ride in the RV with me, partially because she wasn't covered by the insurance, and partially because we were always taping, and a wife and baby weren't part of the shenanigans. So she stayed in the equipment van that followed the RV, and we'd talk by walkie-talkie, and she'd be trying to breast-feed while we screamed down the highway at ninety miles an hour. Not a good situation, but the alternative was being down in Mississippi with her family for thirty days. That would have been easier for all of us, but she wanted to come out. I didn't want to be apart from her either, but I needed her to suck it up.

Halfway through the trip, we arrived in Houston, where the higher-ups had flown out to keep us on track and pat us on the back. In return, we bit the hands that fed us, putting them on camera slamming back shots at a bar, and throwing pies in their faces. We must not have bit too hard, because Bob Pittman oversaw the renewal of my contract, almost doubling my salary. After five years, my role at MTV had finally come into focus. I was the guy who went on the road to do crazy stuff, and I loved it.

By the end of *Amuck,* I was burnt. We ended up in Los Angeles—the idea was that Josie, the crew, and I would kick off that year's Video Music Awards by driving the *Amuck* car onstage. The day before, we filmed some promos for the awards show down by the Santa Monica Pier; I was goofing around on a playground. The director, Ken Ceizler, was in the truck, and I could hear him through the producer's earpiece: "Tell him to just goddamn get on with the segment."

I flexed my ego a little bit. "I'm not fucking ready yet. Tell him I want to do it swinging from the monkey bars."

Ken said, "Tell him that I don't like that—it looks dumb."

I said, "Fuck that. This is what I want." The crew was looking at me, stunned. There were about twenty-five people—a big number for an MTV shoot—but the ones who knew me had never seen me be a diva like that. Ken came storming out onto the set and got in my face. I had a big row with him, and I couldn't believe I was doing that. I wasn't really in control of it, but I also felt righteous about what I was saying. In retrospect, I have no idea which one of us was right, but it felt good to let loose with twenty-five people watching. I could see the allure of being a movie star: You can make millions of dollars, flip out, and tell everybody to fuck off for the rest of the day. I totally understood how stardom makes people lose their minds. I was Alan Hunter, dammit!

I won the argument, not that I was especially proud of it. Later on, I didn't want anyone to rub my shoulders or try to make me feel better. Don't reward me for acting like that.

Mark:

Downtown Julie Brown settled in as the new VJ. I liked her right away—she was cheeky in a British way. She hadn't turned into the "wubba wubba wubba" cartoon character yet—she was saucy and slightly suggestive on the air, but off camera, she was much more conservative. Carol and I had a few dinners with Julie and her hunky boyfriend Chris Breed, who managed a club.

Alan:

Julie had more diva attitude than the rest of us: We had gotten used to the lack of star treatment.

Martha:

I was friendly with Julie. We did a bunch of remotes together, including a spring break and a festival at Knebworth where it was pouring rain. They stuck me out in the audience, with everybody screaming and yelling behind me—I had a yellow slicker on, with my hood up in the downpour. I looked up into the stands, and I could see Julie under a canopy, with lights and makeup people and champagne. I had to laugh. That's always been my gig: I'm not just talking to the fans, I'm one of them.

Alan:

Julie and I cohosted a Mardi Gras together, and I was getting most of the air time—basically because I had been there longer. I overheard her yapping to one of the producers, saying, "Why does he get all the segments? What is he, King Alan?" I was a little offended, but she and I got along fine after that. Hell yeah, I'm King Alan.

Martha:

Not many people have ever had the job title of VJ, and I don't think the job really exists anymore. For me, the only real VJs were the five of us, plus Downtown Julie Brown, Carolyne Heldman, Kevin Seal, and Adam Curry. China Kantner and Dweezil Zappa were there for a little bit, but for me, they were the beginning of the celebrity presence instead of the music-expert presence. It's a small club.

Alan:

Carolyne Heldman lasted only six months.

Mark:

MTV chewed Carolyne up and spit her out. She wasn't super-polished, but she was good; I liked what she did. She was really natural, without any music-business bullshit. Almost childlike, in that way, but a great person. They fired her for wearing shorts, because she didn't shave her legs. Whatever. Or her armpits, either—actually, that I had a problem with.

Alan:

Carolyne and I did a spring break together in Fort Lauderdale. Some guy made death threats, so MTV paid for us to have bodyguards. The network was hush-hush about the situation, but I think Carolyne may have been the focus of the threats; they put us both under protection so she wouldn't get spooked.

I took Jan and Dylan down to Florida, and the whole time we had two bodyguards following us around, which was cool but weird. We were sitting at some party for the affiliates, and this poor sap from the local radio station walked up to me, looking to shake my hand. "Hey, Al, how you doin'?" These two guys jumped in and pinned him against a wall. I told them to back off, but he was pissed. I wondered what it would be like to live like that all the time—after a while, you wouldn't be embarrassed by it. You'd take it for granted.

I did one segment with Hawaiian Tropic girls, ten of them all lined up onstage in their bikinis. A contingent of frat guys was chanting something, but I couldn't understand them. So on the air, I asked one of them, "What are y'all saying?"

He said, "Hunter's got a woody!"

He was correct, but it didn't register at first what he meant—I was on autopilot. "Woody? That's not my name. Oh, crap."

In another segment, I was literally interviewing some girl's boobs, or maybe her butt. Jan was in the VIP area, and I could see her holding Dylan up in the air, making sure I remembered I had a family.

Martha:

In Jan's shoes, I would have been swinging an infant around too. A situation like that is enough to bring out the Glenn Close in anyone.

Alan:

MTV sent me to L.A. for a Rod Stewart video shoot, and while I was there, I went to the Playboy Mansion to interview Hugh Hefner. When I was sixteen years old, the Mansion was probably the most iconic place on the planet to me, so my brain was overloaded—*"Oh my God, there's the Grotto!"*—even without all the Bunnies walking around. I was thinking, Wow, this place exists. It's real.

I interviewed Hugh Hefner, who was wearing his jammies and slippers. We talked about rock 'n' roll, and who his favorite bands were. He said the Stones. Then I could see his brain whirring, trying to think of something hip. He came up with, "And I like that U2."

There was a zoo on the grounds of the Mansion. That was where I interviewed one of the Playmates, who was in her bikini, of course. During a tape change, I made chitchat with her: "So you're a Bunny—does that mean you're in the magazine?"

"I was in just this past November! Would you like to see it?"

"Why, of course. That would be great."

She ran up to the Mansion, about a hundred yards away, while I guffawed with the camera guys, who were freaking out about how hot she was. I told them, "Y'all cool it now. I got to get through this interview."

She came back with the magazine, and opened it up on-camera, just delighted to show me her work. There were five or six very revealing pictures of her, and the only thing I could croak out was, "I see you're a real brunette."

It was a weird day. I interviewed Gene Simmons by the edge of the pool, and then we hung out in the Grotto for a little while, no cameras. Gene was a solid, normal guy. I was telling him about Jan and Dylan, and that even though the Mansion was blowing my mind, I was so happy with my family life. He put his hand on my shoulder and said, "Yeah, man, you just got to work at it. Marriage is a good thing." I loved that he was giving me fatherly advice. Then I asked him to show me his tongue. He stuck it out for me—and it *was* really long.

From the MTV promo for "Hedonism Weekend":

JAMAICAN VOICE-OVER GUY: *"Jamaica! Jewel of the Caribbean! Home of reggae, the limbo, cooked food, and peaceful tropical nights. That's before MTV turned it into—"*

ALL FIVE MEMBERS OF BON JOVI, WITH SCARVES, SUNGLASSES, AND UMBRELLA DRINKS: *"Pleasure Island!"*

JON BON JOVI, POINTING INTO CAMERA: *"Hi, I'm Jon Bon Jovi and I want you to spend a weekend of unbridled hedonism with me and these guys!"*

BAND: *"Yeah!"*

JON BON JOVI, CATCHING COCONUT IN LEFT HAND: *"And by hedonism, do we mean you can do anything you please, no matter how wild, strange, or excessive?"*

BAND: *"Hell yes!"*

JAMAICAN VOICE-OVER GUY: *"And it'll all be exposed on national television. Win MTV's Hedonism Weekend with Bon Jovi and join the biggest brain-frying blowout in the Caribbean since the invasion of Grenada!"*

JON BON JOVI: *"And this one has women!"*

JAMAICAN VOICE-OVER GUY: *"Two guys and two girls who have*

never met before will fly to Club Hedonism in Jamaica to party with Bon Jovi!"

DRUMMER TICO TORRES, BEHIND A RECLINING WOMAN IN A BIKINI: *"We gonna play some music?"*

GUITARIST RICHIE SAMBORA, PULLING OUT A STETHOSCOPE: *"No, we're going to play doctor! Oooh, doc."*

JAMAICAN VOICE-OVER GUY: *"And you'll be part of MTV's Hedonism Weekend broadcast, direct from Pleasure Island. Send a postcard with your name, age, address, and phone number on it, to MTV's Hedonism, P.O. Box 899, Radio City Station, New York, New York, 10101."*

JON BON JOVI: *"You'll give hedonism a bad name!"*

Alan:

After *Amuck,* they wanted me to go down to Jamaica for a week with Bon Jovi. When I told Jan about it, she assumed that she'd be coming along. I asked, but they wouldn't do it. I don't know if they were being cheap, or if they were just tired me of me dragging the wife and kid along all the time. So I had to go back to Jan and say, "Sorry, honey, it would be awful for you and Dylan. It's hedonistic, just a big bacchanal." Every reason for her not to come was a reason for her to be nervous I was going. As it turned out, I hated the resort, Hedonism II—the neighborhood around it in Negril, Jamaica, was unbelievably poor. It's no fun to be surrounded by people in such despair.

The label was hawking *Slippery When Wet,* and it was a big cross-promotion for the band and MTV. Bon Jovi got constant promos—the ads for the contest were in heavy rotation—and we got easy access to the guys who had our number-one video. Once we got down there, the band had a lot of work to do—when MTV said jump, they jumped. They're kazillionaires now, but back then, they were just a bunch of mooks from New Jersey. They hammed it up but managed to keep it casual. One segment, we sat around drinking Red Stripes and singing "Kumbaya."

We staged activities at the resort, like a game where everybody had to crawl under each other's legs and then drink a Red Stripe. I kept cheating: cutting the line and pretending to drink the Red Stripe but actually pouring it onto the sand. Jon—shirtless, and wearing short denim cutoffs—was the referee. He kept yelling at me to get back in line: "Hunter! You're outta here!"

At the end of each day, Bon Jovi went into their own world—they had a house off-campus. One night, drinking my Red Stripe in the bar, surrounded by single people having fun, I thought about hunting down some of the cute girls we used in our TV bits earlier in the day—being on the receiving end of some fan flirtation seemed harmless enough. Instead, telling myself I was tired, I bah-humbugged back to my room. Was I being a good husband, or copping out? Viewers may have thought I was living large, but that week didn't feel glamorous, or even much fun: It was a job for the band and it was a job for me.

42

ı don't wanna lose your love tonight

Martha Finds True Love

Mark:

When I came to New York, I smoked cigarettes. Carol hated it, so I stopped.

As time went on, things between us kept getting worse. I started to miss cigarettes: I never had before, but the stress in my life was mounting. Carol didn't know everything I was doing, but it was clear the marriage wasn't working. We saw a therapist for a while and had a difficult series of sessions. At one point, Carol did something very sweet—even if the American Cancer Society wouldn't approve. She gave me a pack of cigarettes and a really cool lighter. "I want to give you what I took away from you," she said. "I didn't want to take things away from you." She knew I had changed a lot of things in my life for her. It broke my heart.

Martha:

When I was still going out with Stiv, he went out to L.A. for a while to record with Brett Gurewitz, who was in Bad Religion and went on to found Epitaph Records. He had a little studio called Westbeach Recorders. Just for the fun of it, Stiv and I recorded a song together,

273

called "Yesterdays Will Find You." Brett called up a guitarist he knew named Jordan Tarlow, and said, "You've got to come down to the studio—I'm recording Martha Quinn and Stiv Bator."

Jordan came down, and I remember the exact moment he walked into the studio. I thought, "That is the cutest guy I have ever seen in my life." Later on, Stiv said to me, "You have a crush on Jordan, don't you?"

I was like, "Noooo!" But of course, the answer was yes. While Stiv was busy in the studio, I asked Jordan if he wanted to go to the movies with me and Nina—she had moved out west by that point. This was the '80s—what guy wouldn't want to go to the movies with Martha Quinn and Nina Blackwood? But he responded, "What are you gonna see?" Whatever it was, he decided it was a chick flick, and said, "No, thanks." *No, thanks?!* Right then, I put him in my sights. Like Pat Benatar sang, "I'm gonna follow you 'til I wear you down."

I went back to New York, and not long after that, Stiv and I broke up. Then in September 1986, MTV came out to L.A. for the Video Music Awards. We had never done a big production in L.A. before, and we were like country bumpkins. We didn't know who to call to get anything done. We were scrambling for production assistants—or PAs, as they're called—to help out during the broadcast.

I happily piped up, "I know a guy!" I called Brett, got Jordan's phone number, and left him a message: "Hey, this is Martha Quinn, I don't know if you remember me, but we need PAs. Do you want to come work the MTV Video Music Awards?" Jordan came to the Universal Amphitheatre, got his backstage pass, and worked as a PA. We always say that for our first date, he got paid fifty bucks.

Jordan ferried me around L.A. as we prepped the show. At the end of the night, he dropped me off at my hotel and . . . nothing happened, but I knew that I was into him. We stayed in touch as friends. A month later, Brett gave Jordan an advance for a Morlocks record, a band Jordan had played with up in San Francisco. Jordan spent the money on a plane ticket to New York. We had dinner a bunch of times while he was in town, but . . . nothing happened. One night, he walked me home, took me upstairs to my apartment door, stood at the threshold, held my hand, said good night, turned away, and got back on the elevator. I couldn't believe it!

A few weeks later, I visited L.A. and took Jordan out to dinner with J. J. and Nina. J. J. pulled me aside and asked me what the deal was with Jordan.

I told J. J., "I don't know. The guy just doesn't like me."

He said, "Oh, he likes you, MCQ. He's taking his time, but he likes you."

"But J. J., he hasn't even *kissed* me!"

"MCQ, trust me. The guy's just moving slow. I look into those Jesus eyes"—J. J. always said Jordan had "Jesus eyes"—"and I know what's happening."

As usual, J. J. was correct. What I didn't know was that Jordan didn't think I was interested in him. Apparently, while he was driving me around L.A. for the VMAs, I had made a comment to the effect of "What are you, seventeen?" So while I was waiting for a sign from him, he was waiting for a sign from me.

The next morning, Jordan picked me up at the Sunset Marquis and drove me to the airport. Back then, you could walk someone right out to the gate. Brett had advised Jordan, "If she looks in your eyes at the gate, kiss her." I guess I gazed into those Jesus eyes, because yes, he kissed me. My journey with my future husband had begun.

every now and then I get a little bit nervous That the best of all the years have gone by

MTV Changes, Not Always for the Better

Mark:

I did a segment coming out of the George Michael video "I Want Your Sex," where I made a comment about how there was a story in the London tabloids saying that his girlfriend was actually a transsexual. I made a joke about it, I was careful to say that it wasn't from a reliable source, and nobody thought twice about it. Somehow, George Michael's manager saw the segment, and he went ballistic. George wasn't out yet, and they were hypersensitive about people suggesting he wasn't 100 percent heterosexual.

The channel was trying to get George to appear on the VMAs that year, so they fired the producer who had been on the floor during that segment. They were making a point, both to George Michael's people and the MTV staff—he should have made me shoot the segment again. It was a knee-jerk decision: This guy had been doing a good job. I was so flipped out that this thing I said got him fired. I called him up and apologized, but there was nothing I could do to get him his job back. The guidelines for what we could say had moved under our feet, and they were vague to begin with.

It would have been much better if somebody had come and talked to me about the problem and the fallout. That was the flip side of being talent: Sure, you're protected and catered to, but you're also kept in the dark about some things.

Alan:

I went to the Ritz to introduce Los Lobos, who were strangely alternative at the time. That didn't make much sense to me—they were a good band, but they seemed pretty mainstream, musically. Anyway, there was a huge crowd of rabid Los Lobos fans, and all I had to do was come out and welcome people to the show. The announcer said, "And now, Alan Hunter from MTV."

"Boooooo!" The crowd hated me, hated MTV. They were out of their minds. "MTV sucks!"

I ran out onstage and ripped through the introduction as quickly as I could, "HelloeverybodywelcometotheRitzit'sLosLobos," and hustled offstage.

The next day, I told Mark about it: "There's an audience out there that doesn't like MTV." We hadn't experienced that before; for five years, we had been the alternative rebels on the cutting edge, and I thought music fans saw us as pals. Suddenly, we discovered that some people were perceiving us as the corporate giant—The Man.

Martha:

MTV had always had some shows thrown into the mix, like *Friday Night Video Fights,* or the *Friday Night Party Zone,* which I hosted, or the *Liner Notes* interview program. But then they decided they needed to do a lot more of them. It was so they could cater to specific audiences, and so they could sell ads. *Club MTV* was Downtown Julie Brown's dance-music show, *Headbangers Ball* was the heavy metal show, *Yo! MTV Raps* was the hip-hop show, and *120 Minutes* was the college-rock show—people didn't call that kind of music "alternative" yet.

Alan:

We had overseen this video jukebox, where Mötley Crüe and Bruce Springsteen and Howard Jones could appear in the same block of music. But the MTV executives were building a new vision of the future, one based on specialty shows.

Mark:

I hosted *Headbangers Ball* for a little while, but I had no business being on that show—I was not a metal guy. Adam Curry did it after me, and then they handed it off to Riki Rachtman. I hosted *120 Minutes,* but just for a few weeks. I got turned on to some great stuff from that show, like the Cure and the Smiths. I watched the video for the Cure's "In Between Days," with the armoire that falls off the cliff and floats in the ocean. I thought, "What the fuck is this? What's that guy wearing?" It was great to see something new. Our rotations were burning hot—even the lightest-rotation stuff you saw too much.

Alan:

J. J. did some episodes of *120 Minutes,* and then after he left, I became the *120 Minutes* guy. They filmed me in black-and-white—they wanted me to be mysterious and cop an attitude. They definitely didn't want the chirpy me.

Mark:

It was funny that Alan ended up hosting it, because even after five years, he was so not the music guy. The show was produced by this British guy Dave Kendall, who'd been working for the channel for years. Eventually, he ended up hosting it himself. Alan (in his best Cockney accent) used to call the show *Music That Dave Likes.*

Alan:

The MTV corporate offices were over on Sixth Avenue, and that's where a lot of the new shows were created. After a while, we had no crossover with those shows, and I wondered if that was by design—were they trying to keep us apart?

Mark:

The MTV executives revered print; ironically, they thought that was the credible medium. Since the press thought we were lightweights and had slagged off all the VJs pretty regularly, the bosses looked to other people when they started new shows.

Alan:

The programmers were trying to manufacture irreverence, deliberately replicating the chaotic attitude we had stumbled on innocently in the beginning. The short attention span that we inspired and stimulated wasn't just in our audience—it was also in the higher-ups who made a new programming decision every three minutes.

Mark:

I started to say, "What am I doing here? I'm not getting to do interviews, and I'm not getting to host shows."

Alan:

I wanted to get back into acting. I had an offer to be in the movie *Girls Just Wanna Have Fun,* which starred Helen Hunt and Sarah Jessica Parker. Bob Pittman blocked it—he told me that he wanted to find a better project for me to appear in, but really, he just hated the idea of the VJs doing anything that he didn't control. Then Pittman left, and nobody else really cared. I got a part in an independent film called *White Heat,* which starred Danny Aiello and Tawny Kitaen. I had a whole week off, and I devoted it to this movie.

One day, we were in Silvercup Studios in Queens, doing some interior shots on a soundstage. We had lunch: It was me, the actress playing my love interest, a character actor named Cliff Bemis, and Tawny Kitaen. This was after Tawny appeared in *Bachelor Party*, but before she starred in that Whitesnake video, writhing on the hood of David Coverdale's car. Cliff was this roly-poly guy; he was in awe of me because he watched MTV, and he was in awe of Tawny because she was this hot girl saying incredibly ribald things.

The other actress was throwing Tawny softballs: "So, do you like blow jobs?"

"Oh God, yeah," she said. Then she looked at me and asks, "Do guys like it when you take your finger and use that as a ring up and down the shaft?" Cliff was pretty much creaming his pants. Tawny told a story that involved her doing this, and it got more and more salacious.

Finally, Cliff blurted out, "Do you like to get your butt licked?"

Tawny didn't miss a beat. "Oh yeah, I love that." She was going trashy all the way. Cliff just about fell off his chair. Mark told me some lurid rumors involving Tawny, David Coverdale, and a German shepherd, and I totally believed them—from my experience, she was up for anything.

44

The five years we have had have been such good times

Martha Leaves MTV

Martha:

I thought I was going to work at MTV forever. I would watch Mark and J. J. make copies of interviews for their personal archives, and I would just laugh: That's fine for them, but I don't need to do that. Now I wish I had tapes of the interviews I did. But Mark and J. J. had jobs before MTV—J. J. had worked at radio stations where they'd literally changed the locks because the format had changed from rock to country. They'd been around enough to know that this was a great job, but it was another in a string of jobs. One hundred percent of my work knowledge was MTV—I got hired right out of college, and it was the perfect gig on the planet for me. It was a huge drama when I got let go.

Mark:

Martha's last couple of years, everybody loved her the most. But she badmouthed an executive, Les Garland, which is why she got fired. He wanted her to do something, and she said, "I'm not doing that." Guess what? You're done.

Martha:

I don't know why they fired me. I heard later that Tom Freston wanted to can me the night of the 1986 Video Music Awards. It was his first time at the helm; I was in the audience and I was set to interview Robert Palmer. The question that they gave me was "How did your wife feel about you making a video with all of those girls?" But I couldn't bring myself to ask him that, because it had just come out in the news that he was getting divorced. So I tossed that question, and because I was wearing Tina Turner's dress from the "Private Dancer" video, I joked, "Hey, do you think I could've been in your video?" Seemed cute, harmless enough—but apparently Tom Freston was furious. What I heard was that he wanted me fired that night. That was September, and my contract was up three months later. But it might not be true—I sometimes console myself by saying that he was starting a new regime and he wanted to make his mark.

I definitely got cocky. I took my Martha Quinn-ness for granted. That fall, my dad, who was also my lawyer, was calling MTV, saying, "You know Martha's contract is up." And they were saying, "Uh, yeah, okay, call us back next week." But it didn't seem like anything was odd. And then in December, at my grandfather's funeral in Troy, my dad pulled me aside: "I need to talk to you." Being an attorney, my dad had learned to execute justice swiftly. We went onto the back porch and he said, "I talked to MTV. They're not going to pick you up." *Whoosh.* Just like that, my world collapsed. I was already shattered because I was at my grandfather's funeral—now I felt like the earth was giving way. I got my whole family together, including my next-door neighbor Rich, who was at the funeral because he was a sweetheart. I brought them into the basement (the same one the guy in the Human League had slept in!), and told them all the news. I then proceeded to get totally plastered. Rich drove me back to New York City: I was slumped over in the front seat, drunk as a skunk.

The next day, I went into work. I didn't want to leave without saying anything, the way Nina had. I did my shift, knowing what I was going to say at the end. Peggy Polito was the director, and when I finished my shift, I took a deep breath and said, "Peggy, keep the tape rolling." (As long as the tape was rolling, it could be seen on monitors throughout the building.) "I want everyone to know I have not been picked up. I have been let go, and I want you all to know so you can say goodbye. I don't want people to feel weird."

I was shattered. To this day, I have dreams that I've been fired by MTV. In my dream, I'm going to a party. I can see that Mark and J. J. and Al are all having a really good time, but nobody will talk to me because I'm not allowed in that area anymore.

I was offered a job as the morning DJ on WNEW-FM, which was the big rock station in New York, and I didn't take it. I often wonder what I was thinking. I just sublet my apartment and bailed on New York. My plan was that I would go to Los Angeles, be with Jordan, and take Mary Hart's job on *Entertainment Tonight,* but I didn't even have an agent. I had no self-awareness. I was just rolling from one situation to the next, with very limited coping skills. It was like I was in outer space.

So I moved to L.A. Bob Pittman was a total prince and kept me on the payroll for six months, which meant I was able to get a house. For years, people had been telling me that I had to have my wisdom teeth taken out, and I had always delayed it. Just before my extended contract was up, I called Jordan's dentist and said, "I have to have all four wisdom teeth taken out by next week, because I will no longer have health insurance."

When the six months was up, I went on unemployment, because I couldn't pay my rent. That was my lowest point: Less than a year after that Robert Palmer interview, I was standing on line at the unemployment office in Van Nuys, California, praying that nobody would recognize me.

45

THe PARTY BOYS Call
THe KREMLIN

Billy Joel in Russia

Alan:

Mikhail Gorbachev was running the Soviet Union and he was rolling out perestroika and glasnost, opening up the country. Billy Joel decided he wanted to tour the USSR, which had been starved for Western rock 'n' roll. He did shows in Leningrad—it was Leningrad at the time, not Saint Petersburg—and in Moscow. I got to go over for a while, for a documentary on Billy Joel and life behind the Iron Curtain, called *Rock in Russia*. After years of immersing myself in frivolity for MTV, it was satisfying to do something meaningful, reporting on a country in the middle of fundamental change.

The Russian kids had bootleg tapes of MTV, but they were approximately ten years behind on the music and fashion trends. They were making their own clothes, trying to style themselves like Westerners. Metal was big over there, but if they wanted to dress like a headbanger, they glued some studs on a strip of leather. Sometimes all they had was a little photo clipped from a magazine: "I want to look like the guy from Bon Jovi. I have a wristband and a headband." It was primitive, but it was cool.

It was a fascinating time to be in the country. We'd be driving around town, with our translator and our liaison, looking for people to interview. The first day, some guy came up to the van: "I will help you. I am Dmitri. Where are you trying to get?" We told him. "Oh, let me take you there. I will show you how to get to that part of the city."

"Okay, hop in, Dmitri." Dmitri rode around with us all day, showing us how to get where we were going. The next day he was gone, and I asked our liaison, "What happened to Dmitri?"

He said, "KGB."

"What?"

"He was informant." Apparently, the KGB thought we were there for some subversive reason, instead of trying to fill an hour on MTV with a documentary on Billy Joel and Soviet youth culture. After that, it became a daily question: Would we be infiltrated by the KGB that day? The answer was always yes. Another person would show up and offer his services. It was laughable—we were at the tail end of the Communist era, and these guys were still playing their spy games.

I said, "I'm sorry, they're really doing that?"

The liaison shrugged. "Yeah, what else they got to do?"

When we interviewed artists, they were outspoken: "Fuck Communism, I'm going to speak out." They talked mainly about oppression of music and the arts. We talked to some of these guys in back alleys so we wouldn't attract attention; you could feel the nerves everywhere. Little old ladies would be looking out their windows—if I looked up, they'd quickly close the blinds. If we tried to talk to an average citizen, no way. They'd hide their faces and walk away. The whole country was covered with a veneer of intimidation. Gorbachev was promising the Soviet Union that people wouldn't end up in the gulag anymore, but who knew for sure?

I was pumped to interview Billy Joel. He was on the softer side of the MTV playlist, but I was a big fan. When he arrived at the interview, he had huge bags under his eyes. Our producer was hopping around, trying to figure out how to broach the subject, but Billy brought it up himself: "What do you think, guys? These things are killing me."

"Well, do you want to keep your sunglasses on?"

He started telling us he was sick: He was taking all these drugs for the flu, but they weren't working. We suspected he was drinking too much vodka. Christie Brinkley was traveling with him, and we heard rumors they were bickering. But the interview went great, and then we filmed some promos on the balcony of our hotel.

The biggest night was the first concert, at this big coliseum on the outskirts of Leningrad. It was packed, and you could tell all these young people in the audience were really excited about the show. It was a major production like they'd never seen before, with top-notch lights and sound.

The first fifty rows were empty until five minutes before showtime, blocked off by guards: young men in fur hats, standing at attention. And then, just before Billy came on, the occupants of those seats trooped in: the apparatchiks, the old people, the party leaders. It looked like they had all been waiting outside on a bus until they got the signal. There were old ladies wearing mink coats, and guys with the big Brezhnev eyebrows. It was every politburo cliché imaginable.

Apparently, that was the cue for the stage manager to say Billy could hit the stage. The lights went down, and he started hammering out "Angry Young Man." Liberty DeVitto was banging away at the drums, and the volume was like an airplane taking off. I checked out those people in the front rows, and they looked like the Maxell ad where the sound hits the guy in the chair. They appeared to be in a state of shock.

Five songs into the show, all fifty rows left. They couldn't take it. That meant the guards who had been watching their seats could start enjoying the show, and the crowd really rocked out. Billy did great, except he had an abysmal singing voice, either from the flu or the vodka. He croaked his way through the whole show—when he put out the live album a few months later, he had overdubbed all his vocals.

That whole trip really adjusted my perspective. At MTV, we were always closely monitoring the cutting edge, trying to find inventive new ways to be transgressive. In the Soviet Union, we got to experience this immature version of pop culture—as if we had gone into the Amazon and observed people who had never seen a TV set before.

46

I'm a man who doesn't know how to sell a contradiction

Introducing Kurt Loder

Martha:

The first time I met Kurt Loder was in the very early days of MTV, after some industry party, maybe the opening of a new recording studio. MTV staffer Gale Sparrow and I shared a cab home with Kurt. I was jazzed to be hanging out with a guy from the great *Rolling Stone*. Kurt may deny this, but to the best of my recollection, he was totally drunk, sprawled out on the floor of the cab.

Mark:

When I first heard MTV was hiring Kurt Loder, I didn't get it. There were lots of music journalists out there—why him? What made it baffling was that he personally seemed to hate the channel's existence. He could be reviewing a record, and he'd still find a way to slag MTV. Well, whatever his price was, he whored himself out for it.

Nina:

He gave us such a hard time when he was writing for *Rolling Stone*. He's very well read, and he's very knowledgeable, but he was just incredibly mean. And then he ended up working at MTV—what a hypocrite.

Mark:

I think *Rolling Stone* used to be the Word—the authority when you wanted information about rock 'n' roll. And then MTV became the Word, and on some level, that pissed them off. The flip side was MTV constantly longed for the credibility of print—which is how Kurt got hired. He started just after I left, but it was frustrating to see him work. The guy really knew his shit, which is great, but he made crappy television.

First of all, he didn't look like he belonged on the channel. He was also so tight-assed about the whole thing. Sometimes he would crack a wry joke and barely smile, and that was his attempt at lightening things up. It was always heavy, and not fun. And when he interviewed people, he was just a huge suck-up.

I didn't mind playing the fan when I was talking to somebody I really liked. But the way Kurt's enthusiasm would manifest itself was by spilling out how he knew all the minutiae of their career. *Check me out: I know all this about you.* I don't think he ever did anything better in an interview than what J. J. or I could have done. By the time I left MTV, I had lightened up substantially about the whole thing, and was more of the mind-set of "It's rock 'n' roll—let's have some fun."

Kurt's big advantage was that because he was known as a writer, they let him write his own news breaks and his own interview questions. Whereas every single interview that I did, I had to fight with the producers to get the questions that I wanted in the order that I wanted, knowing that we were going to create a show. And Kurt, who knew jack about television, was given carte blanche.

Martha:

At the beginning of MTV, we VJs interviewed millions of luminaries. But then the news department kicked in, and they figured out it was cheaper to have interviews go up to the office, because they didn't have to interrupt the shooting schedule down at the studio. They could just put up a little video camera, and voilà. After a while, it became, "Why do we ever need to go down to the studio?" The new division of labor: The news department were the music experts, and the VJs were the channel promoters.

Mark:

I think the news department ended up being the most important part of MTV. It defined who we were because of its commitment to causes and because of the way it handled news and interviews and events. I can't say enough good things about Linda Corradina, who ran it, and Doug Herzog, who brought Linda in. Linda asked me once, years after we had both left the channel, if I had ever asked to be the face of MTV News. I had never even realized that was an option. The executives weren't going to suggest it, because they thought we were already stretched too thin doing VJ segments. Joining the news department would have meant cutting my salary by two-thirds. I probably wouldn't have been willing to do that, but in retrospect, it might have been a better road for me.

Alan:

I've got nothing against Kurt. I liked his writing, and I felt for him when he was enduring the craziness of Woodstock '99.

Martha:

I pulled a weird thing on Kurt back in 2004. Little Steven hosted an Underground Garage festival in New York, on Randall's Island. I was there because Jordan's band, the Fuzztones, were playing. There was a lot of white wine flowing backstage, and I had quite a few glasses. Kurt Loder was backstage covering the festival for MTV. I completely resented that he was still working for them, and I was not cool about it. For years, whenever I saw him on MTV, it was salt in my wounds. They got rid of me because they wanted fresh young talent, but they kept Kurt Loder on forever?

He got me on camera and asked me what I was doing at the show. In return, I asked him why he hadn't shown up at the memorial service for J. J., who had died earlier that year. What, he had something better to do than go pay his respects? I'm sure they never broadcast what I said. And that was the last time I ever spoke to Kurt Loder.

47

we'll be moving on and singing that same old song

The Departure of Alan and Mark

Martha:

After MTV let me go, I was in a state of shock. My stepmother, Jane, wanted to help me, so she got me into doing speeches on the college circuit. What I should have done was tell funny stories about rock stars, and then answer whatever questions the audience had about MTV. I'm quick on my feet—I could have done that. What I actually did was studiously prepare and deliver a speech about the history of cable television. It was just horrible: "Cable started in rural areas because the antennas could not pick up the broadcast, so they installed cable in order to disseminate the signal, blah blah blah."

I would go to these colleges and get picked up in a ratty station wagon. Dinner would be at the Ground Round or Brew 'n' Burger—the Chili's and the Friday's of the era. The audiences were humiliatingly small, like thirty people. I hadn't been gone long enough for anybody to have any kind of nostalgia. I was just the person who was on MTV, but now I wasn't, so it was very weird.

Around that time, I was also talking to agents in L.A., and I would dress like a secretary for those meetings—I showed up in suits with shoulder pads, looking like Melanie Griffith in *Working Girl*. At lunch with one agent, I looked across the restaurant and I spotted Richard

Grieco, who at the time was on *One Life to Live*—he was wearing jeans and a T-shirt. It blew my mind. I realized that was what I should be doing: embracing my rock 'n' roll background. But I was really floundering.

Alan:

Mark and I were standing in the hallway, just outside his dressing room, discussing Martha's departure and how dramatic a move that was for the company. One of us said, "We can't be VJs forever." We confided in each other that we wanted to get out while the getting was good. We were both eager to move to California, and we liked the idea of leaving of our own volition, instead of whenever the channel got tired of us.

Mark:

When I started at MTV, I was really naïve. It was the biggest job I had ever had in my life, and I didn't realize how insulated I was from the world. Part of the reason I quit was because I was frustrated; ultimately, management didn't believe in us. It went back to the original casting: They selected us as types, not for our knowledge or talent. Anderson Cooper didn't get his gig because he had silvery hair.

The other reason I quit was that I had been bitten by the acting bug. I had a private acting coach, who worked with Stella Adler in her New York studio, and also taught Vincent Spano. I didn't care if I became Tom Cruise or Mel Gibson; I just wanted to appear in a couple of pictures a year, and make a hundred thousand dollars a picture. That seemed reasonable to me.

Alan:

At MTV, I learned how to be a good VJ—which turned out to be a specific set of skills that didn't translate into many other jobs. I left MTV only one year into my lavish three-year contract. My father was pretty incredulous when I told him. He had no expertise in this world, but I ran all that stuff by him, just to get whatever clichéd fatherly advice he might have. "Are you sure?" he asked. "Maybe you just need to stay another year or so."

"No, I'm burnt. And there's going to be life beyond MTV." In hindsight, he was totally right.

I gave notice within days of Mark. My agent, Howard Klein, told me that the day before he was planning to call MTV to inform them of my departure, they called him asking if I'd accept a changed deal: They wanted me to forgo the salary bumps in my contract and work for the same pay. Howard said he chuckled as he told them I was exercising my option to leave after one year. He said there was palpable disbelief—they never suspected I'd leave.

Mark and I high-fived after the official announcement that we were leaving: We were pumped about snatching our own destinies from the jaws of MTV.

Mark:

Quitting MTV was my first real career stumble, and it's weighed on me as the years have gone by. Up to that point, I had no career failures. Everything I set out to do, I did. I never imagined that streak ending. So naïve. I also didn't consider that opportunity still remained for me at MTV. I could have produced shows for them, and I would have continued being on-air talent if they had wanted that. Why didn't I just stay at MTV and pursue my new acting interest on the side?

I left Carol around the same time I left MTV. When I woke up that morning in March 1987, I didn't know I would be leaving that night. Things had been bad between us for a long time. I had a whole part of me that I was keeping hidden—I had been squashing all my genuine feelings. I was depressed about the situation and emotionally spent. I couldn't imagine how I would ever leave . . . ever live honestly . . . ever be happy. But suddenly, I decided I was done. I had heard a line somewhere: "The kindest executioner has the sharpest blade." That night, when Carol got home, I told her how miserable I was, I packed some stuff, and I was out the door in ten minutes.

The situation wasn't wholly of my own making, but I was the source of a lot of our problems—starting with my inability to commit. To this day, I feel guilty about how I handled everything with Carol.

Many times since then, I sent her a letter or an e-mail on Yom Kippur, saying that I was sorry. A few years ago, Carol and I accidentally bumped into each other in the hallways of the Sirius studios. After that meeting, I hoped that maybe time had done what it does best—but when I tried to get in touch with her again, I got no response. I understood.

I moved into my acting coach's apartment, while he stayed at Vincent Spano's apartment—Vince was off doing a movie. A few months later, in July 1987, I moved to California—my agent had convinced me that I had to be in L.A. if I wanted to pursue acting. I felt so guilty, I left virtually everything in the apartment with Carol, including furniture that had been in my family for seventy-five years.

When I arrived in California, suddenly I felt free. I said it over and over again, to anyone who would listen: "I'm jettisoning everything in my life all at once." I quit my job; I quit my marriage; I quit the city that I lived in. I didn't know what I was heading to, but I felt free and excited.

MTV offered me a part-time deal for one year, which I took—I agreed that I would come back to New York one week a month to do VJ shifts, and that I would also do other stuff for them in L.A. as needed. Being a private contractor was a good deal—I ended up making more money that final transitional year, working only one week a month, than I did when I was on staff.

My last show was during a special weekend in La Jolla. I did my final segment with Richard Marx. I made a little speech about leaving MTV, and walked away from the camera, down the beach into the distance. It was beautiful.

Alan:

There's lots of stuff I didn't learn during my time at MTV. Only years later did I figure out that I shouldn't take anything for granted. Weirdly, I wasn't worried about being replaced, maybe because I had never believed that I had a lock on a talent that nobody else did. Adam Curry came along, and he was smooth and hip, and I thought, "Wow, he's good." Julie Brown did her "wubba wubba" thing, and I thought that was valid. I just felt lucky to be one of the first.

Mark was already in L.A. by the time I did my last show. I tried to script out my last thirty seconds on the air, like I was Walter Cronkite signing off for the last time. What was my epitaph at MTV going to be? But I got distracted with our big move to L.A. I had to get Jan and Dylan to the airport that afternoon, and I was going to stay another couple of nights to pack up the house for the movers.

I was on the set, and the crew was moping around, sorry to see me go. I kept trying to move everything along, because we were running late and I didn't want Jan to miss that plane. "That was the Go-Go's, let's go, news, boom, bang, nothing extraneous here." Finally, I got to the last segment. I gave a shout-out to Martha and Mark and Nina and J. J., and then I said my last words, "Well, it's been great here and I hope to see you soon."

It was unsatisfying, but honestly, I could have worked on it for months with a team of writers, trying to make that two-minute segment magical, and there was no way I was going to encapsulate my entire MTV career.

There was no cake, but I hugged every member of the crew. And then I activated the ejector seat—I told everyone, "Hey, I'm just going to the bathroom. I'll be right back." I walked out the door, headed straight into the car that was waiting for me, and never came back.

after the fire, the fire still burns

Life after MTV

Martha:

The loss of MTV may have been more difficult for me than for the other VJs—every last drop of my personal identity was tied up with MTV. Any psychologist will tell you that if you take away a person's identity, it makes them way more vulnerable to depression. Getting humbled not only made me more compassionate, it also made me funnier. I joined an improv comedy troupe and I took a comedy class. Heather Locklear was also in my class, but she showed up only a couple of times. She was married to Tommy Lee, and I was awed by how glamorous and cool she was. After class, we were both driving over the hill—I was in my Honda Accord, and she passed me in her Porsche Turbo Carrera. She was going home to her husband, Mötley Crüe's drummer—I was heading back to Sherman Oaks, where I had a roommate because I didn't have the money to pay the rent myself.

I did a little bit of stand-up. My first real joke was, "I just moved to Los Angeles from New York, and the biggest difference is the driving thing. Here, you can't go out and have a glass of wine, because you have to drive home. You just can't. But in New York, you can go out, have all the drinks you want, and hail a cab. Then a totally drunk stranger drives you home."

Alan:

My first acting coach in L.A., referred to me by my managers—yep, I had a whole retinue of agents and managers—said I had one year to make an impression. After that, I was just another blond guy in Hollywood.

I got a job hosting a brand-new show on the Disney Channel called *Videopolis*—it was a music show for kids, filmed live once a week at Disneyland. I was heading over to the studio for my wardrobe fitting, and my manager called me up: "Don't go to the fitting—you don't have the job anymore."

Apparently, Jeffrey Katzenberg got wind that I was going to be the host and didn't want any element of MTV involved with *Videopolis*—that was way too edgy for them. I was saying, "I don't have to be edgy! I could be different!"

Soon after I arrived in Los Angeles, the writers went on strike, and there was a year where film and TV production pretty much shut down. Movie actors became TV actors, TV actors did commercials, and commercial actors were out of business. It wasn't clear what category I was in, but I wasn't getting any work. I learned to play golf.

Less than a year into my idyllic new Hollywood life, I was panicking, selling my house and telling my agent to send me up on any commercial gig I was remotely right for: Snickers, Budweiser, Dockers, I was there. I got a few, but I was cursed by MTV—it had made me too recognizable. The other reason I didn't get those gigs? I probably sucked. After going to Russia with Billy Joel, it was hard to summon the gee-whiz attitude needed for a Dairy Queen spot.

Martha:

After Jordan and I had been a couple for a year or so, he went on tour in Europe with the Fuzztones. I broke up with him while he was there, using a line we still quote today: "I'm a free woman in L.A.!" As I understand it, he had no trouble finding companionship to console himself. But when he got back to the States, he visited me and saw my datebook, where I had written down dates with A&R exec John Kalodner. His attitude was, "Well, that's enough of that. I'm home now." We had a few more on/off periods, but ultimately we were best and happiest together.

I'm glad I dated Stiv, because that's the path that led me to my husband and my kids. Jordan and I have been together pretty much 24/7 for over twenty-seven years now, and in all that time, I haven't quite figured him out. Being with him still feels a little like walking on freshly fallen snow. When I left MTV in 1991, Jordan started working as a commercial music composer. Between ads for Revlon, Victoria's Secret, and Neutrogena, his music was on MTV more than Nirvana. When we're empty-nesters, our plan is to roam the country in an Airstream, with our vegetarian German shepherd and one CD: *Tea for the Tillerman.*

Mark:

When I left MTV, I was famous for a while. After a couple of years in L.A., however, being a VJ felt like a millstone instead of a stepping-stone. I was always the guy with hair from MTV, and that boxed me in. I would go on auditions, and the roles would always be for a DJ or a drug dealer or a record-company executive—and I wouldn't even get those. I cut my hair short because I wanted not to be sent up for those roles anymore—I look at those headshots and they're terrifyingly awful. Then the money started to run out and I figured out that my acting dreams were not going to come true. The biggest thing that I lost in the years after MTV was my confidence.

Nina was smart to come out first, and book those jobs on *Solid Gold* and *Entertainment Tonight*. If I had gotten those gigs, I believe I would have triumphed. But at the time, I was so adamant about changing everything in my career and not using MTV as a ticket to whatever I was doing next. In 1991, I remarried. By February 1992, my wife was pregnant, while I was broke and out of work—I decided I had better get a job. I opened up a radio trade magazine, checked out stations in cities where I thought I'd like to work, and called them up: "Hey, I'm Mark Goodman, former MTV VJ, would you like me to work for you?"

My daughter Spencer was born on October 5, 1992, six days before I turned forty; I call her my fortieth birthday present. Spencer celebrated her first birthday in Chicago, where I'd gotten a job at Q101, doing the morning show. When I was younger, I couldn't figure out how having a child would work into my plans. Now I know this: Even though I've had a pretty exciting life, if I had done exactly the same things, but without my daughter, I would have felt like a loser somehow. I've always tried to uncover true feelings in the musicians that I love—in myself, the thing that provides the best access is my daughter.

Martha:

After a couple of years, MTV hired me back. In the interim, I'd become the spokesperson for Neutrogena ("All I wanted was a job in rock 'n' roll and clear skin!") and landed the role of Mrs. Bobby Brady on the CBS nighttime Brady revival. MTV gave me a great contract with tons of money—I think I was getting about two hundred thousand dollars a year. They built me a studio out in L.A. and I hosted a bunch of shows, including *Martha's Greatest Hits,* where I played videos from the early years of MTV, and *MTV Prime with Martha Quinn.*

The first year in L.A. was pretty great, and came close to re-creating the family feeling of the early days: If the kid cleaning the studio had gone to the Depeche Mode concert, I'd bring him out on camera and ask him about the show. Then I got the MTV Suit Clampdown: They told me to stop talking to extraneous crew members. I should have fought harder against it—that killed the spark of the show. I also hosted the MTV version of the radio show *Rockline,* which was the greatest: Fans would call in with questions for people like Slash and Bell Biv DeVoe.

Plus I finally got to interview Paul McCartney! MTV did a contest with Paul, and I told executive producer Joel Gallen that if I didn't get to do the interview, I would go crazy—maybe spontaneously combust like a Spinal Tap drummer. On the big day, Jordan came with me, armed with his *Hard Day's Night* LP and my "White Album" for autographs. We met Paul and Linda at the Capitol Records building in Hollywood, and maybe I was amazed. During our interview, Paul sat drinking a cup of tea. When the interview was over and autographs gotten, he and Linda said goodbye and left. While packing up my gear, I looked down and saw Paul's teacup—still half full. I froze, staring at that tea. Paul McCartney's tea. The tea Paul himself had actually been drinking. I picked up the cup and drank the rest of *Paul McCartney's tea*—I didn't care if I got a bacterial infection, if I got it from Paul. I looked around, saw nobody was looking, and put the spoon, the saucer, and the teacup into my bag. Today, it sits behind glass in my dining room—and has never been washed.

My second year back, MTV told me they wouldn't be paying me the raise that was in my contract. Doug Herzog, one of the executives, said, "Well, it's better than the alternative." I should have walked. Every job I've had since then, I've fought for the money. Not to be a prima donna, but because I know that if I don't feel valued, I won't do a good job. And if I'm not doing a good job, then what's the point?

My three-year contract ran out in 1991, and MTV didn't renew it. My final guest on *Rockline* was "Weird" Al Yankovic. Being let go the second time hurt, but not quite as much. Now I had the experience J. J. and Mark had at the beginning of MTV: I'd had gigs, I'd lost gigs. I started my second phase of MTV knowing the sun would surely set on their newfound adoration of me. That time around, I kept copies of my interviews.

Alan:

Jan and I had a baby girl in 1989, who we named Callie. When we were at the hospital for Callie's birth, Martha babysat Dylan.

I did a few game show pilots: *Haywire, Triple Threat, Pure Insanity.* I'd be smiling and tap-dancing and acting like a monkey: "What's behind door number two?" It was the squarest bullshit ever, and they'd always want bigger smiles and more energy. I felt trapped. When you've been at the center of the coolest TV thing ever, it's hard to do an unhip game show.

I also did a pilot for a Fox show called *Malibu Beach Party with Alyssa Milano.* The day before, Ken Ceizler called me up and asked me to host. I was pale to the point of translucent, so I drove around in Ken's convertible with my shirt off, trying to get a quick tan. The next day, I woke up, and because of my little belly rolls, I had red and white stripes across my chest and stomach. The makeup lady came to the rescue with spray tan. Ken put me in a hot tub with Alyssa Milano:

more specifically, a fake hot tub filled with very cold water that they put on the beach. Alyssa was wearing a bikini; she was sixteen, while I was thirty-two and happy for the cold water.

L.A. was an equal-opportunity self-esteem buster. In 1993, we moved back to Birmingham, where I started a film company with my brother. I wanted to produce, I wanted to direct—I wanted to control whatever part of a little empire I could build. I knew that would make me happier, even in occasional failure, than waiting around trying to get a job that I probably wouldn't love.

Martha:

Al and Jan lived down the street from us in the Valley—I was very attached to their family, and shattered when they moved to Alabama. I drove away from their house sobbing, as Alan stood on his front lawn holding Callie, calling out, "We love you."

Al and Jan were paragons of marital bliss—one thing I could count on in life was that relationship.

Mark:

They were the paradigm for all of us.

Alan:

I had visions of being married forever, but feelings morph and things happen; the midlife crisis is a cliché for a reason. I got a motorcycle and had an affair. I went all the way back to my roots, only to dissolve my marriage in the fishbowl of my hometown. Ouch.

Martha:

I went to Atlanta to do a Bell South commercial. Alan and I were starring in it, and his company was producing it. That night, we drove back to Birmingham together, and at one in the morning, I heard Alan storm out of the house. I went downstairs, Jan and I drank some wine, and she told me what was going on. Ultimately, they got divorced, which really shook me up: If they couldn't stay together, what chance did anybody else have?

Mark:

I think Martha took the divorce harder than Alan.

Alan:

My theory is that I needed an excuse to move out of that marriage. I don't think Jan ever would have forgotten, but she was willing to forgive. We probably could have salvaged the marriage, if I had wanted us to. I'm not sorry about the nineteen years we were married, especially because we ended up with two great kids. I do I think it's ironic that I was a faithfully married man when I was a celebrity at MTV with lots of opportunities and a single guy when nobody cared who I was.

Many years later, in 2007, I got married again. Elizabeth was eighteen years younger than me, and had never seen me on MTV because her family blocked the channel on their television. She came down to Birmingham for the summer to do some research on a screenplay she was writing, and we quickly fell for each other. We got married and had two fab little boys.

Nina:

Dennis used to walk around the house singing, "I love my wife, I love my wife." Things were great between us, except I was working so hard. I had three jobs, and I was flying all over the place. One time, we went up to Santa Barbara for a weekend in a B&B so we could have a couple of days to chill out by ourselves. As soon as we got there, my beeper went off, and I drove back to L.A. so I could interview Ray Davies.

Michael Bolton needed a tour manager, so Dennis went on the road with him for a few months. I went out to visit him on the road a couple of times, and he seemed distant, but I chalked it up to the job, which is high pressure. But when Dennis came back home, I saw and smelled a different person. He had even changed his cologne from the lovely Grey Flannel to Eternity. To this day, I gag whenever I smell Eternity.

Dennis never unpacked—he told me that he didn't want to be married anymore. I freaked out and found stacks of women's telephone numbers in his briefcase, and charges for flowers on his credit card. The next day, he drove off in the red Porsche that I had bought him—his dream car—leaving me literally doubled over in pain. Next to my father dying, it was the worst experience of my life.

I went through a really bad period. The *Entertainment Tonight* gig dried up, and *Solid Gold* went off the air. Arsenio Hall, who was my cohost, went on to his own show, but all the work I was getting offered ran against my values. I got offered correspondent positions on *Inside Edition* and on Joan Rivers's talk show—but as the gossip columnist, which I felt betrayed the trust musicians put in me. I actually did a day of work for *A Current Affair,* reporting on the red carpet at the VMAs—but then the show edited together my interviews with Madonna and Cher to fabricate a feud between the two of them, so I quit.

I was also offered an endorsement deal in the "What becomes a legend most" fur campaign—I could have really used the money, but I'm too much of an animal lover. I started seeing a therapist, who told me that I hadn't grieved for my career. She also told me that I'd make a great receptionist. I told J. J. about that. "Bean," he said, "get rid of her." Being a receptionist isn't necessarily a bad job—but it's not what I worked decades to do.

J. J. was a good friend, but he didn't understand depression. I'm not talking about feeling down in the dumps for a day, but the kind where you feel trapped, and you would do anything, even kill yourself, just to get out of the misery. If he ever got depressed, he never acknowledged it. He'd say, "You know, there are people who are suffering and starving." I understood that, but it didn't help—if anything, it made me more depressed, because that's awful.

All my hope was gone. One day, I was driving home with my 149-pound Malamute, KRSNA (pronounced "Krishna"). That dog saved my life, because I was in so much pain, I wanted to drive the jeep into a bridge abutment. The only reason I didn't was because I didn't want to hurt the dog.

I ended up in the suicide ward. I couldn't even get ahold of that terrible therapist. Gradually, I put myself back together and became a stronger person. Three other things changed while I was in the ward. The first was that I stopped drinking. The second was that I started swearing—before, my vocabulary had been strictly G-rated. The third was that I met this guy, Kelly. He was a Shakespearean actor, and a cool guy, and we became good friends. Year after year, we helped each other climb out of hell. We had a real connection of the heart and the soul, and we've been together for fourteen years now. We laugh about how we met: "It was so romantic, with the morning sun glistening on the barbed wire. . . ."

Kelly turned out to be the love of my life. He still lives in L.A., but when the city started to make me nuts in 2007, he was very supportive of me moving to Maine. I live by myself in the middle of nowhere. I do have lots of animals: two Alaskan Malamute dogs (Chinook and Kippen), an African Grey parrot (Einstein), a Red-Lored Amazon parrot (Thoreau), and six cats, all stray or rescue (Tux, Desdemona, Pyewackett, Leara, Nzuri, and Purrrrchouli). I also have regular visitors on my property: flying squirrels, woodchucks, porcupines, and a couple of moose. With all the wildlife and the blossoming trees, it feels like living in a Disney movie by way of Monet.

Driving across the country was an adventure. I flew the dogs out later, but I stacked all the cat crates on top of each other, and had the two parrots in cages in the front seat. Each evening, I'd have to find a pet-friendly motel and unload them all. When the clerk would ask, "What kind of animals? I'd casually say, "Oh, a couple of cats," and ask for a room as far away from the office as possible. In the morning, I'd gather them up—I put each cat in a little harness and leash so I could manage them a bit easier—and roll out before dawn. It would take fifty miles of traveling before the meowing stopped.

Mark:

On New Year's Eve 2001, Randy, my best friend in L.A., hosted a small dinner at his house in the Hollywood Hills. The plan was to drink lots of champagne, barbecue a great dinner, and then take car service to the rave that was happening on Hollywood Boulevard.

I had separated from my third wife a while back, and had been casually dating someone else, who had suddenly refallen in love with her ex-boyfriend. Four days before New Year's Eve, she informed me that we wouldn't be going out as planned. I was happy for her, and fine with whatever happened. I guess that's when the big stuff in life happens. Randy worked for Interscope Records, commissioning videos; he invited this girl Lisa, who was an attorney for the company. Lisa brought her childhood friend Jill, who was visiting from New York. As it turned out, the only people on the guest list for Randy's party were me, Lisa, and Jill.

I hit it off with Jill right away. She was incredibly sexy: a beautiful body, and a great mouth. We laughed a lot, and that night, we kissed. We've been together ever since. The first couple of years, we were on separate coasts, but we managed somehow. I moved back to New York in 2004, and that helped solidify our relationship. Jill's got two great sons, who I love. Once they're both off to college, it will be our time.

Martha:

Jordan and I got married in Las Vegas in 1992, wearing our best blue jeans. We have two kids, a girl and a boy. When I first had my daughter, I disappeared completely into motherhood, even becoming a La Leche League leader, running breast-feeding support groups in Hollywood. Before she was born, I was auditioning for sitcoms and doing infomercials, but when my baby came, my attitude became, *"Career? What career?"*

When my daughter was two years old, *CBS This Morning* tapped me to do a biweekly segment called "Yikes, I'm a Grown-Up!" which I cohosted with Lisa Birnbach, author of *The Preppy Handbook*. It was amazing to be back on television, but it was very hard on my family. When my contract was up at the end of the year, I declined to continue. I was nervous to tell J. J. that I'd quit—he was very proud of me having that gig. But when I explained, "It's too disruptive on my family, and my baby girl's just three years old," he got choked up and said, "I'm so proud of you, MCQ. You're doing the right thing for Jordan and your baby." I was so relieved—J. J.'s opinion carried a lot of weight with me.

Mark:

J. J. got back into radio in Los Angeles. I worked for him at a short-lived radio station called "The Edge"—it was free-form with structure, and he was the program director. J. J. was living with a woman and helping raise her daughter. Eventually, they broke up because she suddenly got into channeling, and he just did not buy into that. He felt like Dr. Mobius, or whoever the fuck she was channeling, was getting more attention than him. He wasn't down with that.

49

Don't you forget about me

R.I.P., J. J. Jackson

Mark:

MTV was a trial by fire. We went through this wonderful, terrible experience together, and it bonded us. It was almost a happy accident that we all liked each other and cared about each other—I've had plenty of coworkers in my life I didn't feel that way about. It had something to do with the circumstances, but it also had to do with the people we became together.

Martha:

Mark and I had our tussles, but we VJs stick together, like brothers and sisters. When my second child was born prematurely, the doctors said he might need a blood transfusion, and that it'd be wise to line up donations from matching friends and family. Mark came to the hospital right away—I remember that more than any arguments we've had.

My son was three days old, so tiny, but Mark took one look at my boy and exclaimed, "Dude! What's up, big guy!" I get a lump in my throat whenever I think about it.

Mark:

We may have been at our closest in Los Angeles, when we were hanging out together by choice. For a while, I lived around the corner from

Alan, and often all five of us would end up at his house—Jan loved to entertain. And after J. J. passed away, that cemented the bond between the four of us.

The last time I saw J. J. was a couple of months before he died. We went to see a *Lord of the Rings* movie together, and afterward, we stood in front of the theater, talking about life and how we had evolved, and the things that were important to us. He smoked a cigarette, and I was pissed at him for that, because I wanted him to take care of himself. At the end of the night, I hugged him and told him I loved him. He was such a caring, sweet guy, and a genuine friend. We got to be very close, especially in those later years in L.A.

Alan:

J. J. died of a heart attack on March 17, 2004. I was immensely sad—we didn't see each other very much, maybe twice a year, but his laughter and wisdom were always comforting. Aside from my father, I had never had such a dear person in my life die.

Nina:

Maybe J. J. didn't get the most fan mail, but I think he was the most respected of any of us, hands down. I was gratified to see how many people came to his funeral.

Alan:

I flew to L.A., feeling calm, which is the opposite of how I normally feel when going there. I was going for one reason: to put my friend to rest. Hollywood could suck it.

The memorial service was quite an affair: a packed house that looked like a movie back lot, with actors and extras in a myriad of costumes. People I never would have guessed that J. J. associated with—and Rod Stewart, quietly sitting in the back, weeping.

The four of us took turns at the lectern, speaking about our dear friend; I could see that Martha, Mark, and Nina had all prepared some notes. I didn't have anything, and I started to have the actor's nightmare: Not only did I not know my lines, I didn't know what play I was in. I worried about how I would be received—would I give the best memorial speech of the day? Self-absorption can be a defense mechanism. But when the moment came, the words flowed easily—it was one of the very few times in my entire life I didn't care about whether I was impressing people. I thank J. J. for my serenity that day.

Martha:

After J. J. died, I got a phone call from one of his best friends, Joe. He told me that he and a friend had a product they were developing that J. J. was involved with, and very excited about, before he passed away. They wanted to know if I would consider taking over J. J.'s involvement.

Joe was like a brother to J. J., and therefore to me. I said, "Joe, whatever you need of me, I will do."

"Can we pitch the product to you?"

"Absolutely."

We met at a café in Studio City. I brought Jordan with me, so he could give me his opinion on the product: I figured it was probably a microphone or something else musical.

Joe showed up with his partner, and said, "I just want to tell you, J. J. really believed in this. It was *blowing his mind*." I couldn't wait to see what they had created. They pulled out a box. Jordan and I were on the edge of our seats. They opened it up for the big reveal. Inside was . . . a glass fishbowl with some sand and a few little plastic plants. They adjusted the plants and argued over who forgot to bring the miniature treasure chest. I was still waiting to see what the product was. Finally, Joe presented the bowl with a flourish. He said, "It's the Invisible Fish."

Blink. "Excuse me?"

"The Invisible Fish. Like the Pet Rock. It's going to be the next big thing. And we want you to be the face of the Invisible Fish. We'll send you to trade shows, gift shows. We'll get you booked on *Good Morning America*. You'll do all of the interviews launching the Invisible Fish."

Jordan could barely speak. He had his face in his hands, trying to act like he wasn't laughing. He said he needed to get some coffee and totally abandoned me. I watched him take off, not believing that he was leaving me to handle the Invisible Fish negotiations by myself. Joe was the sweetest guy, and I didn't want to be rude to him, but I knew there was no way I was getting involved with the Invisible Fish. I came up with an excuse; I said, "Gosh, Joe, I just had a baby. I'm *so* sorry, I can't travel."

That was no problem for Joe: "Oh! You can just do the TV shows, then! Like the *Today* show!"

Now I was sweating, but I said, "Oh, I wouldn't want to say yes unless I could be there one hundred percent for the Invisible Fish."

Afterward, I realized that the night J. J. died, he was driving home from a meeting with these two guys. I knew J. J. loved Joe, and I could picture him wanting to be kind to his friend during the meeting. One thing about J. J.: When he thought something was really funny, he would laugh until tears were rolling down his face. He could get out-of-breath hysterical. Maybe, just maybe, J. J. drove away from the Invisible Fish meeting with Joe and his partner, and busted out laughing after an hour of nodding politely. I imagine that his heart gave out, he pulled over because he felt some pain, and then he died in his car.

When his best friend, Jim Ladd, identified J. J.'s body, he said that his face was very peaceful.

we can't rewind, we've gone too far

Final Thoughts

Alan:

There are days when I can't believe I was at MTV, in the middle of everything. Only when fans come up to me with their own '80s anecdotes does it sink in: That was me, at the best party on the planet.

When I left MTV, I felt like a kid with the rest of my career in front of me. Being a VJ wasn't the sort of job that made you feel grown up. But through all the ups and downs, I've had a charmed life—and I have the Buggles to thank for that.

Mark:

In a lot of ways, I'm happier now than I was in the '80s. My theory is that the best songs come from pain, not happiness. I think the emotional shit I went through during, and after, MTV has made me a better person. I'm a lot more empathetic and easygoing now. I'm grateful to be part of rock 'n' roll history, even if I still don't know quite how to handle it when people come up to me and tell me how much I meant to them when they were younger.

Nina:

At the time, I don't think I realized how much impact we had on people's lives as VJs. Not many people get to be part of something like that, and I'm very grateful.

Martha:

In the beginning, everyone told us MTV wouldn't last. As it turns out, they were right—our MTV doesn't exist anymore. There's no videos on the channel now: It's *Jersey Shore* and *Teen Mom* and *My Super Sweet 16*. Recently, I was shopping at my local farm stand, and the farmer introduced me to a teenage girl. He told her, "This is Martha Quinn—she used to be on MTV."

She said, "Really? What show?"

endnotes

Even though the VJs disagree on some of the particulars, this book is truthful to the best of their memories. There are no composite characters; discretion led us to alter the names of two ex-boyfriends ("Tony" and "Quentin") and one drug dealer ("Peter"). Any dialogue in italics is transcribed directly from video of the event (some of it from the VJs' own collections, some from YouTube). We used many other sources to double-check memories and make this volume as accurate as possible.

The passages in chapter 2 where J. J. Jackson discusses his background and Led Zeppelin's pool party are excerpted and condensed from the e-book *J. J. Jackson Remembers Led Zeppelin: The Music and the Guys Who Made It,* by the very kind permission of author Frank Reddon and editor Lou Anne Reddon. The book, based on a series of 1999 interviews with J. J., tells the story of his relationship with Led Zeppelin in depth, and includes J. J.'s song-by-song analysis of the band's debut album and his memories of their groundbreaking shows at the Boston Tea Party. We strongly recommend it for fans of Led Zeppelin, or of J. J.

acknowledgments

Thanks to everyone who helped us research this book, especially Ken Clark, the VJs' former assistant, who not only stockpiled photographs, memos, press clippings, and videocassettes, but graciously opened up his archives and his Oregon home to Martha and Gavin.

Thank you to Daniel Greenberg, a colossus among agents, who has been a pillar of sanity and wisdom. Thanks also to all his colleagues at Greenberg/Levine, especially Monika Verma and Tim Wojcik.

Thank you, on an epic scale, to Amy Tannenbaum, our exceptionally talented and wise editor at Atria. We are also very grateful to everyone at Atria who worked their magic on this book, including superstar publicity director Paul Olsewski, publicist Ariele Fredman, production editor Carly Sommerstein, designer Kyoko Watanabe, copy editor Polly Watson, managing editor Kimberly Goldstein, and, especially, publisher Judith Curr.

In addition to the individual acknowledgements below, the VJs would like to thank our lawyer, David Fox, for motivating us to just write the damn book already. Huge gratitude to everyone at MTV: the executives, the office staff, the crews at Teletronics and Unitel, and the superstar floor staff. Without your efforts, we wouldn't have had anything to write a book about. Thanks to SiriusXM for valuing our history as much as we do. And finally, we want to send out our heartfelt appreciation to everyone who ever watched or loved MTV.

Nina:

Thanks to my mom and dad, for always supporting my music and acting . . . Danny Sheridan, my longtime manager, who taught me that you really can get paid for being a performer . . . Robert Morton, Sue Steinberg, and Bob Pittman, for hiring me . . . my fellow VJs, for traveling our wacky road together . . . Gavin Edwards, for his talent, insight, and being the calm center of Hurricane VJ—you are indeed the *best* . . . Debbie "Jettz" Fingerman, for saving my life . . . Hank Hojda, for his wisdom and guidance . . . Martine Collette (and the Wildlife Waystation), my hero! For all you have done on behalf of the animals, you are always in my heart . . . Kelly Vincent, for making my life meaningful—I love you eternally. . . .

Alan:

MTV was the start of my career and the beginning of a lifelong friendship with four disparate, unique human beings. Love to my VJ partners in crime and punishment: Martha, Mark, Nina, and J. J., whose hearty laugh and bear hugs I miss dearly. A heartfelt thank-you to Jan, for living those MTV years with me and for giving me Dylan and Callie, the first two VJ babies. To the man who hired me, Bob Pittman—thanks for seeing the potential in an aw-shucks southerner. A snuggly group hug to all the '80s artists, MTV and music biz execs, and the army of production folks—many still my dear friends—who were instrumental in creating the madness we delivered to America's living rooms twenty-four hours a day, seven days a week. And finally, to my wife, Elizabeth, and the last two VJ babies, Parc and Lochran— thank you for your love and patience and for acting totally interested as I relived, reveled in, cried over, and cringed at this chapter of Western civilization's not-so-ancient history.

Mark:

I want to thank Bill Flanagan, David Wild, and Rob Sheffield for all being way too busy to help us with this memoir, and to thank Rob for then pointing us in the direction of Gavin Edwards. It is Gavin's tireless effort and scholarly pursuit, coupled with a mind that is ordered perhaps to the point of excess, that have helped me to organize the holes in my memory into something that is accurate, concise, and bordering on complete. Also, big thanks to Stacy Creamer, whose input was always available to me, but only when I asked. I often did, and it was always helpful.

Huge kudos, heartfelt thanks, and maximum love to Jill Shapiro for accepting me and loving me, even after learning more than she wanted or needed to know about my past. She has been my sounding board and editor, which can't have been easy. Thanks to Spencer, my hormonal teenager (her term, not mine). It's amazing to me, considering what I've been a part of, that the brightest moments in my life have to do with her. I hope she won't ever read this book—for all the reasons that will become obvious once she does.

I have to thank Sue Steinberg, Bob Pittman, the crews at Teletronics and Unitel, and the hugely talented APs, ADs, and directors at MTV, without whom all of this would not have been necessary.

To Nina, Martha, and Alan—I've learned so much more about each of them by doing this book. This VJ thing could have gone any number of ways, but for some reason, we all got lucky. We've been tied by the slender threads of experience that bind our lives together. They are my friends who have become my family.

And, of course, J. J. I miss that guy. I think he'd be proud his story—our story—was finally getting published. I think we all had him in the room as we moved forward with this project, and I hope he'd approve. I'm sorry we all didn't get to hear more from the man himself. It was my great pleasure to know him.

Martha:

My life boils down to two phone calls. One was made by Buzz Brindle to Bob Pittman, telling him I should audition to be a VJ. Because of Buzz, I did indeed find myself at the "center of the universe." To this day, I have the honor of being able to live, work, and breathe music. Because of Buzz, I have the privilege of calling Nina Blackwood, Mark Goodman, Alan Hunter, and J. J. Jackson . . . family. I love you guys so much. It turns out that no amount of time can put asunder what Bob Pittman joined together. For that I am grateful each and every day. (And thank you, Gavin Edwards, for climbing aboard the VJ crazy train!)

The second phone call that changed my life forever was made by Brett Gurewitz to Jordan Tarlow, inviting him to come down to his studio while I was there. Because of Brett, I married not just "the cutest guy I ever saw in my life," but the man who would join me in becoming a vegetarian and support me in breast-feeding and attachment parenting. Who would navigate our family through the neonatal intensive care unit and piece me back together after dark days of postpartum depression. All while remaining the "cutest guy I ever saw in my life."

Gavin:

I am indebted to my brilliant and foxy wife, Jen, for many reasons: The way she made it possible for me finish my work on this book is only the most recent. All my love to her, and to our two boys, Dashiell and Strummer. (And thanks to Strummer for extra inspiration: I was driving around with him when "The Safety Dance" came on the radio. "This song sounds happy," he said. "What's it about?" "Nobody knows," I told him.)

Thank you, Abby Royle, for superhuman feats of transcription, transforming countless hours of conversation into Word files. Thank you, Chris Molanphy and Alan Schwarz, for timely research help. Thank you, my dear friends Jennifer Armstrong, Ted Friedman, and Bill Tipper, for generously offering feedback on early versions of this book.

A special shout-out to Rob Sheffield, whose love of MTV is an inspirational beacon to everyone in the Western Hemisphere. He was instrumental in making this book happen, generously introducing me to both Daniel Greenberg and the VJs themselves (and many months later, offering sage advice on the manuscript). Plus, he's just an outstanding human being.

Most of all, thank you to Nina, Mark, Alan, and Martha, for trusting me with your stories, welcoming me into your homes and your lives, and being the slammingest collaborators around. To adapt an old MTV slogan: With the four of you, too much is never enough.